My French Kitchen

to:
Martha
with
all good wishes.
Denise Khaitman Schorr.

Natick _ MA

My French Kitchen

DENISE KHAITMAN SCHORR

Researched and Illustrated by

Jean Hopley Klein

The Globe Pequot Press

CHESTER, CONNECTICUT 06412

This book is dedicated to the memory of my parents, Anna (Nènètte) and Aaron (Henri) Khaitman, for whom the pleasures of the table were one of the requisites of a good life. It is my deepest sorrow that they are not with us to enjoy its publication.

This book has been produced in the United States of America. It is designed by Susan D. Prindle.

LIBRARY OF CONGRESS CATALOGING IN PUBLICATION DATA

Schorr, Denise Khaitman.
My French Kitchen.
Includes index.

1. Cookery, French.   I. Title.
TX719.S3814   641.5944   81-6621
ISBN: 0-87106-885-0   AACR2

Contents

ACKNOWLEDGMENTS

To my students, family, and friends, who throughout the years have requested that I write this book, I offer my sincere thanks for their faith in me and their encouragement.

Deepest gratitude belongs to my husband, Stanley, for his assistance in bringing this project to fruition.

My family in Paris, Jacqueline, Gary, and Didier Kamioner, and my old friends Marcelle and Henri Lesmayoux and Lucienne Pouli Kaleff were gracious and generous in providing me with information and material promptly when it was needed. *Mes affectueux et profonds remerciements.*

Many thanks to my daughter, Gail Annette, and my friend, Joan Hoch, for helping me with their typing skills.

To: Jean Hopley Klein, my illustrator and researcher, whose drawings make this volume a delightful experience; Dorothy Crandall, who gave never-ending faith and support; and Susan Prindle, editor, whose intelligence and intuitive understanding made a manuscript into a better book, I am indebted.

Denise Khaitman Schorr

Introduction

IN MY FRENCH KITCHEN I hope to demonstrate the pleasures and satisfactions of a good kitchen. By "good kitchen" I mean those extra ingredients brought to the culinary workshop by the cook—the care, love, and joy which play such an important part in turning raw materials into meals which delight the eye and the palate. This is the great lesson of the French kitchen: that attitude and commitment to quality make the difference.

My French Kitchen leads you gently into the art of fine cooking. The recipes are arranged in menu form so that you may prepare and present an authentic French meal. Most are *cuisine bourgeoise*—home cooking. As you progress, the menus become more challenging and lead on to ventures in *haute cuisine*.

In 29 years of teaching and lecturing I have answered countless questions about French cookery. Frequently requested information is included here. As you read, you will find what you need to know within the directions for each recipe—*when* you need to know it!

As a child I loved to read cookbooks (though none was ever explicit enough to satisfy my curiosity); but most of my early training came from my mother, who never used a cookbook. In particular, I remember her insistence on the finest and freshest ingredients and on careful preparation. Many of these recipes are hers. Others are my own and drawn from many sources. Like advocates of *La Nouvelle Cuisine*, I am concerned with presentation, color, and texture, and prefer my sauces to be light and delicate. But like the classic chefs, I often use flour in their preparation.

I hope your visit to *My French Kitchen* will give you the confidence and inspiration to try what's here and to go beyond. In the beginning it is important to follow recipes closely in order to learn the fundamental laws of cooking and to become proficient in basic techniques. Cooking for me is as serious an art as ballet, music, or painting. And, as with any art, one must develop the skills it demands. But the time will come for you to move ahead, to create on your own. Then you may come to feel about your recipes, even the most familiar ones, as I feel about mine: that they are unique, that they bear your own stamp. I like to remember what that French master, Brillat-Savarin, once said: "The discovery of a new dish does more for mankind than the discovery of a star."

As a prelude to the menus you will find notes about the philosophy of French cookery, about how the French plan, prepare, and serve their meals and stock their larders, and about cooking equipment.

Menus for different occasions follow. The combinations have proved popular with my classes and most are traditionally French. None, however, is unalterable. You should feel free to make changes if you wish.

Though I have served these menus time and time again to family, friends, and students, they never lose their luster. Although in general the menus progress from the simple to the complex, they are planned with an eye to the work and time involved. When it comes time to serve, a cook should not feel harassed or exhausted. So, if part of a menu is complicated or exacting, other courses are not. (Unless otherwise noted, recipes will serve 4 persons generously. Directions for increasing or decreasing quantities are given when necessary.)

With each menu I suggest an appropriate wine. Recommendations are limited to the French wines I know well. Although I enjoy many American wines, I prefer to leave their selection to you. Your local wine dealer should have useful knowledge of individual vineyards and the vintages in his cellar.

My French Kitchen closes with some short essays which I hope will enrich your understanding and enjoyment of French meals.

Philosophie de la Cuisine Française

THE PHILOSOPHY OF FRENCH COOKERY

COOKING became an art in France not because of the great chefs, whose efforts were known to turn the tide of politics, but because the French people, from the gentleman in his *château* to the peasant in his *chaumière*, are gourmets by heritage and tradition.

The French predilection for *finesse*, be it in architecture, clothing, or cooking, stems from the days of the Roman occupation. Unlike so many other conquered peoples, the semi-barbaric Gallic tribes welcomed Roman rule and willingly accepted Roman ways. In adapting to Roman culture they Gallicized it; their interpretation of Latin became the French language and their emulation of the ruling class's love for feasting became the average citizen's desire for *la bonne table*. Even after the Roman Empire was defeated by the Franks, the invisible graces of Roman civilization remained impressed upon the Gallic spirit. *Haute cuisine* may be a direct descendent of the grandeur of a Lucullan feast, but *cuisine bourgeoise* inherits the spirit in which it was celebrated.

Today a French day laborer wants a good meal on the table when he returns home. A dinner of steak, *frites* (French fried potatoes), crisp salad, and a *vin ordinaire* makes life worth living and gives him a *joie de vivre* that no meal in a Four Star restaurant could equal. His luxury is a fragrant stew pot on the stove, watched over by a cook whose *talent culinaire* has been passed down for many generations.

In France, watching the pot is a labor of love. Preparation of the simplest meal is done with care and affection. No matter what cut the steak, it is cooked to be flavorful and juicy; potatoes are newly peeled and sliced before frying in fresh oil; salad is crisp; and the dressing, subtly seasoned with herbs and spices, is mixed just before the salad is tossed. Such an ordinary meal of fresh ingredients, carefully prepared and attractively served, makes gourmet dining an everyday affair in the French home. *Joie de vivre,* for the cook, comes from creating *une bonne table* and from the knowledge that such efforts are fully appreciated.

1

When I look back on my own past, it seems inevitable that I should have chosen cooking as a serious pursuit. From the time I was a little child I watched my mother cook. I was drawn to the kitchen by the realization that cooking was an occupation which brought the highest praise, as well as by the warmth and cheer I always found there. My mother was happy in the kitchen, and the sense of contentment and well-being which emanated from that room dominated our whole household. My father, for his part, always responded with appreciation. He could detect subtle differences in herbs or other ingredients, a talent which pleased my mother. Always he ended the meal with a little kiss on her cheek before he retired to read the evening paper.

French daily life has changed since that time. As in America, more women are holding full-time jobs. They shop on the way home from work for the evening meal. Still, the emphasis on fresh ingredients, careful preparation, and attractive service that has been passed down for generations continues to make even the most ordinary meal a special occasion.

The French could never have reached such culinary heights if their land had not been so well endowed. The country lies in the middle of the temperate zone, equidistant between the North Pole and the Equator. Every section is ideally suited to the production of some edible. Shellfish abound in estuaries along the Atlantic. Sun-drenched citrus groves border the Mediterranean. Orchards in Normandy provide the rest of the country with apples, cider, and Calvados (apple brandy). This northern province is also the nation's dairy. From salt-grass pastures in Brittany comes *l'agneau de pré-salé,* tender lamb with an unforgettable flavor; from La Beauce, the flat, fertile center of the nation, comes wheat for bread. Where nothing else survives, on steep stony hillsides and barren mountain ridges, vines flourish and sheep graze, yielding wines and cheeses of unquestioned superiority.

The natural assets of France have given rise to regional cuisines which utilize an area's specialties and reflect the character of its cooks. Each region boasts its unique cooking utensils, its confections, its pâtés, its soups and stews, as well as its wines and cheeses. From Burgundy comes *Le Boeuf Bourguignon,* a glamorous beef stew simmered in a full-bodied red wine, and *Le Coq au Chambertin,* cut-up chicken cooked in a red wine from the great Chambertin vineyard. Languedoc is renowned for its famous *Cassoulet,* a stew made with goose, duck, or lamb with a base of white beans which simmers for hours. Normandy offers *Les Petits Coeurs à la Crème* (cream cheese hearts) of Bernières, displayed in little wicker baskets lined with cheesecloth. Périgord is the home of *paté de foie gras* and *les truffes* (truffles). A dish typical of Provence is *La Soupe au Pistou,* a vegetable soup flavored with garlic, basil, and cheese. And everyone has heard of the famous *Bouillabaisse de Marseille*. The list is endless.

A country in which the names of chefs such as Vatel, Carême, and Escoffier are as familiar as those of statesmen like Robespierre and Richelieu, made its priorities evident long ago. Where but in France would the distillation of a flower's fragrance and the crystallization of its beauty in sugar become big business? What other nation would consider turning the production of truffles or Bar-le-Duc jam, which require hours of hand labor, into multimillion dollar businesses? Where else do street vendors garnish their glistening grey oysters with bright lemons, or farmers scatter daisies among the beans they pack in crates for the wholesale market?

To some, the Frenchman's concern for *la bonne table* may seem a misplaced emphasis. Still, gastronomic refinements have usually advanced with the level of culture. The feasts of Lucullus or the banquets of Carême, for all their numerous and unusual courses, did not reach the heights of refinement found in the farm kitchens of France today. In the United States, cooks are showing more concern for creating fine meals. The recent interest in unprocessed food and home-grown produce has led to a rediscovery of the flavors lost through the use of commercial preservatives and freezing. These fresh ingredients may well provide new inspiration to the American cook, as they have to French cooks for so many generations.

Une Maison Bien Tenue

A WELL-MANAGED HOUSEHOLD

THIS section describes some of the principles of planning and preparing French meals—how the French shop, what they serve to family and guests, and how they set their tables. Of course, any meal begins with marketing.

Allons Faire les Commissions

MARKETING

When I was growing up, peddlers used to set up their stalls along the Rue de Meaux near our home: *les numéros pairs, les numéros impairs*—odd days on one side of the street, even days on the other, so that the street cleaners could do their jobs. Carts overflowed with lettuce, beans, artichokes, beets—all freshly picked before sunrise. Chickens squawked in crates, and you could be sure that the eggs you bought had been laid that morning.

There were special days of the week for everything. The butcher shops closed on Mondays, leaving the field open for *la triperie et la boucherie chevaline*—those that sold innards and horsemeat. Wednesdays, *le marchand de fromage de chèvre*, the goat-cheese man, wandered the streets with his string of goats, a basket of cheeses on his arm. He would milk a goat on the spot into the customer's small tin bucket. Then on he went, calling *"Fromage .. fromage de chèvre ... lait de chèvre. ..."* in cadence to the tinkle of little goat bells.

Les Halles, the central market of Paris, was the most exciting place of all. While the city slept, great trucks rolled through the narrow streets to the marketplace, where buyers and sellers bartered the night away. By 9 A.M. the wholesale selling was over, and Les Halles opened for the retail trade. By mid-afternoon all was

4

quiet, except for sweeping brooms, swooshing hoses, and the clanking of iron gates being shut and locked. For a few hours, until the big trucks rolled in again, all was still.

Among my lasting memories are the sights, sounds, and smells of Les Halles. I can still hear the harsh, dissonant cries of vendors as they hawked their wares, the warning calls of impatient carriers, great loads on their shoulders, as they pushed their way through the crowds to make their deliveries. There were sights and smells from the breadth of France: Bushel baskets of snails, mussels, shrimps, and oysters glistened in the filtered light of the marketplace. Wheels of country cheeses—Brie, Cantal, Reblochon—rose high on the dairy stalls, while moist *fromage blanc* (cream cheese), veiled in cheesecloth to keep off the flies, crowded the counters. Sellers of root crops were half hidden behind piles of potatoes and turnips. Pyramids of oranges, grapefruit, lemons, and melons brightened aisles as far as the eye could see, while bananas, carrots, leeks, onions, and garlic hung from makeshift rafters under the distant, dusty ceiling. On Mondays, Les Halles was transformed into an enchanted garden by the brilliant color and haunting fragrance of the flower market.

Today Les Halles is gone. In the early months of 1969 a new center for the distribution of produce opened its doors in Rungis, near Orly Airport, 5 miles south of Paris. In La Villette, on the eastern border of Paris, another market opened as a meat and poultry center. These modern, efficient markets, accessible by air, rail, and highway, ushered in a new era for the French economy. The acres that were Les Halles have been transformed by urban renewal. The excitement, activity, and sounds of centuries have been stilled. But for those of us who found pleasure there, Les Halles will linger in memory.

Today I still search out markets where I can touch, feel, and smell the things I buy. For me, this is part of the pleasure of shopping. Such markets stimulate my imagination as no supermarket shelf can.

My mother took advantage of the variety of food available in Paris. She shopped three times a day, always with her *filet*—mesh shopping bag. She used a string *filet* for light carrying and an oilcloth bag *en toile cirée* for heavier loads. She made her first trip before breakfast. First she visited the *crèmerie*, carrying her own *boîte au lait* (milk can). On the way home she stopped at the *boulanger* for *pain fantaisie* or *baguette*, and if we were lucky, for *croissants*.

Each morning at 11 she made the rounds of the shops to see what might be available for lunch: to the *boucherie* (butcher shop), *poissonerie* (fish store), *charcuterie* (delicatessen), and *épicerie* (grocery), then back to the *crèmerie* for cheese and butter. After this initial survey, she walked to the pushcarts to take advantage of the best produce of the day.

At 6 P.M. she went out again to shop for the evening meal. This ritual was so ingrained that even after we acquired a refrigerator, she continued to market three times a day.

When company was expected, her routine was the same. However, she often called her butcher a few days before the event to discuss what cuts would be available. She might also consult a *charcutier–traiteur* (delicatessen owner and caterer) about what cold masterpiece she could purchase for an appetizer. Very few Parisians do their own baking, and she was no exception. Instead, she would place an order with the best local *pâtissier–glacier* (pastry and ice cream chef). If our wine cellar lacked what she needed for a special dish, she would order it from the *épicier–marchand de vin*. All these delights were assembled, and her own dishes prepared, on the day the guests were expected.

Projeter un Repas

PRINCIPLES OF MEAL PLANNING

Since in the United States most markets do not receive fresh produce every day, I plan my meals somewhat differently than my mother did. Two or three days before a dinner party, I make the rounds of the markets. I like to have all my ingredients on hand the day before the dinner (except seafood, which I purchase on the day it is to be eaten). I also consider the selection of wines and the table setting well before the dinner.

When planning a meal, it is important to avoid repeating textures, flavors, or colors. I take this principle into account in thinking about a menu. For instance, on a trip to the market I might see plump fresh ducks and decide to serve them. Since I like to prepare duck with an orange sauce, a dessert made with oranges would be unsuitable. I might choose *Crème Renversée au Caramel* as my dessert. My choice means that an appetizer made with cream or eggs would not be appropriate. Oysters might be a good choice, or perhaps a salad of fresh mushrooms or cucumber, or a clear consommé. *Pommes de Terre Dauphine* would be a pleasant contrast following the duck, and would be followed by a simple green salad.

The availability of beautiful vegetables or fruit can be a factor when you are planning a menu. If I see very fresh green beans,

I might decide to prepare a *Gigot,* which goes well with them. Any soup could be served before, and any dessert or pastry could follow the main dish, providing that only one has cream in it.

Usually, however, the main dish—be it seafood, fish, meat, or poultry—is the focus of the meal. If the main dish has no sauce, a wide variety of dishes could precede and follow it. If your entrée does have a sauce, however, you will need to take that into account in selecting your other dishes. Just remember that variety and contrast should be your guiding principles.

What you find in the market is certainly important when you are planning a menu. But price may help you make up your mind, too. If you invite only a few guests, of course, you can be more extravagant than when you expect a crowd. If you do plan a large party, remember that more people mean more work; it is a good idea to simplify your menu. Save the more elaborate dishes for a small, appreciative group. Some guests may have particular tastes or medical needs that will influence your selections as well.

When you are planning for company, especially for a large group, it is advisable to design your menu so that much of the work can be done ahead of time. Your dinner should be enjoyable for everyone, including the cook. In preparing your meal, it makes sense to begin with the most time-consuming dish, and progress to those that are less difficult. However, you cannot expect the same quality in your meals if you prepare everything ahead of time. Some dishes, such as salads, should be assembled at the last minute for maximum freshness. Others require a last-minute touch to the sauce or a final browning if they are to be served *juste à point.* Don't hesitate to spend time in the kitchen when necessary, even though your guests are waiting expectantly at the table. The quality of the dishes you bring to them will make their waiting worthwhile.

Les Repas Français

FRENCH MEALS

LE PETIT DÉJEUNER: Breakfast in France is a simple affair: large bowls of *café au lait* (coffee with milk)* and *tartine de pain grillé*

---

*To make *café au lait,* hot milk is poured into the bowl or cup first, and freshly brewed coffee is added. The proportion of coffee to milk depends on individual taste. For a further discussion of coffee, see pages 352–353.

(roasted slices of buttered French bread—often stale bread for the family). If company is present, freshly baked *croissants* and fine quality jellies or jams would be served in addition to the *tartines,* and the *café au lait* would be served in china cups.

LE DÉJEUNER: In France *le déjeuner* is the most important meal of the day. Many workers in France go home for lunch, returning to work in the afternoon. For the family, lunch might include a platter of *crudités* as an appetizer, fish or meat, a vegetable, salad, bread and cheese, and fresh fruit. A *vin ordinaire* (a non-vintage wine) is served throughout the meal.* A bottle of mineral water is on the table, since the French do not drink tap water. Especially for children, wine may be diluted right in the drinking glass. A demi-tasse of *café noir* (very strong black coffee) might end the meal. This is a hearty lunch, but remember that breakfast was light and that French portions are considerably smaller than conventional American servings.

When guests come for lunch, an *apéritif* is served in the living room or at the dining room table before the meal. *Hors d'oeuvre variés,* a platter of *fruits de mer,* or a selection of delicately flavored cold cuts might start the meal. Next comes a fish or meat course, followed by a vegetable course and a salad.** After the salad, an assortment of cheeses is presented with unsalted butter and French bread.*** A different wine is served with each course, except the salad. Dessert or pastry, *café noir,* and liqueurs complete the meal.

On Sunday, *le déjeuner* may become *un déjeuner–dinatoire.* Guests arrive about 1 o'clock and linger over the meal until dinner time. A homemade ice cream, or one made by the neighborhood *pâtissier–glacier,* may be served after the cheese course. Later in the afternoon, pastries, *petits fours,* or both may be offered with coffee, Champagne and liqueurs. For the hardy guests who linger on into the evening, a light supper would be served.

LE DÎNER: A family dinner is usually a lighter meal than lunch. It always begins with soup. In our home no one could imagine dinner without *une assiette ou un bol de bonne soupe.* Next would come an omelet (plain or filled) or slices of boiled ham, a green salad, cheese, and fresh fruit or a fruit compote. Wine, mineral water,

*A red or white or both might be served, depending on the nature of the main dish and the cheese.

**Salads are discussed in more detail on pages 350–351.

***A selection of cheeses is mandatory; to serve just one is considered an insult to the guest. The varieties of cheeses available in France are described on pages 342–349.

or both were served throughout the meal. Often a *tisane* (herb tea) would be served at the end of the meal. *Tisanes* such as *tilleul* (linden), *camomille,* and *vervaine* were considered helpful for insomnia, nervousness, and indigestion. My mother always purchased the herbs by weight at a shop which specialized in herb teas. I still remember the delightful fragrance *chez l'herboriste.*

A dinner for company is generally more elaborate than a luncheon. *Apéritifs* or Champagne often precede the dinner. The first course may be fish or seafood, perhaps served cold and coated with a jewel-like aspic. It is followed by a delicate *potage* or *consommé,* roasted poultry or meat or—for a very formal occasion—both.* Then come a vegetable course, a green salad, an assortment of cheeses, and dessert or a pastry or both. A different wine is served with each course, and of course French bread is on the table. *Café noir,* liqueurs, and brandy are offered after dessert.

Dressons la Table

TABLE SETTING

For the family, the French table is set simply. The cloth may be linen or even oilcloth. Plates are not changed, but are cleaned between courses with a piece of crusty bread. This is acceptable only *en famille;* it is never done when entertaining guests, or when dining in a restaurant. Each family member has a napkin ring to hold the napkin until the linen is changed (perhaps once a week).

For informal lunches or dinners, a dinner plate of about 10 inches is placed at each setting; it is the all-purpose plate for the meal. If soup is served, it is ladled into an *assiette creuse* (soup dish), which is then placed on the dinner plate.

Knives are placed to the right of the plate and often rest between courses on a *porte-couteau* (knife rest). This may be a small rectangle of glass (3 1/2 × 1 1/4 inches), or a little log made of metal. The *porte-couteau* protects the tablecloth when the knives are not in use.** The soup spoon rests, face down, on the knife rest. Forks are placed to the left of the plate, tines facing down. A dessert spoon or pastry fork, if needed, may be placed, also face down,

*If more than one main course is served, usually a poultry or game dish is followed by a meat course.
**Although these are used generally for informal table settings, I use them for formal meals, too, to keep my tablecloth from being stained.

above the plate next to the glass. The glass may or may not be stemware.

Formal table settings are more elaborate. Dishes are changed for each course. The arrangement of flatware is the same as it is for an informal meal, but there is usually a separate implement provided for each course. If fish or seafood is served first, a fish knife would be placed at the extreme right, next to the soup spoon, and a fish fork would be placed outside the dinner fork.

A connoisseur of wines will know from the French table setting what wines to expect, for there is a different shaped glass for each wine. Glasses may be placed in a semi-circle directly in front or slightly to the right of the plate. White wine glasses are set on the outside, and subsequent glasses are arranged from right to left. There are special glasses for Alsatian, Bordeaux, Anjou-Loire, Burgundy, and Champagne.* After dinner, brandy snifters and liqueur glasses are used.

French homemakers value beautiful linen, particularly linen with embroidery or fine lacework. Long before I married, my mother commissioned a skilled needlewoman from Corrèze to make some tablecloths for me. Linens, plain or fancy, are important as the backdrop for the food, the china, and the flowers of the French table.

A French home is seldom without fresh flowers. A *marchande de fleurs* is usually among the pushcart vendors, and most neighborhoods have a little *fleuriste* where the cut flowers seem just picked. Almost anyone can and does buy flowers in Paris. On the table, they add to the beauty of the setting. An arrangement of flowers for a table need not be large, expensive, or elaborate. Just one flower in the right container may provide a stunning contrast to your china, candles, and linen. Fruits and vegetables may also be used effectively as table decorations. Good taste, flair, and imagination are the important ingredients in setting an attractive table.

Serving dishes, too, are chosen with eye appeal in mind. A black bowl, for instance, might be chosen to lend drama to an endive salad. It is a good idea to picture in your mind the presentation of a dish as you prepare it. Strive for elegance and simplicity; a gracious and inviting table will add to the pleasures of a fine meal and good company.

---

*For any wine, an all-purpose tulip shape is acceptable. Even for champagne, I prefer it to the so-called *coupe de Champagne*. For a more detailed discussion of French wines and wine service, see pages 311–341.

Les Trésors du Garde-Manger

TREASURES OF THE LARDER

HERE are some items I feel are indispensable to the preparation of fine food. I cannot imagine an artist starting a canvas without a variety of paints. The same principle applies to creative food preparation.

Beurre Clarifié

CLARIFIED BUTTER

I begin with clarified butter because I use it in so much of my cooking. For *roux* (a blending of flour and butter used as a sauce base), for sautéing, and in omelets, clarified butter has many advantages. Since it will not burn as rapidly as whole butter, it enables the cook to use a higher heat when sautéing. Clarifying removes both milk solids and water, leaving pure oil. Thus, it is far more digestible than whole butter. Clarified butter will keep under refrigeration for several months without turning rancid.

The process of clarification is a simple one.

INGREDIENTS

butter (either unsalted or salted)

METHOD

Place butter in a saucepan. Melt over low heat, being careful that it does not cook. When butter is completely melted, remove pan from heat. Set butter aside for 5 minutes, then skim off the top foam, which is the casein.

11

Stretch a damp cheesecloth, triple thickness, over a bowl and secure with an elastic band. Pour melted butter through the cheese-cloth to strain out the milky substance which settles at the bottom. This is the whey (*petit lait* in French). If this process is done carefully, the resulting liquid will be perfectly clear.

Clarified butter keeps well, but solidifies upon refrigeration. For accuracy when measuring, it should be in liquid form. Melt the quantity you need in a small double boiler or *bain-marie* (water bath) before measuring.

A NOTE ON BUTTER: In most of my recipes I specify unsalted butter, either in stick or whipped form. The reason for this is that I have found unsalted butter to be fresher and of better quality than the salted variety. It is more expensive, but it is worth it.

Bouquets de la Cuisine

KITCHEN BOUQUETS

What a joy for me, tying a *bouquet garni!* Fresh-scented parsley and pungent bay leaves—so much like sprays of spring flowers!

One thing a French kitchen is never without is a *bouquet garni.* This is traditionally composed of several sprigs of parsley and one or two bay leaves tied together with a string. Dropped into a dish while cooking, it imparts flavor and can easily be picked out before serving.

In France, a sprig of thyme is also added to the traditional *bouquet garni.* However, fresh thyme is not so readily available in the United States. When a recipe requires herbs in addition to parsley and bay leaves, it will specify "*bouquet garni* plus . . ." what-ever other herb is desired.

Some of the herbs commonly used in French cookery are de-scribed below. Many of them can be found either fresh or dried. When I use them fresh, I substitute 1 tablespoon of the chopped herb for 1 teaspoon of the dried herb.

BASIL: Basil is an annual plant of the mint family which orig-inated in India. There are at least five varieties. The baby basil makes a lovely plant on a windowsill, and it is easy to grow. It is a necessary ingredient for the famous Provençal *Soupe au Pistou.* Its peppery scent is just right for many sauces, particularly those with a tomato base.

BAY LEAVES: These are dried leaves of the aromatic laurel bush which grows in the eastern Mediterranean, sometimes to a height of 60 feet. Although the leaves are very much alike, Americans should not confuse this plant with their native laurel, which is poisonous. In France, whole branches of *laurier* are sold in the open markets, or from little pushcarts along the streets of Paris. With shoppers going from cart to cart picking the best herbs at the best prices, I often wondered how these vendors could make a living. In this country, I buy the leaves boxed or bottled. In metropolitan areas, bay leaves are now available by the pound. Used sparingly, they give a marvelous flavor to stews, certain sauces, poaching liquids, and marinades. Its evergreen leaves make bay an attractive pot herb for the windowsill.

CHERVIL: Chervil is an annual herb, much like Italian parsley, but with a more delicate leaf and flavor. Use it fresh when you can find it for flavoring salads and sauces.

CHIVES: This hardy species of onion can readily be found fresh in the spring and summer in American markets. It will thrive as a pot herb on the kitchen windowsill in the early spring. During the winter months I rely upon dried chives. Its slender blades, finely chopped, are used in sauces and salads.

PARSLEY: "... The obligatory condiment of every sauce," wrote the nineteenth-century culinary expert and novelist, Alexandre Dumas. Without being that assertive, one can admit that parsley is wonderfully useful for flavoring and garnishing. Since fresh parsley can be found year-round in the markets, I never use it dried. The more common parsley is the curly-leaf variety. The flat-leaf Italian parsley is sometimes also available, and I prefer it for garnishing. Wash parsley in cold water, drain it and dry it thoroughly with a linen or paper towel. Store it loosely in your hydrator or refrigerator. Or gather the sprigs into a bouquet and place them in a container of very hot water. Stored this way in the refrigerator, they will keep fresh up to 2 weeks.

TARRAGON: Tarragon is another herb found in the vendors' pushcarts of Paris in fresh, fragrant sprigs. In America, it is seldom sold fresh, but I do not mind using it dry. In salads and sauces it should be used sparingly, for a little goes a long way. Combined with other herbs, especially chervil and chives, tarragon creates a virtual symphony of taste. Its fragrance alone is enough to inspire a cook. It is an especially good marriage with cucumber.

THYME: This delightfully fragrant perennial herb of the mint family has an essence all its own. Its small lavender flowers often ornament rock gardens in France. The dried or ground leaves are used in sauces and stuffings.

WATERCRESS: A hardy perennial herb, watercress flourishes from mid-autumn until late spring. Its bright green leaves can often be spied along the edges of rushing spring brooks and ponds by hikers in temperate climates, for it has been naturalized in these areas. One of many "cresses" grown for salad greens and garnishing, it is a member of the mustard family. Its botanical name, *Nasturtium officinalis,* denotes its close relationship to the flowering annual so popular in American gardens, the nasturtium, whose leaves and flowers may also be used in salads. Both cresses have the same piquant flavor.

La Planche aux Épices et aux Farines

THE SPICE RACK AND FLOUR BIN

SALT: Coarse salt is often used for seasoning in French kitchens. It comes in flakes and is less concentrated than recrystallized table salt. I prefer it for boiling vegetables, stewing meats, and preparing stocks—generally, when I am cooking anything with a large quantity of water. There is less danger of over-salting with coarse salt. My favorite table salt is the unadulterated natural sea salt (*sel marin*), which has a unique flavor. To measure sea salt, use slightly less than specified. For 1 teaspoon of table salt, for example, use 1 *scant* teaspoon of sea salt.

PEPPER: Formerly a rare spice from the Middle East, pepper once sold for its weight in gold and was accepted as payment of taxes and court fees. Today the shrub from which it comes is cultivated in the tropical areas of Asia and South America as well. The greenish-black peppercorns used in pepper mills, from which ground black pepper is prepared, are the dried, unripened berries of the pepper plant. Fully ripened berries with the husks removed are used in preparation of the milder white pepper. White pepper is used chiefly to avoid dark specks in white sauces. Fresh green peppercorns, or those preserved in brine, usually come from the island of Madagascar. They give a subtle zesty flavor to eggs, fish, meat, poultry, and sauces.

MY PHILOSOPHY OF SEASONING: The amounts of spices and herbs I recommend in my recipes have been tested for many years. To me, they produce dishes that are neither flat nor overly spicy. Try them, and if you feel differently, you can of course adjust them according to your taste.

GARLIC: Garlic is a pungent member of the lily family whose flavor has been ardently liked, and just as ardently disliked, through the ages. Much of its success as a seasoning depends upon its proper use: It can dominate a dish or be so subtle as to keep its identity a mystery. Although garlic salt and flakes are available, I always use fresh garlic. Inside a papery skin, the bulbous garlic root is divided into cloves which can be used whole, chopped, ground, or squeezed. Frequently, garlic is one of the ingredients in a French dressing. Inserted in small slivers in lamb and pork, it imparts an excellent flavor.

SHALLOTS: The shallot, a must in every French kitchen, was first brought to Europe by Crusaders returning from the Holy Land. A member of the onion family, it is becoming more and more popular in America. It has a mild, delicate flavor which, because of its subtlety, is often preferred to onions or garlic. The pear-shaped shallot should not be confused with the small Italian onion, *cippoline,* which has the same brown skin and purplish flesh. The *cippoline* is perfectly round and does not separate into cloves, as does the shallot. In supermarkets shallots are sold three or four to a package, like garlic. At vegetable markets or food specialty shops, however, they may be ordered by the pint or quart basket. Shallots will keep as long as a year. In France, farmers who grow them hang them from the ceiling in their attics, where it is dry and cold throughout the winter. I have tried doing this, but find that they last longer under refrigeration. When you are keeping shallots for a long period, check them from time to time and discard those that are spoiling. To prepare them, cut off the hairy root section, peel the thin outer skin, and slice or chop. I use shallots most often in salads and sauces.

NUTMEG: Nutmegs are the stones of the fruits of evergreen trees grown in the Dutch East Indies and the West Indies. I seldom use this spice, but when I do, I like to grate the kernels myself rather than using the powdered form. When used in making a

cheese soufflé, nutmeg gives the flavor a *"je ne sais quoi."* It is also good used in a white sauce.

CAPERS: The kitchen shelf of a serious cook should not be without at least one bottle of this condiment. Capers are the green flower buds and young berries of a low-growing Mediterranean shrub. They can be purchased pickled in vinegar and spices or preserved in salt. I always use those preserved in vinegar. They add a delightful flavor to seafood sauces, and are equally good when mixed with homemade mayonnaise and served with cold poultry or fish. Capers can be found in almost any supermarket which has a gourmet food section. The vinegar should be drained off before using.

VANILLA BEAN: Keeping *le bâton de vanille* in the sugar jar is a custom that many French housewives practice. The bean imparts a delicate flavor and aroma to the sugar, just enough for making cakes and cookies. The treated sugar also subtly enhances the flavor of whatever is being sweetened, even tea or coffee. Any flavor can be improved by the use of a little vanilla. Even chocolate depends upon vanilla to bring out its true quality, a fact the Aztecs knew and utilized long before the Spanish conquest. I usually use the bean rather than the extract. Buried in sugar or heated with a liquid, its strength is always right.

The vanilla bean is the dried seed pod of an orchid plant native to Mexico. Most of the real vanilla used in the United States today still comes from that country. Vanilla beans can be found on the spice shelves of most supermarkets or in food specialty shops. Select one that is smooth and about 8 to 10 inches long. The cost ranges from 50 to 90 cents a bean, depending on the size and the store. However, one bean can be used over and over, as long as its aroma lasts. After the bean has been steeped in a liquid, wash it well under running water, rubbing it to be sure that it is free of impurities. Wipe it and allow it to dry thoroughly before storing. If it is stored damp, it is likely to mold.

FLOUR: I generally use unbleached, *all-purpose flour,* since I find that it works well for most dishes. However, I also like *gran-*

16

ulated flour, such as Wondra, which is also called "quick mixing." When sprinkled on foods, it makes a more delicate coating than all-purpose flour, and adheres well. It also is preferable for some crisp *petits fours,* as it makes a lighter pastry.

POTATO FLOUR is a fine powder made from potatoes which is used as a thickening agent. Potato flour gives an appealing gloss to a sauce. When you are using it for thickening, mix it with an equal amount of cold water before stirring it into the sauce. For 3 teaspoons all-purpose flour, substitute 2 teaspoons potato flour.

RICE CREAM *(crème de riz)* is made from toasted, short-grain brown rice. It feels like grainy flour. It is used as a thickening agent to make *roux* and gives certain dishes, such as *Potage Crème de Laitue,* a fine texture and delicate taste. For 1/2 tablespoon all-purpose flour, substitute about 1 tablespoon rice cream.

L'Effort qui Vaut la Peine

A WORTHWHILE EFFORT

There is no good cooking without good bouillon. French cooking . . . owes its superiority to the excellence of French bouillon. This excellence derives from a sort of intuition with which . . . our women of the people are endowed.

Alexandre Dumas

Homemade stock is marvelous to have on hand as a basis for soups and sauces. I use it for my onion soup (see page 64). If you like to make your own jellies and preserves, or to bake your own bread, you will understand the feeling of satisfaction I have about making my own stocks. It is not absolutely necessary to have homemade stock when you are creating a dish for gourmets, but the difference is rewarding enough to make the effort worthwhile.

On the following pages are recipes for three stocks: beef, chicken, and veal. Although all are simple to make, they usually require 2 days to complete, since it is necessary for the pot to stand for several hours to allow the fat to gel.

When one considers that two of these stocks are three recipes in one, they are even more worth the trouble. They provide not only stock for future use, but also, right from the pot, a nutritious soup. Add a little broth and reheat, and the vegetables and meat make a boiled dinner *par excellence.*

I make stocks in large quantities and freeze what I don't immediately need for future use. I sometimes freeze some of the stock in a divided ice cube tray, then store the frozen cubes in a freezer bag. By using the cubes, I avoid unfreezing more stock than necessary when I need only a small amount to strengthen a sauce or deglaze a pan.

Fond Brun

HOMEMADE BEEF STOCK

This recipe will yield about 2 quarts of stock.

INGREDIENTS

2 *large yellow onions, sliced*
2 *carrots, sliced*
2 *pounds beef bones**
3/4 *teaspoon table salt*
several turns of black pepper mill, medium grind
bouquet garni (5 sprigs of parsley and 3 bay leaves plus 3 celery stalks with leaves)
13 *cups cold water*
1 1/2 *pounds beef shank*
4 *to 4 1/4 pounds stew beef, in one piece*
2 *leeks and 3 celery stalks tied together*
1 *tablespoon coarse salt*
1 *pound whole carrots*

METHOD

Preheat oven to 450° F.

Lay a bed of sliced onions and carrots in a roasting pan. (I use a 6-quart Dutch oven.) Scatter on beef bones, sprinkle with salt and pepper. Roast 1 hour, turning occasionally with fork.

Add *bouquet garni* and water. Cover and continue cooking in the oven 2 1/2 hours.

Take pan from oven. Strain off liquid and allow to stand until

*Ask your butcher to cut them into chunks. If you have a few chicken necks and gizzards on hand, they will give added flavor to the stock.

fat has gelled. Skim off fat. There should be about 9 cups of liquid left.

Now place beef shank and stew beef in an 8- to 10-quart pot or canning kettle. Tie leeks and celery together for easy removal and drop in. Add salt and contents of roasting pan. On top of the stove, bring slowly to boiling point, uncovered. Skim off the froth which rises to the surface. Add 1/2 cup of cold water to facilitate second rising of froth. Bring again to boiling point and skim. Repeat, adding 1/2 cup of cold water after each skimming, until only a little froth rises.

Simmer gently with cover ajar 2 1/2 to 3 hours. Add carrots and cook until they are tender.

Turn off heat; remove meat and vegetables and *bouquet garni.* Allow liquid to cool so that fat will gel. Remove fat. Reheat broth and strain through a damp linen towel or several thicknesses of damp cheesecloth. Stock is now ready for immediate use or for storage for future use as a soup or a base for *Sauce Brune.*

The meat and vegetables, with the exception of the parsley, can be combined with a little stock and warmed up and eaten as a boiled dinner. *"Les amateurs de boeuf bouilli"* is an expression often heard in France, where there are many lovers of boiled beef. The French use coarse salt as a condiment with boiled beef, much as Americans use mustard—each forkful being dipped into the salt flakes.

Fond de Poulet

HOMEMADE CHICKEN STOCK

This recipe will yield about 2 1/2 quarts of stock.

INGREDIENTS

1 *large yellow onion, unpeeled*
4 *teaspoons chicken fat or shortening*
2 *pounds of chicken wings, gizzards, hearts, or necks*
1 *pound whole carrots*
6 *to 8 pounds of fowl*
8 *quarts cold water*
16 *teaspoons coarse salt or 8 teaspoons table salt*
bouquet garni (2 leeks, 12 sprigs of parsley, 1 pound of celery with leaves, tied together)
1 *large garlic clove*

METHOD

Preheat oven to 450° F.

Place whole, unpeeled onion in a shallow pan in preheated oven for 15 minutes. The roasted onion skin improves the color of the stock.

Heat chicken fat or shortening in a large roasting pan on top of the stove. Brown chicken parts, remove, and drain well. Next, brown cleaned whole carrots. Remove and set aside.

Place fowl and browned chicken parts in large kettle. Add water, roasted onion, salt, *bouquet garni*, and garlic. Bring slowly to boiling point, uncovered. Skim off froth which rises, and add 1/2 cup of cold water to facilitate second rising. Bring to the boiling point again and skim. Add another 1/2 cup of cold water and repeat the operation until no more froth rises (about three times).

Simmer gently with cover ajar for 2 hours. Add browned carrots and cook until they are tender—from 35 to 60 minutes, depending on their size.

Cool. Remove fat from surface. Remove *bouquet garni*, carrots, and all chicken parts. Warm broth and strain through a damp linen towel or triple thickness of cheesecloth. Stock is now ready for immediate use or for storage.

Here is a base with strength that is good to have on hand. It is a wonderful base for sauces, and can also be used for *Velouté de Concombres* (page 204). Combined with a small amount of the broth, the chicken can be warmed up with the carrots, leeks, and celery, and served as a boiled dinner. It may also be served cold, sliced.

Ne Gâchons Rien

LET'S NOT WASTE ANYTHING

Whenever I have a chicken, I remove all the fat and store it in plastic bags in the freezer. After about 1 1/2 pounds have accumulated, I melt it over a low flame, adding 1 medium yellow onion, peeled and sliced.

When the fat is completely melted, I strain it through a double thickness of damp cheesecloth. This amount yields about 2 1/2 cups of rendered fat. This rendered fat is a limpid oil, excellent for frying potatoes and potato pancakes, sautéing chicken livers, and greasing fowl before roasting.

Rendered fat will solidify upon refrigeration and can be kept for several months in the refrigerator.

Fond de Veau

HOMEMADE VEAL STOCK

This recipe will yield 1 1/2 to 2 quarts of stock.

INGREDIENTS

3 *pounds of veal shank or leftover bones from a roast*
2 *cups dry white wine*
1 *whole medium yellow onion, peeled*
2 1/2 *quarts (10 cups) cold water*
1 1/2 *teaspoons table salt*
3 *celery stalks with leaves*
4 *whole carrots*

METHOD

Place veal shank or bones in a large pot of about 5- to 6-quart capacity; add just enough cold water to cover (about 2 quarts). Bring slowly to boiling point and allow to boil for 5 minutes, uncovered, to blanch bones and reduce the scum. Pour into colander to drain off all water. Run cold water over bones. Return to cooking pot; add wine and onion. Bring slowly to boiling point and simmer 45 minutes, uncovered.

After 45 minutes cover bones with the cold water (there will be little of the wine left). Add salt and celery. Bring to boiling point and, with cover ajar, simmer for 2 1/2 hours. Add carrots and simmer 20 to 30 minutes more, or until carrots are tender.

Remove bones and vegetables. Allow to cool and remove gelled fat. Heat slightly and strain through a damp linen towel or triple thickness of cheesecloth.

Your veal stock is now ready for immediate use or for storage. It is very good as a sauce base or for a good soup. Use it for *Potage Portugais* (see page 192).

La Batterie de Cuisine

KITCHEN EQUIPMENT

PEOPLE have asked how I can stand before an audience in a concert hall, display window, or gymnasium, and proceed with the preparation of a dish as calmly as in my own kitchen. The truth is, take away my wooden spoon or my wire whisk and I feel myself fumble; my confidence fades.

With the gift of a set of *petits-fours* molds or a simple lemon stripper, my husband has learned how to please me most. And while a gold pin or an ounce of perfume delights me, receipt of a copper pan elicits sheer joy—joy which returns anew each time I use the pan.

There is no need to go out and buy fancy utensils before trying my recipes. A few simple tools, however, make the process of cooking more efficient and certainly more fun. They make the difference between a carefree adventure and a laborious job.

Mes Petits Outils

MY LITTLE UTENSILS

WOODEN SPOON: Because of its shape, texture, and stability the wooden spoon does a better job than a metal one in many instances. When you are mixing cream puff paste, it is indispensable in obtaining the right consistency. I like its feel and the muted sound it makes against the side of a pan. For many purposes, a spoon 13 to 14 inches long is most useful.

WIRE WHISK: For blending most ingredients thoroughly and smoothly, a wire whisk does a faster, better job than other implements. In preparing cream sauce it allows complete control over

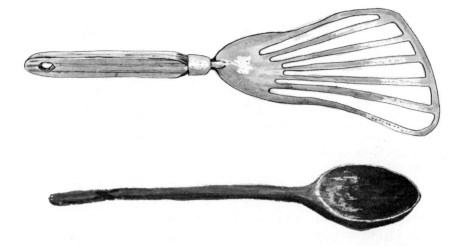

consistency. Any lumps which develop can be whisked away rapidly. The whisk may feel awkward at first, but once you are used to working with one you will probably want a collection in various sizes. A multi-purpose whisk ranges from 8 to 10 inches long.

METAL SPATULA: There are two kinds of metal spatulas I like. One is broad-bladed and can be used to lift omelets, *crêpes,* or fried eggs from the pan. The other, which has a narrower blade, I often use to fold flour into batter or remove pastries from a cookie sheet. Both have flexible blades.

BATTER BEATER: This is a useful implement for lifting vegetables or poached eggs from their water. Shaped like a spatula, it has open spaces which give it flexibility and allow liquids to drain off.

LEMON STRIPPER: Primarily made to strip thin slices of rind from lemons and oranges, this little device does wonders in giving a professional, decorative look to prepared vegetables. In France, an apprentice chef spends many weeks perfecting the skill of fluting mushrooms with a knife. It takes only a little practice with a lemon stripper to attain the same flair. Used along the sides of a whole cucumber, it gives a scalloped edge to the slices. Lemon strippers may be purchased in the housewares section of most large department stores and in food specialty shops.

STRING: A ball of 12-ply string is useful to have in the kitchen for trussing poultry, binding meats, and tying *bouquets garnis.*

Hachons, Hachons, Passons, Pressons!

CHOP, CHOP, STRAIN, AND PRESS

CHOPPING BOWL: In many instances a gently curved bowl is much more convenient to use for chopping than a board and a straight knife. Since the ingredient is confined in a limited area, it can be finely chopped more quickly. Specially designed chopping blades are used with the bowl.

MORTAR AND PESTLE: This is one of the oldest known means of grinding, crushing, and pulverizing. Relics of these bowl-shaped vessels and their stick-like pounders have survived from Stone Age cultures. Once an indispensable part of *la batterie de cuisine,* the mortar and pestle are an oddity in most of today's kitchens, where they have been superseded by the electric blender and the food processor. I keep only a small ceramic set for crushing spices and garlic. I also use the pestle to pound fish fillets for mousse.

CONICAL STRAINER: This is an implement known in French as *le chinois.* Literally translated, this means the Chinese man, perhaps because its shape is slightly reminiscent of a coolie hat. It is a strainer in the shape of a cone with a long handle, made either of solid metal with small holes or of wire mesh. A whisk can be used with *le chinois* to press liquid through the holes. It does the job of extracting juices more efficiently than a wire strainer, and is used mainly when making sauces.

FOOD MILL: This is sometimes found in pot shops under its French name, *le moulin à légume.* It is a device for puréeing. It

resembles a saucepan with holes in the bottom, and is fitted with a rotating blade which is turned by a handle. Food mills can be purchased with interchangeable discs with choices of hole sizes.

LA FUREUR DE L'ÉPOQUE (THE FOOD PROCESSOR): Food processors can be useful machines, especially for chopping large quantities. I find them practical for chopping meat for pâtés, making fish mousse or puréed soups and vegetables, and pulverizing nuts. However, they do not give the proper texture for all foods. In some of the recipes in this book, like *Purée Saint-Germain* and *Bûche aux Marrons,* I prefer the texture that is obtained with a food mill. The processor can also mix pastry dough well, but you should have the feel of making any dough by hand before you let the machine do the job.

KNIVES: It seems too elementary to state, but every kitchen should have proper cutting tools. A cook may avoid many frustrations in the kitchen by using a sharp knife. A good French-made knife is expensive, but considering that it will last a lifetime, it is well worth the investment. It should be sharpened periodically by a professional.

Knives come in many sizes for many uses. Four standard sizes have blades about 4, 7, 10, and 11 inches in length. The 4-inch one is a utility knife, practical for fluting mushrooms, peeling small items, and mincing small quantities of condiments and vegetables. The 7- to 10-inch blades are good all-purpose knives for mincing vegetables, garlic, and shallots. The longer knives are good for chopping large amounts of vegetables, and are adequate to cut meat and poultry. A knife with a 7-inch flexible blade is used for filleting fish.

Boning knives come in various lengths and widths, depending on the job to be accomplished. A good size for a home kitchen has a blade 4 to 6 inches in length. Consult with knowledgeable people at a good kitchen utensil shop before you purchase one.

Do not dull your knives by using them as a hatchet to chop bones. Use a *cleaver,* which is also useful to flatten meat. A good all-purpose cleaver has a blade about 7 inches in length and 2 1/2 inches wide. It should be sharpened frequently, like your knives, by a professional.

Between visits to the knife sharpener, one may use a *steel,* which is a rounded or semi-rounded shaft with a firm-textured, file-like surface. Knives may be sharpened by passing the blades evenly and consistently over and under the steel, using a very light

touch and holding the steel horizontally and the knife at a very slight (15°) angle.

PINEAPPLE CORER: There is a special implement for coring pineapples, a tapered cylinder about 6 to 8 inches long, which, when pressed over the core and twisted with a circular motion, neatly and easily cuts it out. Another implement, which looks like an oversized donut cutter with a long handle, removes the pineapple rind at the same time. If you serve fresh pineapple often, either of these can be a time-saving investment.

POULTRY SHEARS: A glorified pair of scissors with one knife-like blade and one saw-toothed blade, poultry shears are sprung into open position by a strong spring and half closed by a catch. They make cutting up poultry an easy task. Use them with the serrated blade underneath.

La Fierté d'une Cuisinière

THE PRIDE OF THE COOK

I started out years ago with a pan from my mother's kitchen. Gradually, one by one, for presents on special occasions or as a treat to myself instead of a new hat, I have accumulated a battery of pans, enough for most culinary needs. My favorite copper pots and pans were willed to me by one of my aunts. They do take more care than the modern pans, but their attractiveness and usefulness far outweigh the few extra minutes it takes to keep them shiny.

COPPER PANS: Copper is one of the best heat conductors that exists. The advantages of a copper pot are that it quickly spreads the heat evenly throughout, and that the entire pan stays at the same temperature. Copper pots are lined with tin, silver, or sometimes today with stainless steel. This lining eliminates the possibility of a toxic chemical reaction, which can take place if food is allowed to stand for any length of time in contact with copper. Relining should be done by a specialist any time the copper begins to show through. A good copper pot, new or old, should be heavy, with an iron or brass handle. A heavier pan is more rugged, can stand a higher heat, and is steadier than a lighter utensil.

There was a time when a display of copperware was common in the kitchen of the average French home. A visit to the antique shops or *les brocanteurs* (the junk shops) in the back streets of Paris will attest to the former popularity of copperware. When I was growing up, an old copper pot could be picked up for a *sou* at one of these shops. Today, the prices they bring reflect the demand for them, and new copperware is being made all the time. People have discovered not only the good cooking qualities of copper pots, but their beauty when they hang, well polished, in a kitchen.

BAIN-MARIE: This double pan allows the cooking pan to be surrounded by water. It does for baking what a double boiler does when you are cooking on top of the stove. Using a *bain-marie* makes the baking slower and more even and improves the consistency of many delicate baked dishes. A *bain-marie* may be purchased, but any combination of pans will do. In the old days in Paris, our little apartment stove, *la Cuisinière,* had a basin built into the side, always ready with heated water for the gentle preparation of custards and the warming of sauces.

DUTCH OVEN: This is a heavy pot with handles on both sides, usually of enamelware or heavy stainless steel. Dutch ovens come in various sizes; my largest one is a 6-quart pot. They are particularly good for stews, soups, pot roasts, or poaching.

FRYING VESSEL: This can be an electric deep fryer or any pan fitted with a wire basket with a 4-quart capacity. It should have opposing handles for easy lifting and a cover into which the basket fits for draining the food after frying. A large electric skillet can also be useful for frying.

CRÊPE PAN: A good, heavy cast-iron frying pan, 5 inches in diameter across the cooking surface, is the best utensil for making dessert *crêpes*. In France, these frying pans are made with gently sloping, not perpendicular, sides. These make it somewhat easier to flip the *crêpes*, or even to turn them with a spatula. Although any size frying pan can be used, the batter should cover the bottom of the pan to ensure a symmetrical shape. Larger *crêpes* are made in a larger pan.

Inventions Commodes

HANDY DEVICES

SALAD BASKET: Beware when you are strolling through residential sections of Paris during mealtime hours! From balconies above the street and inner courtyards come little showers as homemakers step outside to shake their salad baskets. The salad basket is an adjustable, collapsible wire basket with flexible handles, made for rinsing and drying salad greens. Place the washed greens in the basket, fold the wire cover over the top, and on sunny days, step outside your kitchen door and swirl and twirl your basket round and round. It's a good way to get a little fresh air and exercise, and to get a look at the world if you've been feeling pent up. On rainy or less energetic days, hang the salad basket on a hook over the sink or rest it on the brim of a large bowl, and allow the water to drain off. Although there are many new devices to remove water from salad greens, I still prefer the salad basket.

STEAMETTE: A simple, basket-like device, the steamette is made of small, adjustable pierced metal pieces set on legs, which allow whatever is being cooked to steam above water level. Since I discovered the steamette many years ago, I wouldn't be without one. It helps produce fine steamed vegetables and is well worth the purchase price. I particularly like it for steaming potatoes.

Les Joujoux de la Ménagère

TOYS OF THE HOMEMAKER

PASTRY BRUSHES: I use two kinds of brushes for basting and glazing, but neither of them is the bristle type sold in the United States as a pastry brush. For basting meats and poultry, a flat 2-

inch camel's-hair brush, found in any art supply store, is excellent. For glazing pastries, a goose quill works best. The smooth feathers are a pleasure to work with. Either kind should be cared for like any expensive artist's brush: Rinse it well in hot water, then soak it in hot soapy water. Finally, rinse it again under hot running water, shake it, and straighten the hairs or feathers gently with your fingers. Pat dry and store, handle or stem down, in a jar or glass.

DOUGH SCRAPER: *Le coupe-pâte* is a piece of heavy metal, usually about 4 by 5 inches, soldered to a pipe-like piece of the same metal on one side to form a comfortable handle. It is a most efficient implement for scraping every last particle of dough from a working surface.

DOUGH PINCHER: *Le pince-pâte* is an over-sized pair of tweezers made especially for pinching the edges of dough on tarts or pies to give them a professional look. This job may also be accomplished with a fork or a knife handle.

PASTRY BAGS: These are convenient devices for making decorations—tiny and delicate, large and elaborate—with everything from sweet icings to butter and mayonnaise. They are also excellent for shaping doughs, batters, and puréed foods and for filling pastries. Pastry bags are cloth bags which can be fitted with conical metal tips, either straight-edged or fluted. The tips control and shape the flow of their contents. Both tips and bags come in many sizes. My smallest bag measures 6 inches; my smallest tip is about the size of a pinhead at the point. My largest bag is almost 2 feet long; my largest tip 7/8 inch at the point. A bag 12 to 13 inches in length with a tip of 1/8 inch is fairly versatile. Bags now come lined with plastic for easier cleaning. Tips come with fittings called "couplers" that enable you to change sizes without having to empty the bag.

To Use a Pastry Bag: Fill the bag half to three-quarters full. Twist the top to close out air and seal. If you are right-handed, press the contents from the top of the bag with your right hand, holding and guiding the tip with your left. (Reverse if you are left-handed.)

After each use, clean both the bag and the tip thoroughly: Separate the parts, rinse, wash them with hot soapy water, and re-rinse, making sure that all the odor from the contents has disappeared. Dry before storing.

Pour Faire Travailler l'Imagination

TO INSPIRE YOUR IMAGINATION

Molds, molds, molds! My kitchen abounds in molds. There are *madeleine* molds and *charlotte* molds; *babas* molds and crown molds; *brioche* molds, *kugloff* molds and *petits-fours* molds. There are molds for ice cream and molds for pâtés. There are gigantic molds and tiny molds; plain and fancy molds—they inspire the imagination. By tradition, there is a particular shape for almost every pastry in France, but I will discuss only those specifically suggested for the recipes in this book.

PETITS-FOURS MOLDS: These are the smallest of molds. They come in the greatest variety of forms: round, oval, square or rectangular, heart-shaped, diamond-shaped, leaf-shaped, or triangular. They may be fluted or plain. The sides are no more than 1/4 to 1/2 inch high. They are used to bake a variety of fancy cakes and cookies.

BABAS MOLDS: These are cylindrical molds about 2 1/2 inches high and 2 1/2 inches in diameter, tapering outward slightly toward the top. Their name comes from the little rum cakes, *Babas*, which traditionally are made in them. They are also good for making individual servings of soufflés, timbales, poached eggs, rice, aspics, or molded ice cream.

CHARLOTTE MOLD: This most versatile of molds comes in many sizes. It is round, with high straight sides, double handles and a cover, all of heavy metal. The name comes from the dessert which

is made traditionally in it—a blend of lady fingers and cream molded together. It is also an excellent mold for soufflés, baked custard, rice cake, puddings, and moussaka.

CROWN MOLD: This is a low, circular mold with a hollow center. It can be either plain or fluted. It is also called a ring or *savarin* mold. The dough for *Babas,* when baked in this shape, takes on the name *Savarin.* It is a good, all-purpose mold for gelatin dishes, rice rings, sponge cakes, and other similar dishes.

TART PAN: The traditional French tart pan is tin, with perpendicular sides 3/4 to 1 1/4 inch high and a detachable bottom. It comes in various diameters. Because of the detachable bottom, the tart can be easily pushed from the pan after it is baked, and the fluted sides give the tart an attractive appearance when it is brought to the table. An American tin or pyrex pie pan of the same dimensions can always be substituted in a tart recipe. There are also available glazed earthenware tart pans which are excellent for baking. They have the same straight, fluted sides, but no detachable bottom. However, they are attractive enough to be brought to the table right from the oven.

Outils Spéciaux

SPECIALTY TOOLS

FISH KNIFE AND FORK: These are used much more generally in Europe than in America, and are certainly unnecessary as a special purchase. However, it might be useful to know that they exist, just in case you are ever confronted with them. I still use them in my home. They differ in shape from the traditional dinner utensils: The knife has a broad blade with a pointed tip and a handle that is longer than the blade. The fork sometimes has a broader, flattened first tine, with a slit at the tip.

OYSTER KNIFE: The oyster knife has a thick handle which fits the palm of the hand and a short, pointed, double-edged blade. The better ones have a circular shield between the blade and the handle which protects the hand from the sharp edge of the shell. It is used by inserting the blade between the shells of the oyster at the muscular hinge and gently but firmly working it around to sever the muscles.

OYSTER FORK: The traditional oyster fork is a short-handled, three-pronged fork with the outer prongs wider than the center one. It is used also for clams and shrimp when they are served as appetizers.

FRUIT KNIFE AND FORK: These are handy extra utensils to own if you serve fresh fruit often for dessert, especially for company. The knife looks much nicer on the table than a kitchen paring knife or a steak knife. They have dainty pointed blades and usually come with decorative handles, perhaps ivory, mother-of-pearl, or fancy wood. The matching forks are small, narrow, and three-pronged. They are also used to eat cheese in a formal meal.

MENU I

Quoi Faire pour Vendredi?
WHAT TO COOK FRIDAY?

Potage Cressonnière
WATERCRESS SOUP

Filets de Poisson Frais Grillés Denise
FRESH BROILED FISH FILLETS WITH BUTTER AND BREAD CRUMBS

Carottes Poêlées
SAUTEED GRATED CARROTS WITH GINGER

Salade Verte
GREEN SALAD

Compote aux Trois Fruits
COMPOTE OF RHUBARB, CHERRIES, AND BANANAS

Pouilly-Fuissé

THIS meal is an easy one, perfect for a busy day and attractive enough for a company dinner. One of its advantages is that several of the courses can be prepared ahead, and last-minute preparation is minimal: Just a few minutes under the broiler will produce fillets cooked *à point* (to perfection). The fish should be very fresh; serve it the day it is caught, if possible.

If you would like to serve a green salad after the main dish, in the French manner, you might try the chicory salad on page 44 or escarole salad, page 148.

RECOMMENDED WINE: For accompaniment, serve a dry, chilled white wine. The fresh, fruity, dry aristocrat Mâconnais from southern Burgundy, Pouilly-Fuissé, would be admirable.

ORDER OF PREPARATION: The compote and the soup may be prepared several days in advance. You can grate the carrots ahead, too, and store them, covered, in the refrigerator until needed. Finish the carrots and prepare the fish just before serving.

Potage Cressonnière

WATERCRESS SOUP

Potage Cressonnière is a pale green purée of potatoes and watercress, enriched with butter and cream. It is simple to prepare and delicious served hot or cold.

This recipe will provide 4 generous servings. The soup may be refrigerated or frozen before the cream is added.

INGREDIENTS

3 *cups cubed potatoes (about* 1 *pound)*
1 *bunch watercress (about 4 cups coarsely chopped and loosely packed)*
5 *cups cold water*
1 *tablespoon coarse salt, or 1/2 tablespoon table salt*
2 *tablespoons whipped sweet butter*

2 *tablespoons heavy cream per serving*

METHOD

Wash, peel, and cube potatoes. Wash watercress in several

changes of cold water and drain. Reserve 4 sprigs for garnish.*
Chop remainder coarsely.

Combine water, cubed potatoes, and salt in 3- to 5-quart pot.
Cover and bring to a boil over high heat. Reduce heat and simmer
gently 15 to 20 minutes until potato cube can be pierced easily with
a knife point. Add chopped watercress, cover pot, and cook 5
minutes longer. Drain well in colander, reserving the water.

Purée potatoes and watercress. A food mill, blender, ricer,
food processor, or any other implement that will purée the vegetables may be used. Add a small amount of the hot water to facilitate
the process. Return the remainder of the reserved water and the
purée to the cooking pot. Cover, bring to boil, and simmer 10
minutes. Stir occasionally. Add salt if necessary. Stir in butter, 1
tablespoon at a time. (Adding butter slowly will give you a better
control of the texture.) Once butter is added, do not allow soup
to boil.

TO SERVE: Measure 2 tablespoons of cream per soup bowl.
(If soup is to be presented in a tureen, pour all the cream into it.)
Add soup mixture gradually, stirring with a small whisk or fork.
Ladle into bowls. Garnish each portion with a sprig of blanched
or fresh watercress. The soup thickens as it stands. If it is to be
eaten cold, dilute it by adding a bit more cream.

Filets de Poisson Frais Grillés Denise

FRESH BROILED FISH FILLETS
WITH BUTTER AND BREAD CRUMBS

Presented on individual sizzler platters and garnished with
fresh chopped herbs and lemon wedges, these fillets make a hand-
some and delicious entrée that requires little preparation time. The
fish can also be prepared in a large broiling pan and transferred
to dinner plates.

This recipe is for 4 servings.

*TO BLANCH: The reserved watercress sprigs can be blanched to give
them a more intense color and keep them fresher longer. Blanched sprigs
can be stored in the refrigerator for several days. In a 2-cup saucepan,
bring 1 cup water to full boil. Immerse watercress. Return water to full
boil without cover, and time 30 seconds. Drain watercress in colander and
place under cold running water. Reserve.

INGREDIENTS

2 *teaspoons unsalted butter*
4 *fresh fillets (1/4 to 1/2 pound each)**
1/2 *teaspoon salt*
4 *tablespoons melted butter*
2 *tablespoons unseasoned bread crumbs*

4 *tablespoons fresh chopped parsley or 4 tablespoons mixed*
    parsley, chives, and mint, all fresh and chopped fine
fresh lemons

USEFUL UTENSIL: *Sizzler platters*

METHOD

Rub each sizzler platter with 1/2 teaspoon butter. Pat fillets with paper toweling to remove moisture. Place on platters and salt lightly. Coat each fillet with 1 tablespoon melted butter and sprinkle with 1/2 tablespoon bread crumbs. (When broiling in a large pan, use 2 teaspoons butter for the pan; 1 tablespoon melted butter for coating each fillet. Be sure the pan is large enough and that the fillets are not crowded.)

Fillets may now be covered with storage wrap and refrigerated until ready to broil.

A few minutes before you are ready to serve, preheat your broiler. Place fish on rack in broiler, 6 inches below flame. Broil only on one side. If your oven is too small to accommodate the platters, broil them in batches. The first batch can be kept warm on top of the stove, covered with foil.

For fillets of flounder, bluefish, or trout, broiling time will be no more than 5 minutes. The other varieties may require 1 or 2 minutes more, depending on their thickness. The surface should be medium to golden brown when done.

TO SERVE: Place each sizzler platter on its wooden board. Sprinkle with chopped herbs and garnish with lemon wedges. For a dramatic effect, garnish with a serrated lemon half.** Squeeze lemon over the fish before eating. When serving from a broiler pan, place each fillet on a heated dinner plate and garnish.

*Flounder, cod, haddock, halibut, bluefish, trout, swordfish, or salmon steak may be used.

****TO SERRATE THE EDGES OF LEMON HALVES:** With a small sharp kitchen knife, pierce the center of each lemon at alternate angles until the fruit is cut in half. When separated, each half will have a sawtoothed edge.

Carottes Poêlées

SAUTÉED GRATED CARROTS WITH GINGER

A simple, appetizing accompaniment to many dishes, grated carrots have a distinctive texture and character. Once grated, they take only a few minutes to sauté.

This recipe serves 4. For 6, increase carrots to 2 pounds, use 12 tablespoons clarified butter, and adjust seasoning. For more than 6 people, make in batches.

NOTE: This recipe is also delicious made with fresh grated zucchini. It can be prepared with or without the ginger.

INGREDIENTS

1 1/2 *pounds carrots (enough to make 4 cups, grated)*
8 *tablespoons clarified butter**
3/4 *teaspoon table salt (scant)*
4 *turns of white pepper mill, medium grind*
3/4 *teaspoon grated fresh ginger*

METHOD

Peel carrots; trim the root ends. Carrots may be grated with an old-fashioned hand grater (using side with larger holes), with a hand-operated mouli grater, with a food processor fitted with the grating disc, or with any other device that will cut the vegetables into thin strips, 1 1/2 to 2 inches in length.

Heat butter in a 10- to 12-inch frying pan over high heat for 3 minutes. Butter should "sing" when the grated carrots are added. Shake pan well and stir with wooden spoon or roasting fork (a fork is useful for separating the carrots). After 3 minutes sprinkle with salt, pepper, and grated ginger and mix well. Carrots should be slightly crunchy.

TO SERVE: When you are dining informally, place on platter or dish with the broiled fish. For a more formal dinner, serve on a small heated plate as a separate course after the fish.

*To clarify butter, see page 11.

Compote aux Trois Fruits

COMPOTE OF RHUBARB, CHERRIES, AND BANANAS

Fruit compote is served for dessert in most French homes at least once a week. When fruit is available in great variety, a mixed compote may be served every day. A good way to use overripe or surplus fruit, it is a colorful and healthful way to end a meal.

This recipe serves 4. It may be made ahead and stored in the refrigerator.

INGREDIENTS

1 *pound rhubarb stalks*
1/2 *pound cherries (about 2 cups)*
2 *medium-size, unripe bananas*
1 *tablespoon lemon juice*
1/2 *cup granulated sugar*

METHOD

When buying rhubarb, look for plump, rosy stalks that are free of brown spots. Cut off and discard the leaves, which are inedible. Remove both ends of the stalks and any dark spots, but do not peel the skin, as it enhances the compote's color. Wash in several changes of cold water. Cut stalks in 2- to 3-inch sections and split each section lengthwise into 2 to 4 strips. You should have about 4 cups.

Pie cherries are better than black ones for this recipe, if they are available. Remove cherry stems, but leave pits. (Cooked cherries are tastier when pits are not removed. Just make sure to warn your family and guests!) Wash cherries.

Peel bananas, cut crosswise into 1/2-inch slices, and sprinkle with lemon juice.

Combine fruits and sugar in a 6- to 8-cup saucepan. Cover, bring to boiling point over medium heat, and simmer 7 to 8 minutes, until rhubarb is very soft.

TO SERVE: Spoon fruits and syrup into individual sherbet glasses or dessert dishes, or into a shallow crystal bowl. Serve chilled or lukewarm.

MENU II

À La Fortune du Pot
TAKING POT LUCK

Saumon en Conserve à la Mayonnaise
SALMON WITH HOMEMADE MAYONNAISE

Hachis Parmentier
CHOPPED BEEF WITH POTATOES AND ONIONS

Salade de Chicorée
CHICORY SALAD

Crapiaud du Morvan
PAN-FRIED APPLE RUM CAKE

Mineral Water

T HE unexpected arrival of friends need not precipitate a crisis. With this menu, prepared from items common to most larders, it is possible to prepare a pleasant, informal meal on very short notice.

Though the French pantry does not stock many canned goods, salmon, tuna, and *petits pois extra fins* are the exceptions; they are good to have on hand for an emergency. Served as I suggest here— flaked and then tossed with vinegar, shallots, and homemade mayonnaise—salmon changes from a simple canned food into a delectable dish.

The French usually prepare *Hachis Parmentier* with leftover beef and boiled potatoes. However, in my version, I start from scratch. (The English word "hash," incidentally, is derived from the French "*hachis*"; "*parmentier*" simply means that potatoes are one of the ingredients.)

I like to serve a chicory salad with the *Hachis*, and for dessert, a pan-fried apple rum cake prepared from a traditional *recette paysanne* (country recipe).

RECOMMENDED BEVERAGE: Since the meal is an impromptu one, it would be quite appropriate to serve a chilled mineral water: chic, sparkling Perrier, old-time Vichy, or domestic Poland Spring.

ORDER OF PREPARATION: Prepare the appetizer in advance if you wish, and refrigerate. Assemble the *Hachis* ahead so it will be ready for baking just before dinner. Mix the salad dressing, and wash and chill the chicory. The salad, of course, should be tossed at the last minute. The dessert, too, may be cooked ahead and kept warm.

Saumon en Conserve à la Mayonnaise

SALMON WITH HOMEMADE MAYONNAISE

Fresh or canned, salmon is a delicacy. I like to keep some on hand for company or for a family treat. With homemade mayonnaise, it makes an *hors-d'oeuvre appétissant*.

The recipe will serve 4.

HOMEMADE MAYONNAISE

A few points to remember for successful mayonnaise: The egg yolks and the oil must be at room temperature. The oil should be added *very slowly* at first, and the beating should be vigorous.*

This recipe will make 1/2 cup of mayonnaise, enough for a 1-pound can of salmon, which will serve 4 people amply as an appetizer.

INGREDIENTS

1 *egg yolk*
1/2 *teaspoon Dijon mustard*
1/8 *teaspoon table salt (scant)*
2 *turns of black pepper mill, medium grind*
1/2 *cup salad oil*
1/4 *teaspoon wine vinegar*
1/2 *teaspoon fresh lemon juice*

METHOD

In a 1-cup bowl combine egg yolk, mustard, salt, and pepper. Beat vigorously with a wire whisk, adding oil drop by drop. When the mixture thickens, beat in the vinegar. Continue beating, adding oil more freely. When all the oil has been used up, stir in lemon juice.

*If mayonnaise curdles, it is because too much oil was poured in at once in the beginning or, on rare occasions, because the eggs were too old. To correct, break an egg yolk in another mixing bowl and slowly beat curdled mayonnaise and remaining oil into it.

SALMON MIXTURE

INGREDIENTS

1 *can salmon (about 1 pound)*
2 *teaspoons wine vinegar*
2 *teaspoons chopped shallots*
6 *tablespoons homemade mayonnaise*
10 *sprigs fresh parsley, chopped*

METHOD

Open the can of salmon and discard the liquid. Transfer the fish to a medium-size bowl, flake it, and blend in the vinegar and shallots. Blend in the mayonnaise a tablespoon at a time.

TO SERVE: Arrange attractively in a shallow serving dish (on a bed of lettuce leaves if you wish), or divide portions on individual salad plates or small shallow dishes. Sprinkle with fresh chopped parsley. A fish fork would be appropriate for this course.

Hachis Parmentier

CHOPPED BEEF WITH POTATOES AND ONIONS

I am presuming that most households usually have a few potatoes and onions and some chopped beef on hand. If you do, you can provide unexpected visitors with a simple and substantial meal in a few minutes. *Un plat simple, mais très bon!*
These ingredients will make 4 servings.

INGREDIENTS

1 *pound all-purpose potatoes (3 to 4 medium-sized potatoes)*
2 *cups cold water*
1/2 *tablespoon coarse salt*

1/2 *pound yellow onions (2 or 3 medium onions)*
6 *tablespoons clarified butter*
1 *pound lean chopped beef*
3/4 *teaspoon table salt*

2 *pats butter (about 1 tablespoon)*

USEFUL UTENSILS: *Potato masher, 4-cup casserole*

METHOD

Peel potatoes and cut in 1-inch cubes. Put cold water and potato cubes in a 3- to 4-quart pot. Add salt, cover pot, and bring to boiling point over moderate heat. Boil 15 to 20 minutes. Test for softness by inserting blade of a small knife into a cube.

Pour potatoes into a colander and drain off water. Return them to pot and place over low heat. Using a potato masher, mash a small portion at a time. Set mashed potatoes to one side of pan. (This method will keep them light and fluffy.) When all are mashed, remove from heat.

While potatoes are boiling, peel onions, cut in thin slices crosswise, and loosen them into rings. Cut each ring in half.

Preheat oven to 400° F.

Spoon clarified butter into a 10- to 12-inch frying pan and place over high heat. When butter is very hot, add onions, shake pan well, stir well, and sauté for 10 minutes over medium heat. Mix raw meat into onion–butter combination. Sprinkle with salt and blend thoroughly. Combine with mashed potatoes and mix well.

Coat bottom and sides of a 4-cup casserole with 1 pat of butter. Transfer the *Hachis Parmentier* to the casserole and smooth surface with a rubber spatula. Smear the remaining pat of butter on a piece of waxed paper cut to fit the baking dish. Cover the *Hachis* with the paper (buttered side down) to keep the mixture from drying. At this point *Hachis* may be set aside to be baked later.

Bake 20 minutes if you prefer rare meat, or 30 minutes for medium-rare.

TO SERVE: Spoon portions onto dinner plates.

Though salad is usually served after the main dish, I often serve greens with the *Hachis*. The contrast of texture and temperature makes this a pleasant combination in the style of the *Nouvelle Cuisine*.

Salade de Chicorée

CHICORY SALAD

Chicory, or curly endive, as it is more properly called, grows in a loose head of narrow leaves which curl at the edges. It is a refreshing green with a slightly bitter taste, and makes a particularly good salad to serve with the *Hachis Parmentier.*

This recipe makes 4 servings.

INGREDIENTS

1/2 to 3/4 pound of chicory (a medium-sized head)
1/2 teaspoon chopped garlic
1 scant teaspoon table salt
3 turns of black pepper mill, medium grind
2 tablespoons red wine vinegar
4 tablespoons salad oil

heel or crust from a loaf of French bread (optional)

METHOD

Cut core from chicory; separate leaves and discard imperfect ones; remove any dark spots. Wash in several changes of cold water until clean of all dirt and sand. Drain in salad basket; shake well. Place in clean linen towel and pat dry.

Place all ingredients for dressing in salad bowl in the order listed; stir well.

If desired, in place of the 1/2 teaspoon of chopped garlic, add a *croûton aillé.* This is a heel of French bread rubbed in garlic, then immersed in the dressing. (*Croûton* means "heel of bread" in French.) Cut it into 4 pieces, so that everyone may have a bit with the salad. Or slice long pieces of crust from a loaf of French bread, rub on garlic, and immerse in dressing. The croûton will be saturated with the flavors of the dressing—a tasty change from dry American croûtons.

Place salad utensils in bowl; lay greens on them. Refrigerate until ready to serve.

TO SERVE: Toss well. Since this is an informal meal, I would serve the salad on the same plate with the *Hachis.* For a more formal meal, the salad would be served on a separate plate after the main course.

Crapiaud du Morvan

PAN-FRIED APPLE RUM CAKE

Whenever one of my childhood friends entertained unexpected company (including me), she took out flour, sugar, milk, and apples to prepare her *Crapiaud.* Naturally, I stayed in the kitchen, watching her every step. The recipe was an old one from Morvan, in central France, and had been handed down from generation to generation in her family. *Crapiaud,* in colloquial French, literally means "little toad," but, as you will see, this dessert is far from tiny.

The recipe yields 4 to 6 large servings or 8 small ones. It can be cooking while the main course and salad are being eaten, or prepared ahead of time and kept warm in a slow oven or reheated.

INGREDIENTS

3/4 *cup all-purpose flour*
2 *eggs (jumbo, extra large, or large), slightly beaten with a*
  fork
1/3 *cup sugar (heaping), beaten lightly with 1/2 cup milk*
2 *tablespoons dark rum*
1 1/3 *to* 1 2/3 *cups well-packed apple slices (about 1/2*
  *pound)**

4 *tablespoons salad oil***
confectioners' sugar

USEFUL UTENSIL: 10-*inch frying pan, preferably non-stick*

METHOD

Put flour in a 2-quart mixing bowl. Make a hole in the center and add the lightly beaten eggs and the milk–sugar mixture. Stir well with wooden spoon or wire whisk. Mix in rum, 1 tablespoon at a time.

Peel, core, and slice apples. Add to batter and blend well.

This batter can be used at once or prepared many hours ahead of time and left at room temperature.

When ready to cook, heat half the oil in a 10-inch frying pan, swirling it to make sure it completely coats pan. When oil starts smoking, pour the batter in and reduce heat. Let the cake cook over medium-low to medium heat for 15 to 20 minutes, or until the underside is a dark golden brown. Shake the pan frequently while the batter is cooking to make sure it does not stick, or loosen it with a spatula. When the top appears to have set and the underside is well browned, invert the *Crapiaud* onto a plate large enough to hold it. Add the remaining oil to the frying pan, heat for a few seconds, and slide the cake back into the pan, uncooked side down. Cook 10 to 15 minutes over a medium flame until the second side is golden brown. Make sure to shake the pan from time to time and lift the pancake with a spatula to prevent sticking.

TO SERVE: Transfer the *Crapiaud* to a serving platter and sprinkle with confectioners' sugar. (Do this just before serving, otherwise the sugar dissolves.) Slice it into wedges. It can be eaten hot, warm, or cold; but hot or warm it is the most *savoureux*.

*Use Baldwin, Cortland, or another cooking variety.
**If a non-stick pan is used, reduce to 2 tablespoons.

MENU III

Dînons Légèrement
A LIGHT SUPPER

Potage Velouté Anna
ANNA'S VELVETY SOUP

Soufflé au Fromage
SWISS CHEESE SOUFFLÉ

Haricots Verts Sautés
GREEN BEANS WITH GARLIC AND PARSLEY

Salade Verte
GREEN SALAD

Oranges Rafraîchies au Kirsch
ORANGE SLICES IN KIRSCH

Rosé d'Anjou or Gewürztraminer

HERE is a delightfully light but substantial supper: soup, cheese soufflé, sautéed beans, and orange slices in Kirsch. A welcome change from heavier fare, it is a fine menu for the Lenten season and may be used, too, by those observing dietary laws. A chicory salad (page 44) could be served with this menu or, for a special treat, try endive and beet salad (page 78).

The soufflé is a challenge, but one easily surmounted if the directions are followed carefully.

RECOMMENDED WINE: With the soufflé, a light, mellow wine is desirable—either a semi-dry white or a rosé. My preference for a rosé is a Rosé d'Anjou, a fresh, light nectar from the province of Anjou in the Loire Valley. A white wine suited to this menu would be Gewürztraminer, fruity and rich in bouquet, from the Alsatian vineyards on the eastern slopes of the Vosges Mountains along the Rhine.

ORDER OF PREPARATION: For efficiency in preparation, make the dessert early enough so that the flavors have time to blend; next prepare the beans for the soup, and of course, whip up the soufflé last. The final sautéing of the beans should be done while the soufflé is baking, and the salad should be tossed at the last minute.

Potage Velouté Anna

ANNA'S VELVETY SOUP

This is one of my mother's creations; it was my favorite soup when I was a child. It pleased not only my taste but my early sense of economy as well. Since the vegetable water becomes the soup broth, two dishes are started at once in preparing the vegetable— a saving of both time and vitamins.

Unlike many Americans, the French enjoy tapioca and use it frequently. In fact, it is an important ingredient in many soups, sauces, and desserts of classic French cuisine. Prepared properly, tapioca will not lump, and will give an exquisite texture to your soup.

This soup will serve 4.

INGREDIENTS

1 1/2 *pounds green beans*
6 *cups cold water*
1 *tablespoon coarse salt*
6 *tablespoons tapioca**

4 *tablespoons heavy or all-purpose cream*

USEFUL UTENSIL: *Pressure cooker***

METHOD

Remove tips and strings from the beans. Wash them thoroughly under running water. Slit them lengthwise between string grooves to make them more like the narrow French bean.

Place beans, water, and salt in pressure cooker. Cook under 15 pounds pressure for 1 minute. Remove from heat and reduce pressure immediately by placing pan under cold running water.

Remove beans from water, place in colander, and let drain. Set aside until ready to sauté for vegetable course.

Return cooker to heat, replace cover loosely, and bring bean water to a boil. There will be bean kernels in the water which will add to the flavor and goodness of the soup.

When boiling, add tapioca. To ensure even distribution and no lumping, pour in tapioca from a height of 5 to 6 inches above pot, stirring constantly with a wire whisk. (The whisk will produce a smoother texture than a wooden spoon.) As soon as tapioca thickens (5 to 20 minutes), soup is done.

If you have prepared it before the rest of the menu, the soup may now be set aside and reheated before serving.

TO SERVE: Place 1 tablespoon of cream in each soup bowl. Stir with fork as you add soup. (A fork or a small wire whisk does a better job than a spoon mixing this particular combination.) If a tureen is used, place the full quantity of cream in tureen and add soup gradually, stirring briskly with wire whisk. Serve at once.

*I prefer to use imported small pearl tapioca, available in some supermarkets. If you cannot find it, minute tapioca is an acceptable substitute, but you should use only 4 tablespoons

**Because I want the bean water concentrated in order to give a rich flavor to the soup, I prefer to use a pressure cooker for this recipe. When I am cooking the beans simply for a vegetable, however, I use the method given on page 52.

Soufflé au Fromage

SWISS CHEESE SOUFFLÉ

Few dishes are more awe-inspiring than a golden puffy soufflé right out of the oven. And that is just when it should delight both eyes and palate—right out of the oven. Be sure your guests are already seated and waiting expectantly. *Never* let a soufflé wait for the guests!

For a light moist soufflé this is a virtually fool-proof recipe. I have used it for years.

The recipe will serve 4 persons.

INGREDIENTS

1 *pat unsalted butter*
6 *to* 12 *tablespoons grated Swiss cheese (quantity depends upon individual preference)**
4 *tablespoons clarified butter*
4 *tablespoons flour*
1 *cup milk*
1/2 *teaspoon table salt*
1/8 *teaspoon white pepper*
1/4 *teaspoon nutmeg*

4 *egg yolks*
3 *egg whites*

USEFUL UTENSILS: *A* 6 × 3*-inch Pyrex dish, a* 3*-cup Charlotte mold, or a* 5 1/2*-cup porcelain soufflé mold***

METHOD

There are three keys to a successful soufflé: a smooth thick white sauce, stiff egg whites, and an accurately preheated oven. If you have any doubts about your oven temperature, check it with an oven thermometer.

*Swiss cheese should be bought unsliced for grating.
**The 3-cup Charlotte mold will give the soufflé a more dramatic look, because it will rise above the rim.

Preheat oven to 350° F.

Prepare bottom and sides of mold by coating lightly and uniformly with butter pat and 1 tablespoon of grated cheese.

Heat clarified butter in a 1-quart saucepan. Gradually add flour, stirring constantly with a wire whisk until smoothly blended. Allow flour–butter mixture to cook at medium heat for 1 minute. This will cause the *roux* to moisten and swell.

Now add milk gradually, whisking constantly. Bring to boiling point, lower heat, and cook gently for 2 minutes. A thick white sauce should result. Remove saucepan from heat. Stir in salt, pepper, and nutmeg.

This completes the first step for a successful soufflé.

Now separate the eggs. Eggs separate easier when they are cold, so this operation should be performed when they are first taken from the refrigerator. The whites will rise better, however, when warm, so allow them to reach room temperature before beating.

Beat egg yolks lightly with a fork and mix into white sauce rapidly so that they will not curdle. Stir in 4 to 10 tablespoons of cheese, one at a time, depending upon flavor desired. The egg mixture can be left at room temperature at this point until you are ready to complete your soufflé.

Next, beat egg whites until stiff (about 2 minutes).

Add 1/3 of the whites to sauce, folding in carefully. The object of folding is not to snuff out the air that you have beaten into the egg whites, so you have to be gentle. With a rubber spatula, using a cutting motion, bring sauce from the bottom and fold gently over whites. Continue to cut from bottom to top in this way until whites disappear. Add remaining whites in 2 more batches and repeat folding process.

Pour mixture into the prepared mold or pan and sprinkle top with remaining cheese. Bake in center of oven 35 to 40 minutes. Do not open oven door during baking period, as this will cause soufflé to fall.

After 35 minutes, soufflé can be tested. It is done when testing needle comes out dry. The top of the soufflé should be a nice golden brown, and should feel rather firm to the touch. Do not overbake. It is better to have the center moist and runny than too dry.

TO SERVE: A soufflé should be served directly from the oven to waiting guests in its own baking dish. Spoon from the middle first to delay the falling process.

To savor this delicate, spongy, hot dish fully, it should be served without accompaniment.

Haricots Verts Sautés

GREEN BEANS WITH GARLIC AND PARSLEY

For me, the task of picking out green beans is a long process, and one which sometimes distresses my fellow shoppers. I buy beans only at vegetable stands or supermarkets where they are sold in bulk. I select them one by one, searching out the thinnest ones, and making sure that the tips are unbroken and the beans are dark in color and free of spots.

This recipe will usually serve 4. However, if you make it with beans fresh from your garden, you'd better make extra.

BOILING THE BEANS

INGREDIENTS

6 *quarts cold water*
3 *tablespoons coarse salt or* 1 1/2 *tablespoons table salt*
1 1/2 *pounds green beans*

USEFUL UTENSIL: 8- *to* 10-*quart pot*

METHOD

Remove tips and strings from beans. Wash thoroughly under running water. Slit them lengthwise between string grooves to make them more like the narrow French bean.

Bring salted water to a vigorous boil. I use this quantity of water when cooking beans because I feel that they retain their color and crisp texture better. With so much water, the beans can be boiled rapidly, uncovered.

Drop beans into boiling water. Do not cover. Test after 6 minutes. Beans should be firm but not hard. Remove at once from water. Place in colander to drain.

Beans can be set aside at this point until you are ready to sauté them.

SAUTÉING THE BEANS

INGREDIENTS

1 *medium garlic clove*
6 *to 8 parsley sprigs*

1 1/2 *pounds cooked green beans*

6 *tablespoons butter, salted or unsalted, cut into small cubes, at room temperature*
salt and pepper

USEFUL UTENSIL: 12-*inch skillet*

METHOD

Chop garlic and parsley together and reserve to sprinkle over beans when ready to serve.

Place large skillet over high heat. When a drop of water bounces off surface, pan is hot enough. Put in beans and shake skillet to remove all moisture, being careful not to burn beans. This will take 2 or 3 minutes.

Add butter, distributing evenly throughout pan. Continue to shake uncovered pan until butter is melted and beans are thoroughly heated. Turn heat to low. Salt and pepper to taste. *Caution:* If salted butter has been used for sautéing, little additional salt will be needed. Sprinkle on 3/4 of garlic–parsley mixture. Toss.

TO SERVE: If the French way of serving is to be followed, these beans should be eaten by themselves after the soufflé. Keep them covered over low heat until needed. Then place in hot serving dish. Sprinkle on remainder of garlic–parsley garnish. Serve at once.

Oranges Rafraîchies au Kirsch

ORANGE SLICES IN KIRSCH

This is a wonderfully refreshing dessert. It makes a light, colorful finish to any meal.

If the oranges are peeled, they will absorb the flavor of the Kirsch in an hour. If the rind is left on, however, they should be prepared at least 24 hours ahead, so that they will be flavorful and soft. They can be prepared up to a week in advance.

The recipe will serve 4.

INGREDIENTS

2 or 3 oranges
sugar
Kirsch (a white cherry brandy)

METHOD

Oranges may be used peeled or unpeeled. If you are using unpeeled oranges and would like them to have a serrated edge when sliced, cut out narrow strips of rind from top to bottom around the orange with a lemon stripper.

Slice oranges across sections to make rosettes. If oranges are peeled, they may be as thick as 1/4 inch; if unpeeled, they should be as thin as possible.

Place orange slices in a shallow bowl—one that will hold 3 or 4 slices per layer. Sprinkle each layer with 1 1/2 teaspoons of sugar and 1 tablespoon of Kirsch. Toss to mix well. Refrigerate.

TO SERVE: Serve 2 or 3 slices per person in a dessert dish, spooning juice over them. You can make this dessert even more colorful by adding a touch of bright green angelica (see page 358).

MENU IV

Menu de Gala: 1940–1944
A FESTIVE MENU FOR WARTIME

Salade de Tomates
TOMATO SALAD

Lapin Sauté à la Moutarde
RABBIT WITH MUSTARD SAUCE

Chou-Fleur Cuit à Point
CAULIFLOWER AL DENTE WITH PARSLEY

Salade Verte
GREEN SALAD

Poires Pochées au Sirop
POACHED PEARS IN VANILLA SYRUP

*Premières Côtes de Bordeaux or
Meursault*

DURING the war years in Paris, this simple menu was considered a real treat. The main course, rabbit sautéed in mustard, was my specialty and it is still a great joy for me to prepare. Here, cauliflower, simply cooked, is served along with it, rather than as a separate course. Fresh tomato salad whets the appetite and poached pears provide the finishing touch. If you feel the need for another course, watercress salad (page 178) would be an attractive addition.

RECOMMENDED WINE: A mellow white wine would go well throughout this meal: perhaps a white Premières Côtes de Bordeaux from the limestone slopes bordering the Garonne River; or a light, delicately bouqueted Meursault from the Côte de Beaune district of Burgundy.

ORDER OF PREPARATION: The dessert and the sautéing and simmering of the rabbit may be done in advance. The cauliflower and the tomato salad should be prepared just before serving.

Salade de Tomates

TOMATO SALAD

I will always remember one incident involving *Salade de Tomates*. At the close of each lecture series there is usually a party for which the students bring in one of the dishes they have learned to prepare. For one of these occasions a woman brought in this salad. When I teased her for not bringing something that required more involvement and skill, she replied: "But this dish is so very, very good!" The tomatoes, parsley, and onions had all been freshly picked from her own garden, carefully and attractively arranged on the serving platter. The story illustrates one of the principles I stress to my students: The simplest food prepared to perfection becomes gourmet fare.

Since this salad is so simple to prepare, it should not be made over half an hour before serving time. The tomatoes should be fully ripe, red, and firm. The salad will taste best when native tomatoes are in season.

The recipe will provide 4 servings.

INGREDIENTS

1 *pound fresh ripe tomatoes (about 4 medium tomatoes)*
1 *tablespoon red wine vinegar*
2 *tablespoons salad oil*
3 *teaspoons chopped shallots or white onion*
4 *heaping teaspoons chopped fresh parsley*
table salt
3 *to 4 turns of black pepper mill (medium grind)*

METHOD

Wash tomatoes in cold water; wipe dry. Cut into 1/8- to 1/4-inch slices. Arrange attractively in vegetable dish or on platter. Sprinkle on vinegar, oil, shallots, and parsley. Toss only when ready to serve, adding salt and pepper.

TO SERVE: Spoon onto salad plates; eat with knife and fork. Soak up the delectable dressing with crusty French bread.
Un plat qui ouvre vraiment l'appétit!

Lapin Sauté à la Moutarde

RABBIT WITH MUSTARD SAUCE

Had it not been for rabbit during the bleak days of the German occupation of Paris many of our meals would have been meatless and meager. Rabbit and cream were brought to us by friends from the country in exchange for shoes or other leather goods my father made for them. It not only contributed to our survival, but gave our meals a taste of luxury, for rabbit meat is a delicacy in wartime or peacetime.

This recipe will provide 4 substantial servings.

INGREDIENTS

2- to 3-*pound rabbit* *
8 *tablespoons clarified butter* **
salt and pepper
1 *cup hot water*
7 *tablespoons prepared Dijon mustard*

5 *tablespoons sour cream*
liver of rabbit, chopped raw
3 *teaspoons chopped shallots*
6 *sprigs parsley, chopped*
1/4 *teaspoon salt*
3 *turns of the black pepper mill (medium grind)*

3 *teaspoons chopped fresh or dried tarragon or 3 teaspoons chopped
    fresh parsley*

USEFUL UTENSIL: *Goose-feather pastry brush*

METHOD

Set aside rabbit liver.

Pat rabbit dry with paper towel.

Heat butter until it sings in a pan large enough to hold the
rabbit pieces without crowding. (A 12-inch frying pan is ideal.)
Sauté rabbit on each side until nicely brown, regulating heat as
necessary. Sprinkle with salt and pepper.

Cover and cook over low heat for 15 minutes. Add 1/2 cup
of hot water and simmer another 15 minutes.

Measure mustard into a small bowl and whip it with fork.
Gradually whip into it 3 tablespoons of juice from the simmering
rabbit.

Using a pastry brush, coat each piece of rabbit thoroughly with
mustard sauce. Cover and simmer gently another 15 minutes.

This brings the actual cooking time for the rabbit to 45 minutes. It should be done. Test by cutting a sliver of meat from one
of the legs. If it does not feel and taste tender, cook another 15
minutes.

Remove rabbit from pan to serving platter and place in a slow
oven to keep hot.

---

*Rabbit can usually be found fresh or frozen in today's supermarkets,
cut up like chicken. (If you buy a frozen one, defrost it completely by
placing in refrigerator for a day before cooking.)

**If a very large pan is used, more butter may be needed.

NOW DEGLAZE COOKING PAN: Add the remaining 1/2 cup of hot water, raise heat to high, and stir with whisk for about 30 seconds. Turn heat to low.

Place sour cream in a small bowl; whisk into it 3 to 4 table-spoons of sauce from pan. Pour cream mixture into deglazed pan, stirring vigorously with whisk.

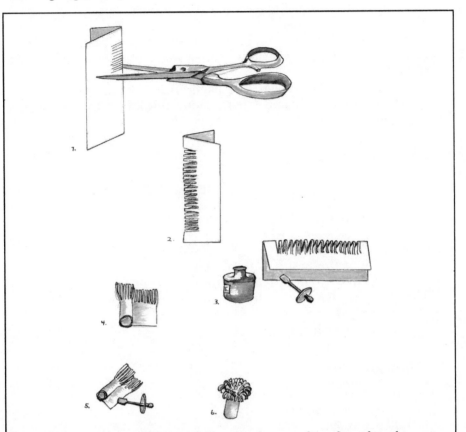

MAKING PAPER FRILLS: Frills may be purchased under the name "paper pants" or "paper frills" in stores that sell specialty foods. Or you can make them yourself easily out of a sheet of plain white paper, 11 inches long by 6 inches wide. Fold it in half lengthwise and proceed as follows:

1) With scissors, cut inward 2 to 3 inches deep along the fold every 1/8 inch, as shown at the top of the illustration.

2) Open and fold sheet in opposite direction; fluff up cut end.

3) Paste solid edges together.

4) Roll into cylinder of appropriate size to fit over bone.

5) Paste end to hold shape.

6) Slit ends may now be cut along fold and the opened ends curled by pulling across the blade of a scissor if desired.

Return rabbit to pan. Sprinkle on liver, shallots, and parsley, all finely chopped; add salt and pepper. Cover and heat through for about 5 minutes. This will be sufficient time to cook the finely chopped liver. Taste and correct seasoning if necessary.

This dish may be prepared in advance. Reheat in a very slow oven or in a double boiler. Watch carefully, or the sauce will curdle. Turn and baste often. Reheating will take over an hour.

TO SERVE: Transfer rabbit to heated serving platter.* Spoon sauce over rabbit. (There will be only a small amount.) Sprinkle on tarragon or parsley.

Put paper frills on legs (see page 59). Serve at once.

See if your family and friends don't think that this is the best four-legged chicken they have ever eaten!

Chou-Fleur Cuit à Point

CAULIFLOWER AL DENTE WITH PARSLEY

Sometimes the best way to prepare a food is the simplest way. This is particularly true when you are preparing an accompaniment for a rich or involved dish. Here is such a recipe: simply cauliflower, perfectly cooked and tossed in butter.

The recipe will serve 4.

INGREDIENTS

1 *cauliflower head of about 2 pounds or 2 smaller ones of equivalent weight***
3 *quarts water*
2 *tablespoons coarse salt or 1 tablespoon table salt*
2 *tablespoons butter at room temperature*

2 *teaspoons chopped fresh parsley*

METHOD

Trim off leaves; break cauliflower into clusters.

Cut stems of each cluster, leaving about 1/4 inch. Slit a cross into the base of each stem so that heat will more easily penetrate it while cooking.

*To warm a silver dish, pour boiling water over it; wipe dry.
**When purchasing, look for a white, firm head, free of spots.

Wash clusters in a pan of cold water, changing water at least three times.

Pour water into a 5- to 6-quart cooking pot, add salt, and bring to a rolling boil, covered. Drop in cauliflower.

When water has returned to a roaring boil, uncovered, time for exactly 5 minutes, leaving the heat as high as possible.

Pour off all water; add butter in small pieces; shake pan to toss. Serve at once.*

TO SERVE: Place cauliflower in a warm serving dish; sprinkle with parsley.

Poires Pochées au Sirop

POACHED PEARS IN VANILLA SYRUP

My husband always requests poached pears for dessert whenever we are having *Lapin Sauté à la Moutarde*. After all these years one seems incomplete without the other. I hope you agree that poached pears make a perfect climax to this menu.

The Bosc pear is my favorite variety for poaching, although, of course, any pear will poach. Boscs are also delicious just as they come from the tree. I can never resist buying some whenever I find them in the market. Poached, they keep well under refrigeration.

This recipe will serve 4. However, the same quantity of syrup will poach 6 to 8 pears and you can have a refreshing dessert on hand for several days.

*ALTERNATE METHODS: Cauliflower can also be cooked in a steamette or a pressure cooker.

To Steam: Place steamette in a saucepan large enough to hold it, and add enough water to come just to the bottom of the steamette. (For a 3-quart pan I use 4 cups of water.) Arrange cauliflower clusters on steamette, cover, and place over high heat. As soon as water boils, time for 10 minutes. Remove clusters immediately, salt lightly, and dot with butter. Serve at once.

To Use a Pressure Cooker: Place clusters on rack in the cooker. Add 1/2 cup water, close cooker, place over high heat. When steam escapes from vent, reduce to medium heat. Close vent. As soon as pressure reaches 15 pounds, remove from heat, place in sink, and run cold water over cooker to reduce pressure immediately. Salt lightly, dot with butter, serve at once.

INGREDIENTS

2 *cups granulated sugar*
3 *cups water*
1 *vanilla bean or* 1 *teaspoon vanilla extract*
4 *Bosc pears**

1 *lemon*

*red food coloring***
slivered or sliced blanched almonds

METHOD

Combine sugar, water, and vanilla in a saucepan large enough so that pears will not be crowded when poaching. (If you have no large pan, plan to poach a few at a time.) Bring liquid to boil over medium heat, stirring occasionally with a wooden spoon, and allow to boil gently 5 minutes.

Meanwhile, peel pears, being careful not to remove stems. Pears may be poached whole or halved. Whole pears look more attractive when served; halved pears are easier to eat. If you halve them, remove the seeds. Saturate each pear with lemon juice to help it retain its appetizing color instead of turning brown.

Syrup is just right for poaching when bubbles burst gently. Plunge pears into syrup and poach about 5 minutes on each side. (Time is the same whether pears are whole or halved.) Stay with them and slowly baste and turn them. When a sharp paring knife glides easily in and out, pears are done.

Remove pears to serving dish; pour in syrup. Allow to cool completely; then cover with storage wrap and refrigerate to chill.

TO SERVE: Place pears in compote or shallow serving dish; spoon on syrup. If desired, place a drop of food coloring on your finger and spread it over each pear, varying depth of color on each fruit for added effect. Sprinkle with almonds. Allow 2 halves or 1 whole pear per person.

Leftover syrup may be stored for future use.

*Pears should feel slightly soft when pressured gently with the fingers. If under-ripe, they will take longer to poach. If very hard when purchased, put them in a drawer to ripen, checking them every day.

**Food coloring is not necessary, but it does make the pears look more appetizing. If you prefer not to use food coloring in your cooking, a little beet juice can be substituted.

MENU V

Un Repas de Dimanche
A SUNDAY DINNER

Soupe à l'Oignon
Comme Aucune Autre
UNPARALLELED ONION SOUP

Gigot Persillé
ROAST LEG OF LAMB WITH A SAUCE
OF CHOPPED PARSLEY, ONIONS, BREAD
CRUMBS, COGNAC, AND WHITE WINE

Haricots de Soissons au Beurre
WHITE BEANS IN BUTTER AND
BOUILLON
GARNISHED WITH PARSLEY AND GARLIC

Salade Verte
GREEN SALAD

Entremets Glacé aux Pêches
MOLDED FRESH PEACH DESSERT

Bourgueil or Saint-Émilion

IN France, Sunday afternoon means good food and time for family and friends. This typical Sunday dinner—steaming onion soup, roast lamb, savory white beans simmered in stock and tossed at the last moment with chopped parsley and garlic, a green salad, and a light fruity dessert mold—is designed for unhurried enjoyment. The cook can plan a relaxed time, too, for most of this meal lends itself to advance preparation.

RECOMMENDED WINE: Choose a fresh, raspberry-scented, red wine from the old province of Touraine, midway along the wine-growing valley of the Loire, a Bourgueil. Or, if you prefer a more full-bodied wine with a strong bouquet, choose a red Bordeaux, a Saint-Émilion from the right bank of the Dordogne.

ORDER OF PREPARATION: Soup, *Entremets,* and. beans may be prepared several days ahead of time. If you are not working ahead, plan to start the beans at least 2 hours before roasting the lamb.

Soupe à L'Oignon Comme Aucune Autre

UNPARALLELED ONION SOUP

Onion soup is a French tradition. A favorite for quiet family gatherings, for formal parties, or best of all for a hearty midnight snack, it is apt to appear on the menu at Christmas and New Year as well. On those special occasions, it is usually preceded by an elegant appetizer of oysters on the half-shell served with fresh lemon or a vinegar–shallot–pepper sauce, thin slices of dark rye bread, and sweet butter.

In Paris years ago, one went to the *Quartier des Halles* after midnight for the color, excitement, and good onion soup always found there. After the theatre or a concert, the best-dressed women of Paris rubbed shoulders with the market's night workers over steaming bowls. Although urban renewal has changed the face of the ancient market, some of the popular soup sellers are still there. The old atmosphere is gone, but the soup is the same.

Preparing it is simple. The secret is in the way the onions are sautéed: They must be properly browned and must *not* be hurried. Reheating the soup improves the flavor, so to have it at its best, make it well in advance.

This recipe will provide 4 servings. The soup may be frozen.

INGREDIENTS

4 *cups hot beef bouillon**
1 1/4 *cups yellow onion, shredded (about 3 medium onions)*
2 *tablespoons clarified butter*
1 *medium garlic clove, chopped or pressed*
1/2 *teaspoon salt*
1/4 *teaspoon freshly ground pepper (medium grind)*
1 *teaspoon tomato paste***

METHOD

Have bouillon ready and piping hot before starting other preparations.

When bouillon is called for, as in this recipe, beef cubes will produce a reasonable result. For the "real thing," however, there is no substitute for homemade stock. (See my recipe on page 18.) In an emergency, cubes are preferable to canned consommés. If you are using the cubes, simply combine water, cubes, and salt in saucepan and boil until cubes dissolve, stirring frequently. Keep hot.

To shred onion, peel and cut into 1/4-inch slices. Halve each slice and separate rings. Do not dice.

For full flavor, it is important that the pan in which onions are sautéed be used throughout, so choose a saucepan large enough to contain the complete preparation (a 2-quart saucepan is ideal).

Now, in this saucepan, heat clarified butter to sizzling over high heat. Add onions. Reduce heat to medium. Watch constantly, shaking pan frequently to prevent burning, until onions are golden to dark brown—the darker the better. This will take from 15 to 20 minutes. *Upon the proper sautéing of the onions depends the ultimate quality of your soup.* Have patience!

When onions are properly browned, add garlic, salt, and pepper. French onion soup is supposed to be peppery, and 1/4 teaspoon may be too much for some tastes. Try less to begin with; later taste, and add more if desired.

Simmer for 1 minute. Add hot bouillon and tomato paste. Cover pan and simmer at least 20 minutes. Stir occasionally.

Now you should have the best onion soup you've ever tasted!

*Use homemade stock or packaged cubes. For 4 cups, use 4 1/2 cups water, 4 beef cubes, 1/2 teaspoon salt.
**Catsup is no substitute here! To keep leftover paste, place in a glass jar, cover surface with liquid vegetable oil, and refrigerate. The oil will flow from the paste as you spoon it out.

CROÛTONS

INGREDIENTS

4 *slices white bread*
butter
1/2 *cup grated Swiss cheese*

METHOD

Croûtons for onion soup are better roasted than toasted. They may be made in advance and stored in a tight tin.

Preheat oven to 450° F.

If you are planning to melt cheese on top of croûtons, it is better to make them from French-style bread. Do not remove crusts; cut into 1/2- to 3/4-inch slices.

Now, butter one side of cut bread, place on cookie sheet, and bake on middle rack of oven from 2 to 5 minutes on each side. (Time depends upon amount of moisture in bread.) They should be golden to dark brown on each side. Watch them.*

Allow one large croûton per serving.

TO SERVE: Although there are several ways of serving onion soup, I prefer this method. It will give a hard, crusty top to your croûton—a pleasant contrast to the soup beneath. Sprinkle a teaspoon of grated cheese on each croûton, and bake on a cookie sheet in a 450° F. oven until the cheese is melted and slightly brown. (This will take 5 to 7 minutes.) Sprinkle 1 teaspoon of grated cheese on the bottom of the bowl, add piping hot soup, and float the croûton on top. The croûton should be sizzling when served.**

*If they should get overdone, do as the *boulangeries* of Paris do: Simply scrape them on both sides with a knife. The important thing is to have them dark enough.

ALTERNATE METHODS: If you want a less crusty croûton, simply place the cheese, without browning, on top of the croûton once it is in the bowl. If you like a stringy topping, cut the cheese into strips, rather than grating it, and brown in the oven as indicated. Finally, if you have ovenproof bowls, you can bake the soup, croûton, and cheese in a 450° oven until the cheese is melted. Your croûton will be crusty on top and soft underneath.

Gigot Persillé

ROAST LEG OF LAMB WITH A SAUCE OF CHOPPED PARSLEY, ONIONS, BREAD CRUMBS, COGNAC, AND WHITE WINE

Roast lamb was a Sunday favorite in my family. When I was a child, one of the chores I liked best was taking the *Gigot* to the local baker for roasting. On the way I met others carrying their seasoned and buttered roasts on earthenware plates to the *boulanger–pâtissier*.

"And what time would you like your *Gigot*, Mademoiselle?" the baker inquired. "Twelve-thirty sharp it will be, then." Our little cut was tagged and ready, roasted to perfection when I returned, for the maker of breads and pastries was also an expert with meats.

The French leave many culinary tasks to the specialist, and roasting is one of them. "One can become a cook, but one must be born a roaster," said Brillat-Savarin, the eighteenth-century *gastronome*, thereby limiting the aspirations of would-be *rôtisseurs* for generations. Inadequate cooking facilities, especially in city apartments where a stove with an oven was a rarity, were also responsible for specialization in France. Today things have changed; modern conveniences are common. But the specialist still does a thriving business.

To serve 4 people, the leg of lamb should weigh between 2 1/2 to 3 1/2 pounds. This recipe will serve for any larger cut, however, and it is always nice to have enough left over for a second meal.

If possible, ask your butcher for a half shank or a "Frenched leg" of lamb. This cut will include the middle haunch but not the upper saddle, which is fattier. It is generally easier to get good slices from this cut. Be sure that there is enough of the end bone sticking out to make it look like a leg on the platter. This extension makes it easier to handle when slicing.

To time a leg of lamb, subtract 1 pound for the bone, no matter what the total weight. Then figure 15 minutes per pound. Thus, a 3-pound roast will take 45 minutes. Turn off the oven and allow the lamb to rest 15 minutes in the oven, leaving the door ajar, so that the juices may set before slicing. Timed this way the lamb will be pink and juicy—the only way, we French insist, to enjoy its true flavor. I have found that Americans usually cook their lamb much longer. If you are skeptical, try it just this once. Taste the difference and choose the way you prefer.

A roast requires less preparation than most things, and this elegant entrée can be prepared in three easy steps.

ROASTING THE LAMB

INGREDIENTS

leg of lamb weighing 2 1/2 *to* 3 1/2 *pounds*
2 *to* 3 *garlic cloves*
8 *to* 9 *tablespoons unsalted butter, at room temperature*
salt and pepper

METHOD

Preheat oven to 400° F. (All roasts should be seared at this high temperature to seal in juices.) Oven should remain at this temperature throughout the cooking.

Remove excess fat from lamb. Absorb any moisture with paper towel.

Peel and cut garlic into slivers. Cut slits around lamb bone on both sides; insert garlic.

Spread on butter like icing to cover lamb. This can only be done effectively with the fingers. Butter will not adhere to ends where meat is exposed.

Place lamb in uncovered roasting pan. After 15 to 20 minutes of roasting, season with salt and pepper on both sides, turning to opposite side for remainder of cooking time.

PREPARING THE SAUCE BASE

INGREDIENTS

1 *medium garlic clove, pressed or chopped*
1/4 *cup unseasoned bread crumbs, fresh or dried*
1/4 *cup chopped white onion**
1/4 *cup chopped fresh parsley*

*White onions are preferable for this recipe because they have a more delicate taste than yellow onions.

METHOD

Five minutes before roasting time is over, remove lamb from oven. Mix garlic, bread crumbs, onions, and parsley with the accumulated juices in bottom of pan. Return to oven and complete cooking time.

Turn off heat. Place lamb on platter and return to oven for 15 minutes to allow juices to set.

DÉGLACER (TO DEGLAZE)

INGREDIENTS

1 *tablespoon dry white wine*
1 *tablespoon Cognac*
1 *cup chicken bouillon**

METHOD

To make sauce from the drippings in a pan in which meat has been roasted or sautéed, is called *déglacer*.

Place roasting pan on stove top over high heat. Add wine, Cognac, and bouillon. Bring to boil, stirring with wooden spoon. As soon as sauce thickens—about 1 minute—all is ready.

TO SERVE: Pour sauce into gravy boat. Keep hot.

Making thin slices, cut off as much lamb as you need, slicing parallel to the bone on the meaty part of the leg. Place slices, with rest of leg, on serving platter.

To garnish your platter, lay down a bed of watercress or parsley. Finish by dressing up the lamb with a paper frill placed over the bone, as described on page 59.

*Use homemade stock (page 19) or 1 chicken cube dissolved in 1 1/4 cups water.

Haricots de Soissons au Beurre

WHITE BEANS IN BUTTER AND BOUILLON
GARNISHED WITH PARSLEY AND GARLIC

Soissons beans are a type of dried bean which takes its name from the city of Soissons, near which a large portion of the crop is grown. They resemble the small white California bean or the American navy bean, either of which may be used for this recipe.

One shouldn't hesitate to buy this inexpensive vegetable; properly prepared, it can be both attractive and delicious.

The recipe will serve 4. Beans can be prepared several days ahead, and can be frozen.

INGREDIENTS

1 *cup navy or California small white beans*
3 *cups lukewarm water*
1/4 *teaspoon baking soda*
1 1/2 *cups chicken bouillon**
4 *to 8 small whole white onions*
3 *tablespoons clarified butter*
1 *bouquet garni (6 sprigs of parsley and 1 bay leaf tied*
   together with string)
1/2 *teaspoon table salt*

1 *medium to large garlic clove, chopped*
4 *to 6 sprigs of parsley, chopped*
2 *to 3 turns of black pepper mill, medium grind*

METHOD

Sort beans to remove any spotted or otherwise imperfect ones.

Combine beans, water, and soda in a 1- or 1 1/2-quart saucepan. Cover and slowly heat to boiling point. Remove from heat and set aside, still covered, to soak for 1 hour. Beans will settle to bottom.

Drain beans by pouring into colander. This first step, in addition to being an important beginning for tasty beans, also makes them more digestible.

*Use homemade stock (page 19) or 4 chicken cubes dissolved in 2 cups water.

If bouillon has been prepared ahead of time, warm it up.

Peel onions. Because the skins of white onions are so thin, they can be more easily peeled if blanched first: Place onions in a colander or strainer and submerge in boiling water 1 minute. Cut off root section and entire skin will slip off. Incise a small x at the stem end to prevent bursting while cooking.

Heat butter in saucepan. Add onions and drained beans; shake pan until both are well coated with butter. Now add warm bouillon, *bouquet garni,* and salt.

Cover pan, heat to boiling point, and allow to simmer gently for 35 to 60 minutes. Beans should be cooked over low to medium heat to prevent bursting. Time does not depend upon size of beans: Sometimes they just take longer. They are done when soft. Chop garlic and parsley and blend together thoroughly with fingers.

TO SERVE: Just before serving, place beans in hot vegetable dish. Sprinkle with pepper and 3/4 of parsley–garlic mixture. Toss. Decorate with remaining garnish.

Serve at once with *Gigot.*

Leftover beans are just as good a second day, as long as they are reheated over low heat or in a slow oven or double boiler. If you have 1/4 cup of bouillon left over, add for reheating. Otherwise add a small amount of water for moisture.

Entremets Glacé aux Pêches

MOLDED FRESH PEACH DESSERT

An *Entremets* is a light sweet dish which may be served after the roast and before the pastry in a formal meal. The climax of our Sunday menu, it is light enough to tempt the most reluctant

sweet tooth. It can be prepared with any fresh fruit juice, and can be made days ahead of time.

The ingredients are for a mold of 4-cup capacity, which will provide 4 to 6 portions. The *Entremets* can also be served in attractive, long-stemmed glasses. If glasses are of 1/2-cup capacity, the recipe will make 8 servings.

INGREDIENTS

2 *pounds fresh peaches (or enough to make 2 cups juice)*
1 *package unflavored gelatin*
granulated sugar
1 *cup heavy cream*

USEFUL UTENSIL: 4-*cup mold*

METHOD

Wash peaches, cut in halves, and remove stones. Extract juice by crushing the fruits, one at a time, through a strainer placed over a 4-cup measure. Two cups of juice should be extracted. If peaches do not render this amount, and you don't have others, add water to make up the desired quantity.

Measure out 1/2 cup of juice and, using a fork, stir in the gelatin. Place the mixture in a 1- to 2-cup saucepan and let it come to the boiling point over medium heat, stirring often to melt the gelatin.

While this mixture is heating, test the remaining juice for sweetness. If it is not sweet enough for your taste, stir in sugar, 1 tablespoon at a time, until you are satisfied. Put the juice in a 2-quart bowl, add the gelatinized juice, and chill until the dessert is just beginning to set. (This takes about 40 minutes; check closely during the last 10 minutes or so.)

Chill a 1-quart mixing bowl and beaters.* Beat heavy cream about 30 seconds at low to medium speed and 4 minutes at high speed, then fold it into the dessert slowly and carefully in small amounts.

Now rinse out the mold without drying it or coat it inside with salad oil. Fill it with the *Entremets* mixture and smooth the top with a rubber spatula. Cover with storage wrap and let set for several hours until firm.

*This chilling makes the beating more efficient. It is especially important in the summer.

OPTIONAL CREAM TOPPING

INGREDIENTS

1/4 *pint heavy cream*
2 *tablespoons confectioners' sugar*
crystallized flowers and mint leaves (optional)

METHOD

Chill bowl and beaters in refrigerator. Whip cream until stiff. Fold in confectioners' sugar.

TO SERVE: Loosen *Entremets* all around gently and carefully with a knife. Place a serving platter on top of mold, turn upside down, and shake gently. If dessert does not unmold on the platter, cover with a hot moist towel for a few seconds. Repeat if necessary until *Entremets* comes out.

Decorate top and base of dessert with rosettes of whipped cream or top off with crystallized flowers and mint leaves.

Cut in wedges and serve on dessert plates.

ALTERNATE PRESENTATION OF ENTREMETS: If you do not wish to mold the *Entremets,* you can place it in sherbet glasses or long-stemmed drinking glasses. Swirl the surface with a fork to create a design. Or, when it has gelled, top it with whipped cream and crystallized flowers and mint leaves.

Menu VI

Soupons Après le Théâtre
AFTER-THEATRE SUPPER

Les Huîtres
FRESH OYSTERS ON THE HALF-SHELL

Croque-Monsieur
SAUTÉED HAM AND SWISS CHEESE
SANDWICHES

Salade d'Endives et Betteraves
ENDIVE SALAD WITH BAKED BEETS

Tuiles aux Amandes
SMALL, TILE-SHAPED ALMOND PASTRIES

Chablis Grand Cru or Premier Cru
or Muscadet-sur-Lie

IN France, *le souper* is a meal close to midnight. The little supper that follows is an ideal repast to come home to after a special evening out shared with good company. It is an occasion for starched linen, glistening crystal, silver, and candlelight.

RECOMMENDED WINE: When serving Chablis, my preference is for a Grand Cru or a Premier Cru. These are the wines made from the finest growths of certain vineyards. They are more expensive than other Chablis, which may be made from inferior grapes and even bottled outside the region. If you prefer a less expensive dry white wine, a Loire wine such as Muscadet-sur-Lie would be preferable to another Chablis.

ORDER OF PREPARATION: The beauty of this menu is that all can be organized ahead of time: the oysters and sauce waiting in the refrigerator, the salad crisp, the wine chilled, the *Croque-Monsieur* ready for sautéing, the *Tuiles* in a tight tin box.

Les Huîtres

FRESH OYSTERS ON THE HALF-SHELL

During the cold months in Paris, baskets of oysters are displayed on the sidewalks, bright whole lemons scattered among their greyish shells. If you live in the neighborhood of an *écailler,* oyster vendor, and bring him a platter, he will return it at the specified hour to your door filled with freshly opened oysters—*marennes, claires, portugaises,* or the aristocratic *belons*—garnished with lemon wedges.

In the United States, I buy oysters in either a fish market or supermarket, where they are sold by the dozen or by the pound. There is usually no choice of variety.

Oysters must be fresh to be good. If the flesh moves at a touch, the oyster is alive. A bad oyster has a bad smell!

Often I have made a meal of oysters and Westphalian pumpernickel bread, accompanied by Chablis or Muscadet. Even when I eat them as an appetizer, I am satisfied only after at least a dozen. However, for some persons, half a dozen may be plenty. You must use your own judgment.

The traditional dressing is *Sauce Échalote*—simply shallots, vinegar, and black pepper. The following recipe is for a dozen oysters.

INGREDIENTS

12 *oysters*

1 *teaspoon chopped shallots**
4 *turns of the black pepper mill, medium grind*
4 *tablespoons red wine vinegar*

USEFUL UTENSILS: *Oyster knife, oyster fork*

METHOD

To open oysters, hold shell in an old turkish towel. Using an oyster knife or any thin-bladed knife, insert point into center of muscular hinge and gently but firmly work blade around shell, severing the muscles. Be careful not to let the juice run out as you are opening them.

Oysters may be opened several hours before serving. Retain juices, cover with storage wrap, and refrigerate.

Combine sauce ingredients as listed in a small bowl or cup; stir with a fork.

TO SERVE: Arrange oysters in shells on a bed of chopped ice on individual platters or large plates. Place small cup of dressing in center of each plate.

To eat, loosen oyster from its shell with oyster fork; spoon on a teaspoon of *échalote* dressing; swirl oyster gently in sauce before raising it to your mouth. Sip the juices that remain from the shell. Wedges of Westphalian pumpernickel spread with whipped sweet butter, a glass of chilled Chablis . . . *et la vie est belle!*

Croque-Monsieur

SAUTÉED HAM AND SWISS CHEESE SANDWICHES

Among the *bon vivants* of Paris, the *Croque-Monsieur* is almost as traditional as onion soup for a snack after the theatre. Served on a bed of watercress with a glass of chilled white wine, it seems a most appropriate way to end a pleasant evening.

Croque-Monsieur may be served as an appetizer or, as in this menu, as the main course of a light meal. It is simple to prepare, since all but the final sautéing may be done ahead of time.

*Chopped red onion may be substituted if necessary.

INGREDIENTS

8 *slices white sandwich bread with a firm texture*
8 *slices imported Swiss cheese*
4 *slices boiled ham*
10 *tablespoons clarified butter*

watercress for garnishing

METHOD

Trim crusts from bread by stacking 4 or more slices together and cutting with a sharp bread knife.

Trim cheese and ham to fit bread slices.

On one slice of bread place a slice of cheese, then a slice of ham, then another slice of cheese; top with second slice of bread. Press sandwich with your hand to make it as compact as possible. Make other sandwiches the same way. If they are to be stored in refrigerator, wrap carefully with storage wrap.

The final step will take only 3 minutes. Just before serving time, heat butter over medium heat in a 12-inch skillet. In a regular frying pan this takes from 30 to 60 seconds.*

Once butter starts to crackle, retain medium heat, and sauté sandwiches for 1 to 1 1/2 minutes on the first side, until light golden brown. Turn carefully, using 2 spatulas, and sauté again until golden brown on second side.

TO SERVE: Place on platter on a bed of watercress, or place individual portions on dinner plates garnished with watercress. Sandwiches should be eaten with a knife and fork.

Salade d'Endives et Betteraves

ENDIVE SALAD WITH BAKED BEETS

The vegetable for this salad is marketed in the United States under the name French or Belgian endive, although it is actually the forced, bleached shoot of a plant in the chicory family. Its elongated, whitish leaves fold loosely together, unlike the plant we call chicory in France and America, which has a curly green head.

*If an electric frying pan is being used, set dial at 400° F. and use 2 additional tablespoons of clarified butter.

I always have the feeling that I am getting ready for an elegant dinner whenever I prepare endives. In a salad they are a delicate change from other greens; as a cooked vegetable they are an epicurean delight. Although they are usually more expensive than most vegetables, there is little waste to endives.

Prepared in this way, combined with a few slices of baked beets, endives are pleasing to the eye and to the palate.

The recipe will serve 4 persons.

INGREDIENTS

3/4 *to* 1 *pound of endives*
1/2 *teaspoon table salt*
5 *turns of black pepper mill, medium grind*
1 *teaspoon Dijon mustard (optional)*
1/2 *teaspoon chopped garlic*
1 *tablespoon red wine vinegar*
2 *tablespoons salad oil*
1/4 *cup sliced baked beets (optional)**

METHOD

Remove any imperfect outer leaves; clean root ends by scraping; cut out any brown parts.

Endives are easier to clean than most leaves. To facilitate washing, slice each spear lengthwise into three or four sections, depending upon size. Swish up and down in cold water, changing the water three or four times. Place in salad basket, drain, then shake as much water out as possible. Wrap in clean linen towel and pat gently to absorb remaining moisture.

If the leaves are prepared just before serving time, leave in towel until ready to mix with dressing; otherwise remove from towel and store in hydrator. If leaves have been thoroughly dried, they will keep crisp and fresh for several days.

In a 2-quart salad bowl, combine salt, pepper, mustard, garlic, and vinegar. Mix well with a fork. Add oil and stir. If beets are to be a part of your salad, add them now and mix into dressing.

Place salad fork and spoon in bowl, then cut endive leaves into about 2-inch pieces and allow them to rest on salad implements until the very last minute when you are ready to toss and serve.

TO SERVE: Toss. Serve after the main course on individual salad plates.

*See instructions for baking beets on page 80.

Betteraves au Four

BAKED BEETS

In Paris, our neighborhood vegetable seller used to bake beets for her special customers at no extra charge.

Even today, I still feel that beets have a more interesting flavor and texture when they are baked rather than boiled.

METHOD

Preheat oven at 450° F.

Select large beets of uniform size, if possible. Scrub with a vegetable brush under running water. Cut off leaves, leaving about 1 inch of stem. Do not cut root end or peel, as beet will bleed.

Place on cookie sheet and bake until tender. Test by inserting small-bladed knife. Baking will take from 40 minutes to 2 hours, depending upon size. Skins will be wrinkled.

Allow to cool, then peel and slice about 1/4 inch thick. If you have large beets, you can give them a more elegant touch by shaping each slice with a cookie cutter.

Sprinkle with salt and add to the salad dressing before adding greens.*

Tuiles aux Amandes

SMALL, TILE-SHAPED ALMOND PASTRIES

This thin crisp *petits fours* is much like a potato chip in texture and in its addictive qualities. At parties I have catered, I am always amused to see guests going back to the tray of *Tuiles* again and again.

LA GOUTTIÈRE: If you want to give the traditional shape to these *petits fours,* you may flip them, while still hot and soft, over a rolling pin which has been covered with waxed paper. There is also a special device, called a *gouttière,* sold for giving *Tuiles* this curved shape. The name literally means "rain gutter" in French. It is simply a 10 × 10 metal sheet with accordion ridges about an

---

*Baked beets also make an excellent salad by themselves, tossed with a vinaigrette dressing.

inch high onto which the pastries are flipped. Some of my students have improvised a *gouttière* of aluminum foil.

A NOTE ON ALMONDS: Slivered almonds may be purchased in cellophane bags or in tins in almost all supermarkets. It takes about 6 ounces to make the 1 1/4 cups required for this recipe.

Almonds also may be purchased whole, unshelled or shelled, in which case they will need to be blanched and chopped.

To Blanch: Drop kernels into boiling water and allow to steep until skins slip off or can be easily removed with the aid of a paring knife. Pat dry, or spread out on a cookie sheet and place in a slow oven to dry.

To Chop: Use a chopping bowl, or put in an electric blender or food processor for 1/2 second.

This recipe will make 3 to 4 dozen *Tuiles*. If you wish to make more, they should be made in batches.

INGREDIENTS

3/4 *cup granulated sugar*
1 1/4 *cup chopped blanched almonds*
1/4 *cup granulated or sifted pastry flour**
4 *egg whites*
3 *tablespoons melted unsalted butter***

1 *stick unsalted butter wrapped in cheesecloth*

USEFUL UTENSILS: *Blender, food processor, or chopping bowl; wire cake rack; gouttière or rolling pin*

METHOD

This is a simple recipe, made of the simplest ingredients, but there are four points to remember as keys to success:

1) This confection is temperamental and behaves badly in

*If pastry flour is used, sift once again after measuring.
**Two tablespoons solid butter melted slowly over low heat.

damp weather; therefore, always make it on a dry sunny day. *Tuiles* will keep well for weeks stored in a tight tin box, so choose your day.

2) Be sure to stir the batter each time you spoon some onto the cookie sheet.

3) If you have difficulty removing *Tuiles* from the cookie sheet, return sheet to the oven to re-soften, then loosen them without removing the sheet again from the oven.

4) Grease your cookie sheet between each baking.

If you want the *Tuiles* to have a shiny surface, make the batter 2 days in advance of baking and store in the refrigerator.

Combine sugar, almonds, and flour in a small mixing bowl.

In another bowl, beat egg whites lightly with a fork. Add them a little at a time to the dry ingredients, mixing well. Stir melted butter in slowly with a rubber spatula. Then stir this batter with spatula for 2 minutes.

If you are going to let batter stand so that *Tuiles* will be glossy, cover bowl and place in refrigerator. If you can't wait to taste one of these confections, go ahead and bake them.

Preheat oven to 350° F.

Wrap waxed paper around rolling pin to receive *Tuiles* or have a *gouttière* ready.

If you have more than one cookie sheet, prepare them all by greasing 3 or 4 round areas on each sheet with the stick of butter wrapped in cheesecloth. Use them alternately when baking. At the beginning, it is enough to make 3 or 4 *Tuiles* at a time because of the rapidity with which they must be taken off the sheet. However, as you gain experience and confidence, you may be able to make as many as 5 or 6 at a time.

Stir batter; then drop 3/4 of a teaspoon onto each greased area. Place on middle rack of oven. Bake from 4 to 8 minutes, until edges are a medium to dark brown. It takes careful watching.

Quickly remove each *Tuile* with a wide metal spatula and flip onto rolling pin or *gouttière*. If any cool and stick to the cookie sheet, return to oven, re-soften, and without removing sheet again from the oven, loosen with spatula.

Re-grease sheet with butter stick after each baking. Stir batter again before spooning out next batch.

When *Tuiles* have cooled into curved shapes, remove to wire rack. Repeat process until all batter has been used. When *Tuiles* are completely cooled, store in tight tin box.

TO SERVE: Arrange *Tuiles* on serving platter so that they overlap as do the ceramic roof tiles of a French house.

MENU VII

Un Vrai Favori
A REAL FAVORITE

Salade de Concombres
MARINATED CUCUMBERS WITH TARRAGON

Boeuf Bourguignon
BEEF IN RED WINE WITH GLAZED ONIONS AND MUSHROOMS

Pommes de Terre Vapeur Persillées
PARSLEYED STEAMED POTATOES

Salade de Romaine
ROMAINE WITH MUSTARD AND SWISS CHEESE DRESSING

Oranges en Surprise
FRESH ORANGE SURPRISE TOPPED WITH WHIPPED CREAM

Châteauneuf-du-Pape or Morgon

L E *Boeuf Bourguignon* is usually the first dish I prepare for my lectures, and over the years I have found it to be popular among my audiences and students. For most people it seems the epitome of good French cooking; the aroma that arises from the pot is irresistible. Yet it is an easy dish to prepare. I accompany it with marinated cucumbers and parslied steamed potatoes, a Romaine salad with a dressing of mustard and Swiss cheese, and a fresh orange dessert.

RECOMMENDED WINE: This hearty meat dish needs a full-bodied red wine, both in its preparation and as its companion. A vigorous Châteauneuf-du-Pape is an excellent choice. This wine is from the lower Rhône Valley near Avignon, where the Popes lived in the fourteenth century—hence the name, "new castle of the Pope." An equally good selection is Morgon, an unusually robust Beaujolais with an earthy flavor.

ORDER OF PREPARATION: Cucumbers, beef, and dessert may all be prepared well ahead of time if desired. Potatoes may be peeled and shaped as much as 2 days in advance if they are immersed in water, covered, and stored in the refrigerator. Begin steaming the potatoes 1/2 hour before serving time. The salad should of course be tossed at the last minute.

Salade de Concombres

MARINATED CUCUMBERS WITH TARRAGON

This is the French way of preparing cucumbers. It gives them an entirely different quality and flavor from the usual fresh slice of cucumber served in the United States. In France, when cucumber salad is served as an appetizer, a leafy green salad is still served after the main course. The first step, extracting the water from the cucumbers, should be done several hours to a day ahead.

The recipe makes about 4 cups—more than enough for 4 persons. The salad will keep well in the refrigerator for several days. For more servings, make in batches.

INGREDIENTS

5 *medium cucumbers (about 1/4 pound each)*
table salt

2 *to 3 turns of black pepper mill, medium grind*
2 *tablespoons red wine vinegar*
4 *tablespoons salad oil*
1 *teaspoon tarragon**

METHOD

Peel cucumbers. Slice 1/8 to 1/4 inch thick into a bowl, sprinkling each layer lightly with 1/4 to 1/2 teaspoon of salt. Thinner slices become too soft upon standing. Place in refrigerator.

After cucumbers have been allowed to stand for at least 2 hours, drain off water which they have rendered. Taste cucumber. If too salty, rinse in cold water, changing water several times if necessary to reduce saltiness. Drain again and squeeze in clean linen towel or other cloth to remove excess water. Really wring the towel to squeeze them dry.

Place slices in a bowl. Add pepper, vinegar, oil; toss well. Sprinkle with tarragon and toss again. Salad may now be refrigerated or used immediately.

TO SERVE: Bring to the table in a vegetable dish from which each person can help himself to a serving on a small salad plate.

Boeuf Bourguignon

BEEF IN RED WINE WITH GLAZED ONIONS AND MUSHROOMS

This dish is an appealing one for a buffet supper; unusual in that very little fat or shortening is used in its preparation. You can make it a day or two in advance, since the flavor of the wine sauce will improve upon reheating. If you make it in advance, however, do not add mushrooms or onions until final heating. It may be frozen, too, without the onions and mushrooms.

Remember, only a good wine makes a good sauce. For this

*If fresh tarragon is available, use one sprig, chopped.

particular dish I suggest Morgon or Châteauneuf-du-Pape. Serve whichever wine you use in the sauce as an accompaniment at the table.

This recipe will serve 4 when made with 2 pounds of beef, or 5 or 6 persons made with 3 pounds.

THE BEEF

INGREDIENTS

2 1/2 *cups hot beef bouillon**
2 *to* 3 *pounds beef cut into* 1- *to* 2-*inch cubes***
salt
pepper
3 *tablespoons unsifted flour*
2 *cups dry red wine*
1 *teaspoon thyme*
4 *bay leaves*

METHOD

There is but one secret here: *The perfect wine sauce must be simmered gently and evenly throughout.* Never let the sauce stand without cooking; never boil it vigorously. (An electric frying pan is not appropriate for this recipe because its heat varies too much.) I prefer cooking *Le Boeuf Bourguignon* on top of the stove where I have greater control over the simmering of the sauce.

Have bouillon ready. If you are using cubes, combine water, cubes, and salt, bring to boiling point, and simmer 5 minutes, stirring occasionally until cubes are dissolved. Keep hot.

Heat an empty 4-quart pot until hot enough to sear meat. (If the pot is too small, the meat will not brown properly.) Test with one cube of meat; if it sings, temperature is right.

Brown meat evenly on all sides, keeping heat high. This should take only about 5 minutes.

Reduce heat. Sprinkle meat with salt and pepper. Sprinkle on flour, 1 tablespoon at a time, tossing meat between each addition to coat evenly. Add wine, hot bouillon, thyme, and bay leaves. Cover

*Use homemade stock (page 18) or 2 beef cubes dissolved in 2 1/2 cups water, with 1/2 teaspoon table salt added.

**Preferably top of the rib; otherwise, chuck, brisket, or bottom round.

and, when liquid has reached boiling point, allow to simmer gently, covered, for 2 1/2 hours. Check from time to time to regulate simmer and to turn meat.

GLAZED ONIONS

Peeled onions may be added directly to simmering pot 15 to 20 minutes before cooking time is over, depending upon their size. Both for looks and taste, however, I prefer to glaze the onions. They should be cooked as close to serving time as possible.

INGREDIENTS

10 *to* 20 *small white onions*
1/4 *cup cold water*
1 *teaspoon sugar*
2 *tablespoons unsalted butter*
1/2 *teaspoon table salt*

METHOD

Because the skins of white onions are so thin, they can be more easily peeled if blanched first: Place onions in a colander or strainer and submerge in boiling water for 1 minute. Cut off root section and entire skin will slip off. Incise a small x at the stem end to prevent bursting while cooking.

Combine all ingredients in a l-cup saucepan. Bring liquid to a roaring boil, uncovered, then reduce to boil gently 15 to 20 minutes. Shake pan from time to time to prevent sticking and to give an even glaze to the onions. When done, onions will be tender and most of the liquid will have evaporated. Keep warm until ready to serve.

THE MUSHROOMS

INGREDIENTS

1/2 *to* 3/4 *pound fresh white mushrooms*

USEFUL UTENSIL: *Lemon stripper*

METHOD

Now prepare mushrooms to be added during the last few minutes of cooking time. Mushrooms are a spongy vegetable which soaks up and retains moisture, so the less contact with water the better. They should never be washed, peeled, or overcooked. To clean, wipe with a damp sponge. I reserve a little sponge especially for this purpose.

Cut off tips of stems. Reserve largest and firmest mushrooms. Slice remaining ones lengthwise about 1/4 inch thick.

The large mushrooms which you have reserved whole may be fluted for added attractiveness. With a lemon stripper, cut a radial groove from top center of cap to edge, twisting the mushroom slightly clockwise under the pressure of the stripper to curve the groove.

Add whole mushrooms to the pot 5 minutes before the end of cooking time. Add sliced mushrooms 2 to 3 minutes before you remove beef from the stove. Taste and correct seasoning if necessary.

TO SERVE: Place beef and sauce with sliced mushrooms in shallow platter or chafing dish. Arrange onions around edge. Top with whole mushrooms. Serve at once with steamed potatoes.

Pommes de Terre Vapeur Persillées

PARSLEYED STEAMED POTATOES

By using a steamette for this recipe, you will be able to get a perfectly white, deliciously moist, steamed potato.* But it is the

*If you don't have a steamette, any device which will allow potatoes to steam above water can be substituted.

shaping, as well as the cooking, which give this vegetable its appeal. The amount given will allow 2 potatoes per serving, plus extras.

INGREDIENTS

8 *to* 10 *potatoes**
water
table salt
chopped parsley

USEFUL UTENSIL: *Steamette*

METHOD

Wash and peel potatoes. With a potato peeler, mold potatoes to the size and shape of a large egg. Large potatoes can be cut in half or quarters before shaping.

Leftover shavings may be used for potato soup, as an addition to vegetable soup, even for mashed potatoes. Don't throw them away! Store them in cold water and refrigerate for future use.

Place enough cold water in pan to come just below bottom of steamette. Put in potatoes, cover, and when water reaches boiling point, time for 20 to 30 minutes. Test for softness by inserting small knife blade into potato.

TO SERVE: Sprinkle with salt and chopped parsley just before bringing to table in serving dish. Never add parsley while potatoes are still in pan, as it loses its fresh appearance.

Salade de Romaine

ROMAINE WITH MUSTARD AND SWISS CHEESE DRESSING

Romaine is distinguished by its elongated dark green leaves and its crunchy texture.

A 1/2-pound head of Romaine will be sufficient for 4 servings.

*Use red Bliss potatoes when available; otherwise Maine or Long Island.

INGREDIENTS

1 *head of Romaine (about 1/2 pound)*
1 *teaspoon chopped garlic*
1/2 *teaspoon salt*
1/8 *to* 1/4 *teaspoon fresh ground black pepper (medium grind)*
1 *heaping teaspoon Dijon or Meaux mustard*
1 *tablespoon red wine vinegar*
2 *tablespoons salad oil*
1/3 *cup cubed imported Swiss cheese (about* 1 *ounce)*

USEFUL UTENSIL: *Salad basket*

METHOD

Cut off root end of Romaine, separate leaves, remove the imperfect ones. Wash each leaf under cold running water, then place in a bowl or pan and wash again several times. Drain in colander or salad basket, shake well, and allow to finish draining in refrigerator until ready to use. Pat dry between paper or linen towels.

In a salad bowl of 1 1/2- to 2-quart capacity, mix the garlic, salt, pepper, mustard, and vinegar in the order listed; mix well with a whisk or fork. Add oil, beating continually. When all the oil has been incorporated, add the cubes of Swiss cheese.

When ready to serve, gently break the leaves into bite-sized pieces, put them in the bowl and toss well.

TO SERVE: Place portions on small salad plates.

Oranges en Surprise

FRESH ORANGE SURPRISE TOPPED WITH WHIPPED CREAM

The most flattering adjectives may be used to describe this dessert—superb, delicious, refreshing, colorful, attractive. And yet, *Oranges en Surprise* is so simple to make! There is just one thing to remember: For that divine, subtle flavor you *must* use fresh orange juice.

The recipe will serve 4.

INGREDIENTS

4 *large navel oranges*
2 *cups fresh orange juice**
1 *package unflavored gelatin*
5 *tablespoons sugar***

METHOD

Cut a slice off the navel end of the oranges to flatten them so that they will stand upright. Next, slice enough off the other end so that the pulp can be scooped out with a spoon. Remove entire pulp.

Strain this pulp to obtain juice. This will never give enough for 2 cups, so squeeze additional oranges until you have the required amount.

Measure out 1/2 cup of this juice and add gelatin, to soften.

To remaining 1 1/2 cups of juice, add the granulated sugar. Place in saucepan and bring to a boil over high heat, stirring with whisk. Boil 1 to 2 minutes. Add softened gelatin, stirring constantly with whisk. As soon as juice has returned to boiling point—no longer than a minute—remove from heat. Allow to cool several minutes so that it will be easier to handle. Remove foam from surface.

Ladle mixture into orange shells. This amount will fill four large shells half way. (If you want to fill shells to the top, simply double the recipe.) When cool, place in refrigerator. Oranges will gel in about 2 hours.

*Any type of orange can be squeezed to make up the necessary amount of juice.
**This dessert will also come out well when made without sugar, especially if the oranges are particularly sweet.

In summer when it is hot, or when you are in a hurry, 1 1/2 packages of gelatin may be used to hasten gelling. The less gelatin, however, the better, for too much is apt to make the consistency rubbery.

TO MAKE TOPPING

INGREDIENTS

1/4 *pint heavy cream*
2 *tablespoons confectioners' sugar*
grated orange peel
candied mint leaves or angelica, if desired

METHOD

Chill bowl and beaters in refrigerator for efficient whipping. (This is particularly important in the summertime.) Whip cream until stiff. Fold in confectioners' sugar.

When orange filling has gelled, or just before serving time, spoon on cream attractively. If you have a pastry bag, fit with desired tip and squeeze out cream.*

TO SERVE: Place oranges in dessert dishes. Decorate top of cream with a sprinkling of finely grated orange peel or with candied mint leaves or angelica (see page 358).

*ALTERNATE TOPPING: In place of whipped cream an extra amount of orange gelatin may be made, chopped, and either spooned on or squeezed through a pastry bag for a decorative topping.

MENU VIII

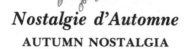

Nostalgie d'Automne
AUTUMN NOSTALGIA

Potage Parmentier
LEEK AND POTATO SOUP

Côtes de Porc Sauce Poivrade
MARINATED PORK CHOPS SAUTÉED
WITH A TANGY SOUR CREAM SAUCE

Chou Vert à la Denise
SAUTÉED SAVOY CABBAGE
WITH SHREDDED ONIONS

Salade Verte
GREEN SALAD

Gâteau aux Raisins
BUTTER CAKE WITH RUM-SOAKED
RAISINS

Mâcon Rouge or Crozes-Hermitage

HERE is one way to take the chill from a brisk autumn evening: hot soup, one popular among country people everywhere, followed by pork chops, prepared with a marinade often used for venison or other game. A cabbage dish, my own creation, and perhaps an endive and beet salad (page 78), would provide pleasant accompaniments. Complete this fare before the rosy glow of a fire with a slice of plum cake, and the memories of crisp air, savory food, and contentment may bring *nostalgie d'automne* to you, too.

RECOMMENDED WINE: Augment this meal with a bottle of Mâcon Rouge. *"C'est là que la grappe distille à l'automne son breuvage embaumé,"* said the poet Lamartine, a nineteenth-century native of Burgundy. "It is in the Mâcon region ... that the grape exudes its scented nectar in the autumn." Or try another wine of excellent body and bouquet, a Crozes-Hermitage from the upper Rhône valley. The vineyards of Hermitage take their name from the fact that the steep hills bordering the river here were once the home of religious hermits.

ORDER OF PREPARATION: The cake should ripen for 24 hours, so plan to make it at least a day ahead. The pork chops, too, should marinate 24 hours. The soup and the first steps for the cabbage may also be done in advance if you wish.

Potage Parmentier

LEEK AND POTATO SOUP

There is no substitute for leeks. Onions or scallions will not do for this recipe.

I always get comments when serving this soup: It is so green!

The color comes from using as much of the leafy part of the leek as possible.

This is a wonderful party recipe, served either hot or cold. The ingredients will serve 4. The soup may be frozen before adding the cream.

INGREDIENTS

2 *cups cubed potatoes (about 3/4 to 1 pound)*
2 *to 2 1/2 cups diced leeks (3 or 4 leeks, depending upon size)*
5 *cups cold water*
1 *tablespoon coarse salt or 1/2 tablespoon table salt*

4 *tablespoons heavy cream*
croûtons (optional)

METHOD

Wash and peel potatoes; cut into cubes.

Cut off hairy roots from leeks. Discard outer leaf if imperfect. Cut away 2/3 of the green portion and slit remaining leaves many times lengthwise so that they flop to facilitate cleaning. Wash well under cold running water. Dice into 1/4-inch pieces.

Combine all ingredients except cream in a 4-quart pot, bring to a boil, covered, over high heat, then simmer gently for 20 to 25 minutes, or until vegetables are tender.*

After vegetables have been cooked, purée them a small quantity at a time in a food mill, food processor, blender, or ricer. Add a bit of the liquid to facilitate the process. Return liquid and purée to cooking pan, cover loosely, and simmer for 30 minutes. Stir from time to time. Correct seasoning if necessary.

TO SERVE: If soup is to be served in individual bowls, place a tablespoon of cream in each bowl and stir with small whisk or fork when adding soup.

If the soup will be brought to table in a tureen, put the full quantity of cream in tureen and whisk while adding soup.

Serve at once.

*TO PREPARE IN A PRESSURE COOKER: Combine all ingredients except cream in cooker, using only 4 cups water. Seal, cover, and place over high heat. When steam escapes, in about 10 minutes, lower heat, cap vent, and continue cooking over medium heat until 15 pounds pressure has been reached (about 7 minutes). Reduce heat to low and cook 15 minutes.

Reduce pressure immediately by holding cooker under cold running water.

This soup thickens as it stands. If it is to be served cold, dilute just a bit with a little milk. Top with *croûtons* if desired.

TO MAKE CROÛTONS: With a 2- to 4-inch cookie cutter, cut circles from the center of several slices of bread. Cut circles in half. Croûtons may be fried or roasted. To fry, melt clarified butter in a small pan and heat croûtons on each side until golden brown. This does not take long, so watch the pan closely. I prefer my croûtons roasted, however. To do this, preheat oven to 450° F. Butter one side of cut bread, place buttered side up on a cookie sheet and roast for about 2 minutes. Turn and brown on the second side for 1 minute. Croûtons are tastier if made just before serving.

Côtes de Porc Sauce Poivrade

MARINATED PORK CHOPS SAUTÉED
WITH A TANGY SOUR CREAM SAUCE

This recipe is best if the chops can marinate for at least 24 hours, so plan to begin preparations a day ahead.
The recipe will serve 4 generously.

MARINATING THE CHOPS

INGREDIENTS

*4 to 6 rib pork chops, 3/4 to 1 inch thick, weighing about
      1/4 pound each*
salt and pepper
2/3 cup dry white wine
2/3 cup red wine vinegar
2 bay leaves
1 teaspoon dried thyme
3/4 cup chopped onion (1 medium onion)
1/2 cup chopped raw carrot (1 medium carrot)
1 teaspoon table salt
1/4 teaspoon freshly ground black pepper, medium grind

METHOD

Trim excess fat from chops. Sprinkle both sides with salt and pepper.

Using a dish large enough to spread chops in without crowding (8 1/2 × 8 1/2 × 1 1/2 inches), combine marinade ingredients and stir well.

Plunge chops into marinade and cover well. Refrigerate for 24 hours, basting and turning several times.

SAUTÉING

INGREDIENTS

5 *tablespoons clarified butter*

METHOD

When ready to cook, heat butter to sizzling in a skillet large enough to accommodate chops without crowding (a 10-inch pan). Rather than crowd them, do a few at a time.

Take chops from marinade and pat with paper towel to remove moisture. Sauté 5 to 6 minutes on each side over medium heat until golden brown.

Cover skillet and let simmer 15 minutes over low heat.

Transfer chops to serving platter, cover (if you don't have a fitted cover use aluminum foil), and keep warm either in a slow oven or on a hot tray.

COMPLETING THE SAUCE

INGREDIENTS

3/4 *cup hot bouillon, either chicken or beef**
3 *tablespoons sour cream*
1 *teaspoon potato flour***
2 *tablespoons cold water*

2 *tablespoons chopped fresh parsley*

USEFUL UTENSIL: *Chinois (conical strainer)*

*Use homemade stock (pages 18–20) or bouillon cubes. If using cubes, combine 1 cup of cold water and 1 cube and simmer for 5 minutes.

**Potato flour gives more body and a finer gloss to your sauce, but if you do not have it on hand, you can substitute the same amount of all-purpose flour.

METHOD

Pour remaining butter from skillet and put in liquid from marinade. Boil over medium heat for 5 minutes, uncovered. Add hot bouillon.

Reduce this liquid over high heat for 3 to 5 minutes, stirring and scraping skillet with wooden spoon.

Spoon sour cream into a bowl. Add several tablespoons of liquid from skillet and whisk. Slowly add this mixture to skillet, whisking vigorously.

Measure potato flour into a cup or small bowl; add water 1 tablespoon at a time, stirring well. Stir several tablespoons of liquid from skillet into this mixture; then add mixture to skillet, whisking well. The flour will cause the sauce to thicken slightly and give it an appetizing lustre. Taste and correct seasoning if necessary.

TO SERVE: Strain sauce over chops on platter, using a *chinois* (conical strainer) or ordinary strainer; press vegetables to extract all juices.

Sprinkle with parsley. Serve at once.

Chou Vert à la Denise

SAUTÉED SAVOY CABBAGE WITH SHREDDED ONIONS

The loose-headed Savoy cabbage, with its yellowy-green, crimped leaves, has a more interesting texture and appearance than the more common smooth-leafed, tight-headed cabbage. However, since it is not always available, ordinary green cabbage may be substituted.

The recipe will serve 4.

INGREDIENTS

2 *pounds Savoy cabbage*
5 *quarts cold water*
4 *tablespoons coarse salt or 2 tablespoons table salt*

6 *tablespoons unsalted butter*
1 *cup shredded yellow onion, well packed*
salt

METHOD

Remove any imperfect outer leaves from the cabbage. Cut into quarters lengthwise and cut away some of the core, leaving enough to hold the leaves together. Immerse in cold water, changing water several times.

Using a large pot (about 9 quarts), add water and salt; bring to boiling point. Plunge cabbage into pot, lower heat, and when water just barely comes to boiling point again, time for 10 minutes, cooking gently, uncovered.

Drain cabbage at once through a colander and hold for several minutes under cold running water. Cut quarters in half lengthwise and gently squeeze out as much moisture as possible, creating neat little pear-shaped bundles with your hands. Squeeze any loose leaves into similar bundles. Secure each bundle with toothpicks to retain shape during further cooking.

Thus far, cabbage may be prepared ahead of time, wrapped well, and stored in refrigerator until needed. It will keep several days.

For the final step, melt butter over medium heat in a skillet large enough to hold the entire amount of cabbage without crowding. (Use two skillets if necessary.) Do not brown butter. Add onion and stir with wooden spoon until glossy (about a minute). Add cabbage, cover skillet, and heat thoroughly, checking from time to time to baste and to make sure cabbage is not browning. Heating will take about 10 minutes on each side.

TO SERVE: Sprinkle cabbage with salt. Transfer to heated vegetable dish. Remove toothpicks. Serve at once.

Gâteau aux Raisins

BUTTER CAKE WITH RUM-SOAKED RAISINS

Prepare raisins a day to a week in advance—the longer the better. The cake itself should be prepared at least a day ahead in order to ripen. It will keep over a week wrapped well and stored in a bread box. Do not freeze.

INGREDIENTS

1 *cup raisins, currants, or a mixture of both*
1 *cup lukewarm water*
3 *tablespoons sugar*
1/4 *cup plus 2 tablespoons rum*

1 *pat unsalted butter*
8 *tablespoons (1/4 pound) whipped sweet butter**
1 *cup granulated sugar*
3 *eggs, extra large or jumbo***
1 1/2 *cups granulated flour*
1/4 *teaspoon baking soda*
1/4 *teaspoon table salt*

USEFUL UTENSILS: 8 3/4 × 4 3/4 × 2 1/2-*inch loaf pan, electric mixer*

METHOD

The day before, or as much as a week before the cake is to be made, the raisins should be prepared: Combine raisins, water, and sugar in a small saucepan, bring slowly to boiling point, simmer 20 minutes. Cool. Strain off raisins, pat dry. Place in a 2-cup bowl, add rum, cover, and allow to soak at least 24 hours.

The day of preparation, preheat oven to 450° F; grease a loaf pan with butter pat.

Cream butter with electric mixer. Add sugar gradually and cream until pale in color, scraping bowl sides often with a rubber spatula. Add eggs one at a time, beating well each time.

In another bowl, combine dry ingredients. Lift raisins from rum bath and distribute them through the flour mixture with your hands or a rubber spatula.

Add dry ingredients to the egg batter, blending together thoroughly with the fingers.

Pour into prepared pan; smooth out surface. Bake on middle rack of oven for 8 minutes at 450° F.

Then, using a long carving knife, cut a cross through length and width of cake, a step which helps this cake to rise. Reduce heat to 300° F. and bake 1 hour. Cake is done when testing needle or knife comes out dry.

Remove from oven and cool on wire rack; unmold. When completely cold, wrap well and allow to ripen at least 24 hours.

TO SERVE: Cover narrow rectangular platter with a paper doily; place cake on platter. Slice as many pieces as desired. The recipe will provide 10 to 12 slices.

*Remove from refrigerator at least 1/2 hour before using.
**Take from refrigerator at least 1 hour before using.

MENU IX

Recevons à la Bonne Franquette
A PARTY FOR 12 WITH LITTLE EFFORT

Filets de Harengs Fumés Marinés
SMOKED HERRING MARINATED
WITH CARROTS AND ONIONS

Poitrine de Boeuf Braisée
BRAISED BRISKET OF BEEF
SMOTHERED IN ONIONS

Purée de Pommes de Terre
WHIPPED POTATOES WITH SWISS
CHEESE

Salade de Chou de Chine
CHINESE CABBAGE SALAD

Tarte aux Pommes
PLUMP APPLE TART WITH COMPOTE
AND APRICOT GLAZE

A domestic dry red wine

ONE of the simplest menus I know for entertaining, this one will serve 12 with ease. Much of the preparation can be done ahead so that on the day of the party the hostess will be able to get things together with a minimum of fuss.

The meal—marinated herring, braised beef brisket, potato purée, Chinese cabbage salad, apple tart—is sure to please.

RECOMMENDED WINE: A good imported wine for 12 will take a big chunk out of any budget. Try a domestic dry red wine which can be purchased by the gallon. Sample some first in smaller bottles so you will know which you prefer. Pour into decanters or pitchers for serving.

ORDER OF PREPARATION: Marinate herring at least 4 days in advance. The compote for the tart should be prepared in advance, too. The tart may be baked and the potatoes peeled and cubed a day ahead. Even the brisket is excellent reheated. As usual, put the salad together at the last minute.

Filets de Harengs Fumés Marinés

SMOKED HERRING MARINATED
WITH CARROTS AND ONIONS

In our home Mother used to serve marinated herring at least once a week, either as an appetizer or as a light supper with *pommes de terre en robe des champs*—potatoes in their dress of the field, that is, boiled in their skins. *Quel bon petit plat!* What a good little dish!

It was not until one of my mother's visits to the United States in the 1950's that I was able to work out this recipe. We were browsing through a supermarket one day when we both exclaimed aloud, *"Harengs à mariner!"* You'd have thought we had discovered a precious jewel! I had never seen the right kind of herrings to marinate before in the United States. They come in a cellophane package labeled *Smoked Herring Fillets.*

Two fillets per serving is plenty for an appetizer. When herring is served as a main dish for a light meal, plan more generous portions.

Prepare the herring at least 4 days ahead of time. They will keep well for several weeks in a cool dry place. If there is no such spot in your home, refrigerate them. Since the oil will gel, you should plan to remove them from the refrigerator at least an hour before serving time.

This recipe will serve 12 as an appetizer or 4 for a light meal. To increase number of servings, make separate batches.

INGREDIENTS

1 *pound smoked fillets of herring*
2 1/2 *cups cold milk*

1 *medium carrot, scraped and sliced into circles*
1 1/2 *cups yellow onion rings (about 1/2 pound)*
5 *bay leaves*
3 1/4 *cups salad oil*

METHOD

Use a dish large enough so that herring can be laid out without crowding. Cover with milk. Allow to soak a minimum of 8 hours in a cool place or in refrigerator.

Place a double layer of paper towels on a cookie sheet. Remove herring from milk one at a time; pat with paper towel, then lay on cookie sheet. Discard milk from soaking dish (sorry, this is one waste!). Rinse dish, dry, and again spread fillets in it. Scatter carrot slices, onion rings, and bay leaves over fillets; add oil.

Marinate for a minimum of 4 days before serving.

TO SERVE: If you are serving this meal buffet style, present herring on a large platter; otherwise, place 2 fillets per person on small salad plates. Fish knives and forks are appropriate to use. Serve thin slices of rye bread, either light or dark, spread with sweet butter to accompany herring.

Poitrine de Boeuf Braisée

BRAISED BRISKET OF BEEF SMOTHERED IN ONIONS

Brisket is the cut of beef from the breast of the animal, the part between the front legs. It is the cut put down in brine to make corned beef.

A whole brisket is made up of two parts: a single brisket, sometimes called a "brisket straight cut," which is the thinner, leaner half; and a double brisket, which is thicker. To feed 12 persons buy a whole brisket, which will weigh from 8 to 12 pounds. You'll probably have to order it ahead of time from a butcher shop or supermarket.

You'll be amazed how easy this meat is to prepare. Again, it is attention to detail that counts.

INGREDIENTS

1 *whole fresh beef brisket (8 to 12 pounds)*
14 *or* 15 *cloves of garlic*
salt and pepper
6 *cups shredded yellow onion (about* 2 1/2 *pounds)*

METHOD

Trim fat from brisket. The butcher will have trimmed some, but there is always more to come off.

Peel garlic and cut each clove into slivers.

With a sharp knife make slits on all sides of the meat; insert slices of garlic.

Heat a roasting pan (one with a cover) or a large Dutch oven on top of stove for 5 minutes. You may have to place roasting pan over 2 burners. *Use no shortening and no rack.*

Brown brisket on one side; it will take about 10 minutes. Turn and brown on second side, sprinkling first side with salt and pepper. When second side is brown, turn and sprinkle again with salt and pepper. During browning move meat in pan to prevent sticking.

Scatter onions over the top of meat; sprinkle well again with salt and pepper. Cover pan and simmer gently over medium heat for 2 hours, basting often. Turn 2 or 3 times during cooking. Pan gravy should bubble gently at all times; it may be necessary to adjust heat now and then.

Cut off a sliver; if it is tender, meat is done.

Place meat on a cutting board to slice. Remove all garlic. If carved in advance, return slices to pan to keep warm in juices.

TO SERVE: Arrange slices on heated platter (over a bed of watercress, if available). Pour juices into gravy boat.

To eat, spoon gravy over meat.

Leftover meat may be reheated or eaten cold.

Purée de Pommes de Terre

WHIPPED POTATOES WITH SWISS CHEESE

For puréed potatoes the ingredients are few, the method easy; all that is needed is care in the preparation. The comments of your guests when they taste this dish will be a delight to your ear!
This recipe will serve 12.

INGREDIENTS

10 *to* 11 *cups cubed potatoes, preferably Maine or Long Island (about* 5 1/2 *pounds)*
6 *cups cold water*
3 *tablespoons coarse salt or* 1 1/2 *tablespoons table salt*
3/4 *pound whipped sweet butter (at room temperature)*
2 *cups warm milk*
3 *cups (about* 3/4 *pound) grated imported Swiss cheese*

USEFUL UTENSILS: *Potato masher, electric mixer*

METHOD

Peel potatoes and cut into 1-inch cubes. Drop into large pot with cold water. This may be done a day ahead and the potatoes stored in the refrigerator.

To cook, add salt, cover pot, and bring to boiling point over moderate heat. Boil 20 minutes. Test for softness by inserting blade of small knife into a cube.

Pour contents into colander to drain off water. Return potatoes to pot; place over low heat. Using a potato masher, mash a small portion at a time and set to one side of pan so that they will be light and fluffy. When all have been mashed, remove pot from heat. Add butter, a tablespoon at a time, mixing in with wooden spoon. Next add milk and cheese alternately, a little at a time, stirring well after each addition with wooden spoon. *It is important to add these ingredients slowly, otherwise texture will be runny.*

When all ingredients have been carefully incorporated, keeping mixture over very low heat, whip with electric hand mixer at high speed for 1 minute.

TO SERVE: Transfer potatoes to a heated covered vegetable dish; swirl fork over surface in a decorative pattern.

For this dinner potatoes should be eaten with the meat. They are especially delicious with the natural juices of the brisket spooned over them.

Salade de Chou de Chine

CHINESE CABBAGE SALAD

A Chinese cabbage salad is ideal for a large number of people. If it must stand for a time after it is tossed, it retains its crispness. It is always refreshing.

This recipe will provide 12 servings.

INGREDIENTS

2 1/2 *pounds Chinese cabbage (usually* 1 *medium-sized head)*
2 *teaspoons table salt*
12 *turns of black pepper mill, medium grind*
2 1/2 *teaspoons chopped garlic*
3/4 *cup red wine vinegar*
2 *cups salad oil*
24 *large black olives (optional)*

METHOD

Separate leaves from cabbage. Remove brown parts, if any. Wash well under running cold water. Drain in salad basket. Pat dry in a clean linen towel. Split in half lengthwise and cut across to make pieces about 2 inches in length. When properly dry, greens may be stored in hydrator until ready to use.

Choose a large salad bowl, one of 5- to 7-quart capacity. Mix in it the salt, pepper, garlic, and vinegar and stir well. Add oil, a small amount at a time, stirring well. If olives are to be used, drain them and add at this time. Dressing may be made in advance; cover bowl with storage wrap. Be sure to stir again before adding salad greens.

When ready to serve, place salad fork and spoon in bowl. Add cut cabbage leaves to salad bowl, allowing leaves to rest on salad implements until ready to toss and serve.

TO SERVE: Have guests help themselves from the bowl; provide small salad plates. There should be two olives per serving.

Tarte aux Pommes

PLUMP APPLE TART WITH COMPOTE
AND APRICOT GLAZE

A Parisian would find it hard to imagine a pastry shop window without an apple tart on display. It has always been a favorite and a specialty of mine and it is one of the first pastries my students learn to make. The sight of the finished product gives them a sense of artistic accomplishment, as it will to you!

This French specialty is made with a *pâte brisée,* one of the basic French pastry doughs. The filling is an apple compote, topped with crescent apple slices, then glazed with apricot preserves.

The French tart pan has straight fluted sides with a detachable bottom; it is about the same height as the American pie pan. The following recipe is for a 12-inch tart pan or a deep 10-inch pie pan.

This recipe is especially useful because it provides the basis for three additional desserts: 1) an apple gelatin made of the juices drained from the apples; 2) dough enough for two more tarts, or one large tart and a dozen tartlets; 3) leftover compote, a delightful dessert served as is in sherbet glasses. Even if I plan to make a smaller tart, I always prepare this amount of compote so that I will have enough for a separate dessert.

THE COMPOTE

INGREDIENTS

6 *pounds apples (Cortland or Baldwin)**
1/2 *cup water*
2 *teaspoons vanilla extract or a vanilla bean*
1/2 *cup sugar*

*This amount of either of these varieties will make 4 cups of drained compote, enough for a 12-inch tart pan or a 10-inch American pie pan. An 8-inch or 9-inch tart requires 1 1/2 to 2 cups of compote.

METHOD

Plan to start compote at least a day ahead, if possible, because the apples should drain many hours.

Pare, core, and quarter apples. Place in a large pot, one of 5- to 6-quart capacity. Add water and vanilla. Cover and bring to boiling point over high heat. Reduce heat to medium and cook gently for 20 minutes. Do not stir, but shake pan occasionally to prevent sticking.

After 20 minutes, add sugar, fold in gently with wooden spoon, and cook another 5 minutes. Remove from heat. If vanilla bean has been used, remove, wash, dry, and store for future use.

Place colander over a large bowl. Pour compote into colander. (If metal colander is used, line with double thickness of cheesecloth to prevent discoloration of fruit.) Set aside to drain. Refrigerate, if desired, when compote has cooled completely. From time to time gently press fruit with wooden spoon to squeeze out as much liquid as possible.* Be careful not to mash the apples. Allow to drain until ready to put in crust.

THE CRUST

INGREDIENTS

1 2/3 *cups flour***
4 *tablespoons granulated sugar*
1 *teaspoon table salt*
9 *tablespoons unsalted butter (1/4 pound plus 1/2 ounce)****
1/3 *cup cold water*

USEFUL UTENSILS: *Coupe-pâte (dough scraper), pince-pâte (dough pincher)*

METHOD

Many really good cooks become frantic at the thought of handling dough; they bring themselves to the task as if getting ready for battle. I am pleased to say that many of my students have overcome that fear. There are just two important keys to remember: 1) Never start dough on a damp day; it is apt to become too moist,

*The juice recovered from the compote can be used to make an apple gelatin dessert. The recipe is on page 111.
**Any flour can be used, but for beginners pastry flour is best.
***Take from refrigerator 30 minutes before using.

limp, and difficult to work. 2) Allow dough to rest at least 2 hours in the refrigerator. Return it to the refrigerator for 1/2 hour anytime you begin to have trouble rolling it out.

Remember these pointers, follow directions carefully step by step, and success is assured!

Start well in advance, as dough should rest at least 2 hours before being rolled out. It may be stored in the refrigerator several days, or frozen if kept for a longer period.

Measure flour into a medium-sized mixing bowl (about 1- to 2-quart capacity). Make a well in center of flour; place sugar, salt, and butter in well, cutting butter into small pieces. Gradually add water. Then, working fast, mix lightly with fingertips until dough is sufficiently moist to hold together. Form into loose ball, remove from bowl, and place on a lightly floured board or table top.

The next step is to distribute the butter more thoroughly by a procedure known as *fraisage:* With the heel of the palm, press a section of dough against board and away from you. Repeat until all dough has been treated in this manner. Do not over-work, as butter should not be too soft.

Scrape dough together and form into a ball. Sprinkle lightly with flour. Wrap in waxed paper or freezer wrap. Refrigerate at least 2 hours to permit dough to rest.

ROLL OUT DOUGH: When dough has rested, remove from refrigerator. After 2 hours, dough should be just right to roll out. If it has rested overnight or longer, it will have to stand at room temperature for about 1/2 hour. Dough is workable when it rolls out easily and can be flipped from side to side without difficulty.

Place dough on a lightly floured surface. Beginning from the center, roll with brisk motions into a circle approximately 19 to 20 inches in diameter. Turn dough several times so that it does not stick; this is most easily accomplished by flipping it over the rolling pin as you go along. Dust working surface with flour each time; do not be afraid of disturbing the proportions of the dough.

Invert tart or pie pan on top of dough and cut out a circle at least 2 inches larger than pan.

Turn pan upright, flip dough onto rolling pin, then flip into pan. Press it smoothly to shape of pan. Push dough upward around sides; when it overlaps rim, trim off excess by pressing rolling pin around rim. Again push dough upward around sides. This time flute excess to make decorative rim with either a fork or a *pince-pâte*.

Roll remaining dough into a ball, wrap well, and either refrigerate or freeze for future use.

BAKE DOUGH: Prick bottom and sides of dough with fork. Cover entire surface with foil. Place in refrigerator for 1 hour or more.

Preheat oven to 425° F.

Place a weight such as dried beans or coins on top of foil to prevent blistering. Bake dough 10 minutes. Remove foil carefully. If dough has shrunk away from sides, press it to fit firmly again; it will still be workable at this point. Bake another 3 to 5 minutes. Watch carefully. Dough should be golden brown. If it is not, bake a few more minutes. Place on wire rack to cool.

ASSEMBLING AND BAKING

INGREDIENTS

2 *pounds raw apples*
confectioners' sugar (optional)

METHOD

When crust is cool, fill shell with compote to the rim. Smooth top with rubber spatula.

Peel and core remaining apples; cut into semicircular slices 1/8 to 1/4 inch thick. Arrange around top in three circular rows. Overlap slices of first row in a clockwise direction; overlap slices of second row in a counterclockwise direction; use clockwise direction again for third row. It is important that slices overlap as much as possible, as they will shrink in the baking.

Place in preheated 425° F. oven and bake 30 minutes. Turn pan to make sure cooking is proceeding evenly and bake another

15 minutes. Cool slightly on wire rack.* Sprinkle with sugar while still warm and serve, or cool and glaze.

GLAZING

INGREDIENTS

2 12-*ounce jars apricot preserves*

METHOD

When tart is cold, place preserves in a small saucepan and boil gently 5 minutes, stirring constantly. Remove from heat and cool 1 minute. Pour immediately onto tart and spread over entire surface, using a goose-feather or other pastry brush. Be sure to use glaze immediately, as it hardens when cooling. Excess glaze may be returned to jar.

TO SERVE: Cut wedges with sharp knife and lift out with cake server.

*If you wish to serve the tart at another time, let it cool completely, wrap it, and freeze it. When you are planning to serve it, remove from freezer and defrost. Preheat oven to 425° F., cover tart with foil wrap, and place it in center of oven, reducing heat to 300° F. Allow tart to heat through (this can take as long as 45 minutes). Then proceed as if freshly baked, sugaring or glazing as described.

APPLE GELATIN DESSERT: From the juice recovered from the compote, you can make a delicious dessert. This amount will be enough for 4 to 8 servings, depending upon the size of the portions.

INGREDIENTS

2 *cups apple juice*
1 *package unflavored gelatin*
1 *to 2 drops red food coloring (optional)*

sweetened whipped cream (optional)

METHOD

Set a small pan of hot water over low heat on the stove.
Dissolve gelatin in 1/2 cup of apple juice in a 1-cup measure. Place in pan of hot water and stir 5 minutes until gelatin completely dissolves.

Stir mixture into remaining juice. Add food coloring if desired.

Rinse a 2-cup mold in cold water. Pour juice in; place in refrigerator for at least 2 hours.

TO UNMOLD: Loosen top edge with a small knife. Slip mold into basin of hot water for 10 seconds. Invert onto a serving platter and shake. If gelatin does not slip out, hold again in hot water for 3 seconds. Wipe away any liquid spotting platter.

TO SERVE: Decorate with sweetened whipped cream, squeezed through a pastry bag to suit your fancy. Bring platter to table. Cut *gelée* into servings and place on individual dessert dishes.

MENU X

Un Air de Provence
A BREATH OF PROVENCE

Soupe au Pistou
VEGETABLE SOUP WITH
TOMATO, GARLIC, AND BASIL

Maquereaux au Chambertin
MACKEREL SIMMERED IN RED WINE
WITH SHALLOTS

Salade de Pissenlit au Lard
DANDELION SALAD WITH BACON

Beignets Soufflés
PUFFED FRITTERS WITH ORANGE ZEST

*Chambertin or Clos de Vougeot
and Sauternes*

ALTHOUGH only the soup in this menu is truly a specialty of Provence, its aroma and flavor will linger on—*un air de Provence*— throughout the meal. The main dish, *Maquereaux au Chambertin,* is a favorite in the Côte de Nuits where Chambertin originates, and wherever fresh mackerel is found. The salad is an interesting combination of dandelion greens and bacon, and the dessert, tangy, orange-flavored fritters.

RECOMMENDED WINE: Serve a velvety Chambertin, the "jewel of Burgundy," or its close cousin, a Clos de Vougeot, another full-bodied red wine from the Côte de Nuits, with the mackerel. For the fritters choose a sweet dessert wine, any of those from the Sauternes region of Bordeaux.

ORDER OF PREPARATION: Soup and paste for the fritters can be made ahead. The mackerel and salad should be prepared just before serving. Fry the *Beignets* while your diners wait.
Quel bon diner pour faire oublier les soucis!

Soupe au Pistou

VEGETABLE SOUP WITH
TOMATO, GARLIC, AND BASIL

This soup is a symphony of vegetables, harmoniously blended with a *pistou* made by crushing tomatoes, garlic, basil, and oil together. It is a specialty of Provence in southeastern France.

My younger son, who is not too fond of soups, has eaten this one for breakfast!

No other vegetable need be served with the meal when this soup is the appetizer. A crisp salad after the main course is sufficient.

This recipe will serve 4 amply. The soup can be prepared several days in advance, but the cooked dry beans and cooked macaroni should be added when soup is being warmed.

INGREDIENTS

1 *cup lukewarm water*
1/4 *cup dry white beans (navy, California, or Italian cannalenni)*
1/8 *teaspoon baking soda*
1/2 *teaspoon table salt*

1 1/2 *cups lukewarm water*
1/2 *teaspoon table salt*

1/2 *to 3/4 pound shell beans (optional)*
1/2 *cup lukewarm water*
1/2 *teaspoon table salt*

4 *cups lukewarm water*
1/2 *tablespoon coarse salt or 1/4 tablespoon table salt*
1 *cup (about 1/2 pound) peeled cubed potatoes*

1/4 *pound summer squash, peeled and cubed*
1/4 *pound zucchini, washed and cubed, but not peeled*
1/2 *pound tomatoes*
1/4 *pound green beans*

1/4 *cup elbow macaroni*
1 *cup boiling water*
1/4 *teaspoon table salt*

USEFUL UTENSIL: *Pestle*

METHOD

Blanching the white beans in baking soda makes them more digestible. Begin the day before, if possible, or at least several hours ahead of time, so that they may soak.

Combine beans, 1 cup water, soda, and salt in a 4-cup saucepan; bring slowly to a boil, covered; then remove from heat. This should take about 20 minutes. Set aside and allow to stand with lid on for at least 1 hour, or overnight.

After soaking, drain off all water. Add the 1 1/2 cups of water and 1/2 teaspoon of salt. Cover pan, bring to boiling point, and simmer 25 to 30 minutes. Test after 25 minutes, beans should be soft but not mushy. Some beans require longer cooking. Also, some beans, like the *cannalenni*, soak up more water as they cook. Add water as needed. Set aside until needed.

While white beans are cooking, if you are going to add the shell beans, combine them with water and salt in a quart saucepan. Cover, bring to boiling point, then simmer for 20 to 30 minutes.

Test after 20 minutes; beans should be soft, but not mushy; drain.

Meanwhile, combine water, salt, and potatoes in a 4-quart pot—one large enough so that all vegetables may be combined together in it at the end. Cover, bring to boiling point, and simmer 20 minutes.

PREPARE VEGETABLES: Peel and cube summer squash; wash and cube zucchini. Skin tomatoes,* cut them in half crosswise, and squeeze gently to remove seeds and juice. Remove tips and strings, if any, from green beans; then wash and cut into about 2-inch pieces.

Add squash and tomatoes to boiling potatoes. Cover pan and, when again boiling, time for 5 minutes. Drop in beans, cover, and time again for 7 minutes.

Meanwhile, bring salted water to rolling boil in a 1-quart saucepan. Pour in macaroni, stirring constantly with a fork. Allow to come again to rolling boil, then time for 10 minutes. Drain.

Add white beans, macaroni, and shell beans to vegetables 5 to 10 minutes before soup will be served.

THE PISTOU

INGREDIENTS

1/4 *pound tomatoes, peeled*
salt
1 *large garlic clove (about 1/2 teaspoon, minced)*
3/4 *tablespoon dried basil or 1 1/2 tablespoons chopped fresh basil*
2 *tablespoons olive oil*

1/4 *cup (about 1 ounce) grated imported Swiss cheese*

METHOD

Le pistou must be made right in the soup tureen or a large bowl, for soup is always added to the *pistou,* never the *pistou* to the soup!

Place tomatoes in tureen; sprinkle with salt; add garlic, and crush with pestle or mash with fork. Crush in basil. Add oil a little at a time, stirring with whisk.

*If skins do not peel off easily, plunge them into boiling water for 60 seconds; skins will then slip off.

Stir hot soup into *le pistou* a little at a time. Taste and add more salt if necessary.

TO SERVE: Sprinkle cheese over the top. Serve at once.

Maquereaux au Chambertin

MACKEREL SIMMERED IN RED WINE WITH SHALLOTS

Here is one time that red wine is used in a sauce for fish. This recipe calls for Chambertin, a fine red Burgundy, but any good dry red wine may be substituted.

Prepared in this way, the mackerel may also be served as an appetizer if desired.

The recipe will serve 4 as a main course or 8 as an appetizer. For more servings, make in batches.

COOKING THE MACKEREL

INGREDIENTS

*4 large tinker mackerel fillets or 4 regular fillets**
pat of unsalted butter
salt and pepper
main bones of the mackerel
2 cups dry red wine
2 beef cubes
5 teaspoons chopped shallots

METHOD

Ask to have the mackerel filleted by your fish seller. He will remove the head and main bones and cut the fish in half, providing two fillets per mackerel. The skin is almost impossible to remove. Be sure to ask for the bones!

Pat fillets with paper towel to remove moisture. Make several

*A tinker mackerel is from 8 to 13 inches long, and weighs no more than 1 pound. Anything larger is simply called a "mackerel," although those over 2 pounds are sometimes called (or miscalled) "king mackerel."

thin cuts slant-wise across the flesh grain in each fillet to prevent curling while cooking. Sprinkle both sides of fillets with salt and pepper. Use a 12-inch frying pan or one large enough so that mackerel will not be crowded. Rub butter on bottom of pan.

Arrange fillets in pan; add fish bones, breaking them into pieces if necessary. Add wine; crumble in beef cubes; stir. Sprinkle on shallots. Cover pan and bring to boiling point over medium heat. (This will take about 4 minutes.) Remove immediately from heat and set aside for 3 minutes. (Fish will crumble less if allowed to relax before being moved.) Using a large metal spatula to prevent breaking fillets, transfer them to heated platter and keep hot in a warm oven.

PREPARING THE SAUCE

INGREDIENTS

2 *tablespoons granulated flour**
1 *tablespoon soft butter (preferably whipped sweet butter)***
2 *to 3 drops red food coloring (optional)*
1/2 *teaspoon Worcestershire sauce****

3 *to 4 teaspoons chopped fresh parsley*

USEFUL UTENSIL: *Chinois (conical strainer)*

METHOD

Bring liquid with bones to a boil, uncovered, over high heat. Boil vigorously for 2 minutes.

Strain liquid into a saucepan. (A conical strainer is handy for this.) Press bones against strainer with a wooden spoon to extract as much juice as possible. Place pan over medium heat.

Make a *beurre manié* by mixing flour and butter together with your fingers into a thick paste. Add it, small amounts at a time, to the liquid while constantly moving the pan on the burner in a circular motion. (This action, called *vanner,* will gradually incorporate the paste into the liquid and thicken it, and the sauce will

*I prefer to use granulated flour to make *beurre manié,* because it mixes more readily. All-purpose flour can be substituted if you wish.
**Take from refrigerator an hour before using.
***Worcestershire sauce, like food coloring, enhances the color of the sauce, but its use is optional.

be much shinier than if stirred with whisk or spoon.) Do not let sauce boil.

When sauce has thickened, add red food coloring and Worcestershire sauce, if desired; blend well with wooden spoon. Taste and correct seasoning if necessary.

TO SERVE: Transfer mackerel to a warm serving platter. (I use an oval silver platter and arrange fillets diagonally.) Pour on sauce; sprinkle with parsley. Serve at once.

These mackerel need no accompaniment except a glass of Chambertin or the same wine used in the sauce, and some crusty French bread.

Salade de Pissenlit au Lard

DANDELION SALAD WITH BACON

Dandelion salad is served traditionally with bacon in many French homes. The marriage provides an appealing contrast of textures, and the slight bitterness of the greens combined with the smoky taste of fried bacon is unique.

If cultivated or wild dandelions are not available, you can substitute chicory.

These ingredients will provide 4 generous (or 6 medium) portions.

INGREDIENTS

1/2 pound dandelion leaves, cultivated or wild
1/2 pound bacon (preferably slab)
4 turns black pepper mill (medium grind)
1 teaspoon chopped garlic
4 tablespoons red wine vinegar
8 tablespoons rendered bacon fat

METHOD

Trim bottoms of dandelions and discard imperfect leaves; remove any dark spots. Wash in several changes of cold water until free of all dirt or sand. Drain well in salad basket or colander. Shake well. Place on clean linen towel and pat dry.

Slice bacon into 1/2-inch cubes. Fry in an 8- or 10-inch frying pan over medium heat. Slab bacon will take 10 minutes to cook; sliced bacon will take 5 (3 minutes over high heat, then 2 minutes over low). Stir bacon occasionally until well browned.

While bacon is frying, place pepper and garlic in bottom of a 1 1/2- to 2-quart salad bowl. Cut dandelion leaves into bite-size pieces. Place greens and fried bacon in salad bowl. Add vinegar and rendered bacon fat. Toss well. (This way of adding shortening and vinegar to a green salad deviates from the traditional method, but it allows the fat to mix more thoroughly with the greens.)

TO SERVE: Toss well again. Present on individual salad plates and savor after the main course.

Beignets Soufflés

PUFFED FRITTERS WITH ORANGE ZEST

For the French, *Beignets* of all kinds are a festive dessert. They are associated with the *Mardi-Gras* and *Mi-Carême* holidays when, after parades and costume parties, they are served to the delight of children and adults alike.

The base of *Beignets* is *pâte à chou*, cream puff paste, one of the easiest doughs to make. Although a fried confection, the *Beignets* are not greasy when they are properly made.

This is a good recipe to keep in mind when unexpected company drops in. Within half an hour you can have a pyramid of puffs ready to put on the table. The paste can be made in advance and refrigerated. The recipe makes 1 1/2 to 2 dozen *Beignets*.

INGREDIENTS

1 *cup cold water*
1 *teaspoon table salt*
2 *tablespoons granulated sugar*
1/4 *pound (8 tablespoons) unsalted butter*
1 *cup all-purpose flour*
4 *jumbo eggs**
3 *teaspoons finely grated orange rind*

6 *cups salad oil*
confectioners' sugar

*Remove from refrigerator 30 to 60 minutes before using.

USEFUL UTENSIL: *Frying vessel or a pan of 3- to 6-quart capacity*

METHOD

Combine water, salt, sugar, and butter in a 2-quart saucepan; bring to a boil over high heat, stirring constantly so that butter is dissolved and well combined. Reduce heat to medium and add flour all at once. Stir vigorously with wooden spoon. *The wooden spoon is indispensable to obtain the right consistency of cream puff paste!* Mixture will form a paste which will leave the sides of the pan.

Remove pan from heat and add eggs, one at a time, stirring each one vigorously until it is well blended before adding the next. Stir in orange peel.

Batter is now ready to fry. It should be smooth and shiny and have the consistency of thick mayonnaise.

TO FRY: A frying vessel is ideal, but any pan of 3- to 6-quart capacity may be used. Just be sure *Beignets* are not crowded when frying. Pour in 2 inches of oil. It will take about 10 minutes over medium heat to reach the right temperature; a frying thermometer should read between 360° F. and 380° F. Test with a drop of batter, if it sizzles and colors quickly, oil is ready.

Drop paste into oil a heaping teaspoonful at a time, allowing enough room so that the *Beignets* may swim and twirl freely by themselves. Fry 5 to 7 minutes. When they give the appearance of being firm, turn them, if they have not already turned by themselves, so they will cook evenly to a golden brown. Tap them. If they feel firm, they are done. The whole process should take about 10 to 12 minutes.

Remove *Beignets* from oil onto wire rack and allow to drain. Sprinkle with confectioners' sugar while still hot. Lay a bed of crumpled paper towels on a cookie sheet in a warm (not hot) oven; transfer *Beignets* to cookie sheet to keep hot until all are ready to serve. They may be kept this way for as long as an hour and still be crunchy and light.

When oil is cold, strain through a double thickness of cheese-cloth into a jar which can be tightly closed. Stored in a cool place, it will keep almost indefinitely.

TO SERVE: Place a linen napkin in the bottom of serving bowl or on a platter;* arrange *Beignets* in a pyramid. Sprinkle again with confectioners' sugar. Or place three or four beignets on individual dessert plates; sprinkle with sugar.

*Instructions for folding the napkin are on page 122.

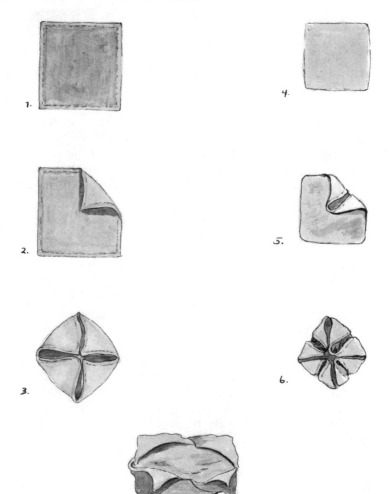

TO FOLD A CLOTH NAPKIN: To make an attractive presentation of fried food, use a luncheon napkin about 18 inches square, and proceed as follows:

1) Place it flat on a table.

2 and 3) Fold each corner to meet in the middle, forming a smaller square.

4) Turn over the napkin without losing the square shape.

5) Repeat the first process, having the corners meet in the middle, forming a smaller square.

6) Turn it over again. From the center roll the corners back to form petals.

7) Put the prepared napkin on the service dish as an attractive bed for the food.

MENU XI

Le Menu de Lundi
A MONDAY MEAL

Pommes de Terre en Salade
HOT POTATO SALAD WITH
WINE VINEGAR DRESSING

Coeur de Veau en Tranches
VEAL HEART STEAKS
WITH GARLIC AND PARSLEY

Pâtisson Blanc Américain
CROWN SQUASH AU GRATIN

Salade Verte
GREEN SALAD

Visitandines
ALMOND PASTRIES

Rosé de Tavel or Rosé de Béarn

IN France, *le coeur de veau*, veal heart, often appears on a Monday table, for that is the day the butcher shops close and one must buy from *les triperies*, shops which specialize in innards. Veal hearts make a wonderful, simple luncheon dish served with a salad, crusty French bread, and a little wine. For this menu they are introduced by a simple potato salad and followed by crown squash *au gratin*, a dish exquisite to both eye and palate. A green salad, such as the chicory salad on page 44, would be an appropriate third course. The dessert is a delicate almond pastry, *Visitandines*.

RECOMMENDED WINE: You might serve Tavel Rosé, a dry, fresh rosé with character, from the southern Côte du Rhône; or a pleasant, fresh Rosé de Béarn from the southwestern tip of France.

ORDER OF PREPARATION: *Visitandines* can be made several days ahead and stored in a tight tin. The first steps in the preparation of the squash can be done a day in advance, if you like. Prepare potato salad just before eating if you plan to serve it warm; otherwise, it can be made 2 or 3 days ahead of time. Sauté the hearts just before serving.

Pommes de Terre en Salade

HOT POTATO SALAD WITH WINE VINEGAR DRESSING

For this menu potato salad is served as an appetizer, but this recipe is also marvelous as part of a cold buffet or as picnic fare. I prefer to eat this salad while the potatoes are still warm, but, of course, it may also be served cold.

The ingredients here make about a quart, enough for 4 persons.

INGREDIENTS

4 *cups cooked sliced potatoes (about 3 large ones)*

1 *to* 1 1/2 *teaspoons table salt*
3 *turns of the black pepper mill, medium grind*
1 *heaping teaspoon chopped garlic*
2 *tablespoons red wine vinegar·*
2 *tablespoons salad oil*

4 *tablespoons warm white wine or boiling water*
2 *teaspoons chopped fresh parsley*

METHOD

Wash potatoes* under running water. Do not peel. Cover with lukewarm water in 4-quart saucepan and bring to boiling point—slowly, so that potatoes will not burst—with pan covered. Boil gently over medium to low heat for 35 to 40 minutes. Glide blade of a small knife through to center to test if they are done.

Remove potatoes from water and allow to cool slightly for easier handling. Peel while still hot, using a potholder or two-pronged fork to hold them; then cut into 1/3-inch slices on a cutting board.

In a large salad bowl (about a 2-quart one), arrange half the slices in layers; sprinkle on half of dressing ingredients in order listed; toss, being careful not to break potato slices. Add remaining potatoes, then sprinkle on remaining dressing ingredients and toss again. Mix in white wine or water; toss again. If you are serving the salad immediately, sprinkle on parsley.

If this salad is made in advance, be sure to remove from refrigerator at least 1/2 hour before serving time. Toss again. Sprinkle on parsley.

For a variation, add fillets of drained anchovies or black Greek olives before tossing final time.

TO SERVE: Salad may be brought to the table in the bowl in which it has been mixed or spooned onto a bed of lettuce on individual salad plates.

Coeur de Veau en Tranches

VEAL HEART STEAKS WITH GARLIC AND PARSLEY

Most people enjoy veal hearts. Their flavor is mild, not at all like that of liver or kidney, and they have the delicate texture of sautéed mushrooms when they are properly cooked. My youngest daughter, Patti, who could eat them every day, cooks them to perfection.

Veal hearts are best very fresh. If you do purchase them ahead, wrap them in storage paper and freeze.** I like to keep some on

*I prefer baking potatoes for this recipe, as they do not crumble as readily when sliced.
**Frozen hearts should be defrosted completely before preparing, either overnight in the refrigerator or several hours at room temperature.

hand in the freezer; they are inexpensive, freeze well, and with 2 or 3 minutes of preparation, are ready to bring to the table.

INGREDIENTS

2 *pounds of veal hearts**
8 *tablespoons clarified butter (or about 2 tablespoons per slice)*
salt and pepper

1 *teaspoon chopped garlic*
8 *to 10 sprigs of fresh parsley, chopped*

METHOD

Trim fat from top of hearts. Halve each heart, cutting through horizontally, and remove all blood vessels. Cut again horizontally into 1/4-inch thick steaks and score them with a knife so that they do not curl.

Using a 12-inch frying pan, one large enough to take all pieces uncrowded, heat butter over high heat until sizzling.** Reduce heat to medium and sauté meat, 2 minutes on first side, 1 minute on second side. Hearts should be nicely browned on both sides; center will be rare to medium rare. Do not overcook or meat will be tough. Sprinkle both sides with salt and pepper.

Chop garlic and parsley together. (This can be done in advance.)

TO SERVE: Transfer hearts to heated serving platter. Sprinkle with parsley–garlic mixture; pour on pan juice. Serve immediately.

How can such a simple dish be so good?

Pâtisson Blanc Américain

CROWN SQUASH AU GRATIN

I love to purchase crown squash when I find them in the market. They are such attractive little vegetables to look at and can be made so simply into this tasty dish. They are sold under the name crown or white button squash.

*Some hearts are small; others will weigh as much as 2 pounds.
**It is important that the pan be large enough and hot enough so that the hearts will brown properly.

This recipe is a good one to follow any main dish which does not contain cheese. It will serve 4.

BOILING THE SQUASH

INGREDIENTS

2 *pounds crown squash**
3 *quarts cold water*
1 1/2 *tablespoons coarse salt or 3/4 tablespoon table salt*

METHOD

Wash squash in cold water, changing water several times. Stems are short, so do not remove them; they add to the attractiveness of the finished dish.

Bring salted water to a rolling boil with cover on. Drop squash in; bring again to rolling boil and boil uncovered over high heat for about 7 minutes. (If squash are large, cooking time will be longer.) When small knife blade glides in and out easily, they are done.**

At this point, squash may be stored in refrigerator, well wrapped, for several days. The final baking should be done just before you are ready to serve.

*Try to buy squash that are between 2 and 3 inches in diameter, as they are prettier and tastier.

**ALTERNATE METHOD: If you prefer, squash may be cooked in a pressure cooker: Combine 1/2 cup cold water and 1/2 teaspoon salt in the cooker; place squash on rack. Cover and seal. When steam escapes, cap vent and continue cooking over medium heat until 15 pounds pressure has been reached. Cook for 3 minutes, then reduce pressure immediately by running cold water over cooker. Lift out squash and drain.

BAKING THE SQUASH

INGREDIENTS

1 *pat unsalted butter*
salt and pepper
1 1/2 *to* 2 *teaspoons grated Swiss cheese per squash*
1 *to* 1 1/2 *teaspoons unsalted butter per squash*
6 *to* 8 *teaspoons chopped parsley*

METHOD

Preheat oven to 450° F.
Coat a baking dish, large enough to hold squash uncrowded, with butter.
Cut squash in half horizontally; scoop out seeds with spoon. Place bottom halves in baking dish, cutting a bit off bottoms if necessary to make them rest evenly.
Sprinkle with salt, pepper, and cheese; dot with butter. Place stem halves on top; sprinkle with cheese; dot with butter. Bake 12 minutes.*

TO SERVE: If you have baked the squash in an attractive dish, bring it to the table right from the oven; otherwise, transfer it to a heated serving platter.
Sprinkle with parsley.
Vraiment très bon!

Visitandines

ALMOND PASTRIES

Visitandines are little pastries made of sugar, flour, almonds, butter, and egg whites, and baked in *petits-fours* molds. Traditionally they are rectangular in shape, about 4 × 2 × 1/2 inches. However, any shaped *petit-four* or tart mold will do as long as the depth is not more than 1/2 inch. This is important, for the delicate texture of the pastry is lost if the molds are too deep.
The simplest of recipes, *Visitandines* may be made as much as

*If more convenient, squash can be broiled, 5 to 6 inches from the heat source, for 10 minutes.

a week in advance, for they keep well stored in a tight tin box. This recipe makes enough for 2 1/2 to 3 dozen when made in *petits-fours* molds, or for 13 to 15 when made in traditional molds. For larger amounts, make in batches.

INGREDIENTS

8 *tablespoons unsalted butter*
2/3 *cup pastry, cake, or granulated flour*
1/2 *cup powdered almonds**
2/3 *cup granulated sugar*
4 *egg whites*
1/2 *teaspoon vanilla extract*

USEFUL UTENSIL: *Petits-fours molds or tart molds no deeper than 1/2 inch*

METHOD

Preheat oven to 400° F.

Melt butter slowly over medium heat until golden brown to obtain *beurre noisette,* butter with a nutty flavor.

Using a pastry brush, coat molds generously with some of this melted butter; drain the excess from the molds back into the pan.

In a 2- to 3-cup mixing bowl blend together flour, almonds, and sugar with your fingers.

Beat 2 egg whites lightly with fork and pour slowly into dry ingredients. Stir thoroughly with a rubber or plastic spatula until mixture forms a paste. Repeat with other 2 egg whites. Then stir vigorously for 2 minutes. Batter should stick to bowl.

*For this recipe, I buy packages of already chopped nuts, then powder them in my blender or chop them very finely in a food processor or chopping bowl. A more economical way is to buy nuts in the shell by the pound. One-half pound of nuts will yield 3/4 of a cup when chopped. The almonds do not have to be blanched.

Stir in remaining *beurre noisette,* then vanilla.

Place molds on a cookie sheet for easier handling. Fill them with a teaspoon. *Be sure to stir the batter before filling each mold.* This step is important in retaining the consistency of the mixture. Bake on middle rack of preheated oven for 6 to 7 minutes. If you are using the larger *Visitandines* molds, they may take up to 12 minutes. Check after 5 minutes to see that they are baking evenly. Turn if necessary.

When done, *Visitandines* should be a dark golden brown. Set molds on wire pastry rack to cool. If the molds have been carefully buttered and the pastries baked sufficiently, they will slip easily from the molds when cool. If they do not, return to the oven for a few minutes or loosen by running a knife gently all around and underneath the pastries.

TO SERVE: Place in little paper cups, unmolded side up.

Menu XII

Quand Mon Mari est Chef
WHEN MY HUSBAND IS CHEF

Poireaux à l'Huile et au Vinaigre
LEEKS VINAIGRETTE

Coq au Vin
CHICKEN IN RED WINE WITH ONIONS AND MUSHROOMS, SERVED WITH CROÛTONS

Pommes de Terre Duchesse
BRIOCHE-SHAPED DUCHESS POTATOES

Salade Verte
GREEN SALAD

Omelette à la Confiture
OMELET FILLED WITH APRICOT PRESERVES

Aloxe-Corton or Volnay

FUN to plan and prepare, this menu, once accomplished, gives one a sense of what it is to be a competent *cuisinière*, or *cuisinier*, as the case may be. *Coq au Vin*, the main course, is one my husband enjoys preparing.

With simple leeks vinaigrette as appetizer, delicate Duchess potatoes to follow the *Coq*, and a dessert omelet filled with preserves, the meal is elegant but simple. A *salade verte* such as the escarole salad described on page 148 would be a pleasant addition.

RECOMMENDED WINE: Serve an Aloxe-Corton or a Volnay, two delicate, smooth red Burgundies, with the main course and use the same wine in preparing the *Coq*. As a finishing touch, serve the good French Cognac used in the entrée, after the coffee.

ORDER OF PREPARATION: First prepare the leeks; next, the potatoes except for the final glazing and browning; then the *Coq*. (All of this may be done ahead.) Finally, gather and ready the ingredients for the last-minute cooking of the omelet.

Poireaux à l'Huile et au Vinaigre

LEEKS VINAIGRETTE

The French buy leeks the way Americans buy potatoes; as a basic ingredient to have on hand. King of vegetables in the French kitchen, leeks are used in countless ways: in soups and salads, as a vegetable, as a flavoring for stocks and broths.

The long and slender leek belongs to the onion family. It is thicker than its relative the scallion; its roots are bushier and its flavor milder. Most American markets carry leeks. Ask for them if you don't see them.

This recipe will provide 4 portions. For more servings, two bunches of leeks may be cooked in the same amount of water. Divide the cooked leeks into two vegetable dishes and toss each with the amount of dressing given.

INGREDIENTS

3 *quarts water*
1 *tablespoon coarse salt or* 1 1/2 *teaspoons table salt*
4 *to* 8 *leeks, depending upon size*

1/4 *teaspoon table salt*
1/8 *teaspoon freshly ground pepper, medium grind*
2 *teaspoons chopped shallots or chopped red onion*
1 1/2 *tablespoons red wine vinegar*
2 *tablespoons salad oil*

METHOD

Add salt to water; bring to boil.

Cut hairy roots and outer leaves from leeks. Then cut off two-thirds of the green, leafy portion. Slit remaining green leaves lengthwise so that they flop to facilitate cleaning. Wash well under running water.

Drop leeks into water and boil, uncovered, for 10 to 20 minutes. Leeks are done when white part feels soft under probing knife. Drain. Cut crosswise into inch-long pieces. Place in vegetable dish; sprinkle with salt and pepper. Add shallots, vinegar, and oil in order. Toss.

Leeks may be eaten hot, warm, or cold. They keep well several days under refrigeration.

TO SERVE: In France, leeks prepared this way often appear as an appetizer. Usually they are presented in a vegetable dish and each person helps himself to a serving on a small plate.

Coq au Vin

CHICKEN IN RED WINE WITH ONIONS AND MUSHROOMS, SERVED WITH CROÛTONS

Usually red wine is not used with chicken, but this recipe is a brilliant exception. Choose a smooth red wine, preferably a good Burgundy, for your cooking wine, and serve the same at the table to accompany the *Coq*. Elegant as it is, this dish is not difficult to prepare. My version uses very little fat.

This recipe will serve 4, and double of the amount of chicken

may be used with the same quantity of the other ingredients. It is delicious the second day.

INGREDIENTS

2 1/4- to 3-*pound broiler or roasting chicken*
flour
salt and pepper
20 *small white onions*
8 *tablespoons clarified butter*
3 *tablespoons flour*
1 *garlic clove, chopped*
1/4 *cup Cognac*
1 *bottle dry red wine (about 3 1/2 cups)*
bouquet garni (5 to 6 sprigs of parsley and 2 bay leaves tied together)

1/2 *to* 1 *pound fresh white mushrooms*

USEFUL UTENSIL: 12-*inch frying pan or Dutch oven*

METHOD

Cut chicken into quarters or smaller pieces. Dry with paper towel, coat with flour. Sprinkle each piece with salt and pepper.

Peel onions. The skins of white onions are so thin that they can be peeled more easily if blanched first. Place onions in a colander or strainer and submerge in boiling water for 1 minute. Cut off root section and entire skin will slip off. Incise a small x at the stem end to prevent bursting while cooking.

Heat butter in large frying pan or Dutch oven. Place onions and chicken in pan and brown over medium heat. Remove onions and chicken; discard butter.

Return pan to stove, reduce heat to simmer, and replace chicken in it. Sprinkle flour and chopped garlic over chicken.

Now pour on Cognac and ignite, holding match at arm's length. *Whenever you put flame to a dish step back to avoid accidents. It may flare high.*

While Cognac flames, turn chicken with tongs. When flames die out, add wine and season to taste with salt and pepper. Add *bouquet garni.* Cover and bring liquid to boiling point. Lower heat and cook gently, covered, from 35 to 45 minutes, basting and turning several times. At this point *Coq* may be refrigerated for several days or frozen.

Add onions after 15 minutes of cooking.*

Now clean mushrooms: Mushrooms should never be washed, peeled, or overcooked. They are a spongy vegetable which soaks up and retains moisture, so the less contact with water the better. To clean, mushrooms should be wiped with a damp sponge. I reserve a little sponge especially for this purpose. Cut off tips of stems.

Set aside 8 of the largest and firmest mushrooms to be added to the pot 5 minutes before end of cooking time. To add a professional touch, these large mushrooms may be fluted. With a lemon stripper, cut radial grooves from the top center of cap to its edge, twisting the mushroom slightly clockwise under the pressure of the stripper to curve the grooves. (See drawing on page 88.)

Slice remaining mushrooms lengthwise and add 2 minutes before end of cooking time. Taste sauce and correct seasoning if necessary.

PREPARING THE CROÛTONS

INGREDIENTS

4 *slices firm white sandwich bread*
2 *pats unsalted butter, at room temperature*

METHOD

Croûtons may be sautéed in clarified butter, but I prefer them baked, as they are less greasy.

Preheat oven to 450° F.

Planning 2 croûtons per person, cut slices of bread with cookie cutter into desired shapes. Butter one side. Place buttered side up

---

*If you are planning to refrigerate or freeze your *Coq,* the onions should be cooked just before serving.

on pie pan or cookie sheet; brown in oven. Turn and brown other side. Browning will take about a minute on each side. Watch them closely.

TO SERVE: Remove *bouquet garni*. Transfer chicken to heated serving platter. Pour sauce over chicken, arranging onions and fluted mushrooms appealingly. Decorate outer edge of platter with croûtons.

The Way of Tradition: The traditional way of savoring most French dishes is to serve them singly. *Coq au Vin* needs no accompaniment. The delicate flavor of sauce and mushrooms should be enjoyed for themselves alone.

All one should ask in addition is some crusty French bread to soak up the gravy and a glass of smooth Burgundy to sip.

Pommes de Terre Duchesse

BRIOCHE-SHAPED DUCHESS POTATOES

Duchess potatoes are important to French cuisine. Piped through a pastry tube or formed into attractive shapes, they make a delicious garnish for roasts and other meat dishes. When *Les Pommes de Terre Duchesse* are served as a separate course, as in this menu, I think the *brioche* shape is the most appealing.

L'appareil à Duchesse, as the mixture is called in French culinary language, is made of mashed potatoes, butter, and egg yolks. No milk, please! A well-made *Duchesse* will be light in texture, but will have enough body to hold its shape. Follow the directions carefully; I find that they are foolproof.

This recipe makes 8 small *brioche* shapes.

These potatoes may be prepared as much as a day ahead of time, except for the final glazing and baking.

MASHING AND SHAPING THE POTATOES

INGREDIENTS

2 1/2 *to* 3 *cups cubed potatoes (about* 3 *medium potatoes)*
water
1/2 *tablespoon coarse salt or* 1/4 *tablespoon table salt*
3 *tablespoons whipped sweet butter*
2 *egg yolks*
1/8 *to* 1/4 *teaspoon salt*

flour

METHOD

Peel potatoes; cut in small cubes. Cover with cold water in saucepan. Add salt. Heat to boiling point, reduce heat, and boil gently, covered, for 15 to 20 minutes, until soft.

Drain potatoes and dry for 1 minute by shaking pan gently over low flame. Mash and add butter in small pieces. Mix until melted. Remove pan from heat.

Add egg yolks one at a time. This is important, for if all yolks are added at once the mixture will be too thin and liquid. Mix thoroughly with a wooden spoon. Add salt if necessary. Allow to cool.

Preheat oven to 450° F.

Now you are ready to shape potatoes. Coat your hands and the surface on which you are working with flour to prevent sticking. (For this purpose, I prefer granulated flour.)

I make a traditional *brioche* shape. A *Brioche* is a French roll whose shape can be imitated as follows:

Roll one handful of potato mixture into a ball about 2 inches in diameter. Press a dent into the ball with your thumb. Then, take a teaspoon of potato mixture and roll it into a cone shape. Place the small end of the cone into the dent in the ball. Repeat with remaining potato, placing forms on a buttered pyrex dish or cookie sheet.*

---

*If these forms are being made much in advance, stick toothpicks into them so that wrap will not stick, cover with storage wrap, and refrigerate until ready to coat and bake.

DORURE (GLAZE)

INGREDIENTS

2 *egg yolks*
2 *teaspoons water*
1/4 *teaspoon salt (1/8 for each yolk)*

USEFUL UTENSIL: *Goose-feather pastry brush*

METHOD

Combine egg yolks, water, and salt. Mix with fork to form a *dorure* or glazing mixture. With a pastry brush, glaze each potato form carefully just before baking. (If the glazing is done ahead of time, the *dorure* hardens and makes the outside too crusty.) Remove any drippings from the pastry sheet, as they prevent the potato from puffing freely.

While the *Coq* is being served and savored, bake potatoes from 15 to 20 minutes, until nicely browned.

TO SERVE: *Les Pommes de Terre Duchesse* constitute the third course of this menu. They should be served directly from the oven, for if they are allowed to stand they lose their slight puffiness.

Omelette à la Confiture

OMELET FILLED WITH APRICOT PRESERVES

. . . you may travel around the world, but you will find no professional cook, whether Cordon Rouge or Cordon Bleu, who can make an omelet like the French housewife preparing dinner for her children.

Alexandre Dumas

There is nothing like a freshly made dessert right off the fire. Many cooks hesitate to serve such delectables to guests because they require last-minute attention. This omelet is simple, however, and much of the preparation can be done in advance. You needn't be away from the table more than 5 minutes before you return bearing this lovely hot surprise.

This recipe serves 2. This is the quantity most easily controlled for best results. Even some of the most experienced cooks prefer not to tackle a larger omelet than this. If you are planning to serve 4, as in this menu, you should make two omelets.

INGREDIENTS

2 *tablespoons apricot preserves**
3 *eggs*
1/2 *teaspoon table salt*
1 *tablespoon sugar*

1 1/2 *tablespoons clarified butter*
stick of unsalted butter

USEFUL UTENSIL: *A 7-inch skillet (measured across cooking surface)*

METHOD

Two things to remember about omelets: The eggs should not be beaten too much, neither should they be cooked too much. Overbeaten eggs produce a heavy omelet; overcooking will destroy the delicate texture. Remove the omelet from the stove when it is still moist, fluffy, and soft on top.

Some people swear it is the pan that makes the difference. A mystique has grown up about the omelet pan; to wash it or not to wash it has prompted heated discussions. I do not have a special pan; to me, it is far more important for the pan to be clean and free from any rancid taint than for it to have a seasoned finish.

Whip preserves with fork so that they will be easier to spread. If you are planning to make two or three omelets, prepare enough for all.

Break eggs into small mixing bowl. Add salt and sugar. Stir with fork or wire whisk merely enough to combine whites and yolks. If you will be making 2 or 3 omelets, prepare ingredients for each in separate bowls.

These first steps can be done before you sit down for your appetizer. Have clarified butter in frying pan ready to go for last step.

When ready for dessert, heat butter in frying pan over medium heat until it turns brown and has a nutty aroma. Pour in egg

*Any type of jam may be used, although I prefer to avoid grape because it takes on an unattractive color when spread on the omelet. Jellies are unsuitable because they do not have enough body and make the filling runny.

mixture. When setting begins, loosen edges with a spatula and tilt pan to permit unset egg to flow onto hot pan. Remove pan from heat before the top of your omelet is dry. A gourmet defines an omelet as done when the egg still retains a little flow in the center and is smooth and soft at the outer edges. *Never turn an omelet to cook on both sides.*

Spread whipped preserves over the center and fold omelet in half or in thirds. If you are preparing a second omelet, place the first in a slow oven to keep warm.

When you have become a confident omelet-maker, you may want to try working with 6 eggs. This is the maximum number of eggs that can be used satisfactorily. Increase the other ingredients proportionately, and use an 8- to 10-inch frying pan. If the larger size pan is used, the omelet will be larger and thinner and take less time to cook.

TO SERVE: Flip folded omelet onto warmed serving plate: Grasp frying pan in your left hand so that handle lies across your palm, with your fingers and thumb opposing each other over the top of the handle. Bring the platter up to the edge of the pan and turn out omelet. Holding the pan in this way allows you to use your whole arm, not just your wrist. It is the professional way of getting an omelet neatly and easily out of a pan.

For a glossy effect, run a stick of butter over omelet. Carry to the table immediately. Cut into 2 portions.

MENU XIII

Un Plaisir Pour les Yeux
A FEAST FOR THE EYES

Carottes en Vinaigrette
SHREDDED CARROT SALAD

Escalopes de Veau Liégeoise
SAUTÉED VEAL CUTLETS GARNISHED WITH LEMON, CHOPPED EGG, PARSLEY, OLIVES, AND ANCHOVIES

Céleri Braisé
CELERY BRAISED WITH STOCK AND VEGETABLES

Salade d'Escarole
ESCAROLE SALAD

Bananes Flambées au Rhum
BANANAS FLAMED IN RUM

Sancerre or Pouilly-Fumé

THIS menu consists of dishes that are colorful as well as interesting in texture: crunchy shredded carrots, veal cutlets carefully garnished and presented, and tender braised celery. The crisp escarole salad leads to the climax of the meal—bananas flamed with rum.

RECOMMENDED WINE: *Un bon petit vin de la Loire*—a good little dry white wine from the Loire—like a Sancerre or a Pouilly-Fumé, chilled, goes well with this meal from beginning to end.

ORDER OF PREPARATION: This menu is a good one to plan for company when you want to have most of the work done ahead of time. The carrots can be prepared as much as two days in advance, and the cutlets and celery can be started the day before. The bananas may be sliced and ready for sautéing an hour or two before dinner is served.

Carottes en Vinaigrette

SHREDDED CARROT SALAD

This refreshing, colorful appetizer is popular with my students. A convenient addition to any cold buffet or picnic lunch, it can be made an hour or two ahead and will be crisp and fresh. Made a day or so in advance, it will have a marinated quality.

The recipe will serve 4 generously.

INGREDIENTS

4 *cups grated carrots (1 to 1 1/2 pounds)*
1 *teaspoon table salt*
1/4 *teaspoon freshly ground white pepper or 12 turns of the
    pepper mill, medium grind*
2 *tablespoons red wine vinegar*
7 *tablespoons salad oil*
3 *tablespoons fresh lemon juice (about 1/2 a lemon)*

fresh parsley sprigs (optional)

METHOD

Wash carrots and scrape with potato peeler. Grate, using the large holes of a hand grater, the grating disc of a food processor, or a Mouli grater. Measure into a 6- to 8-cup mixing bowl, sprinkle with salt and pepper, toss well. Add remaining ingredients in order listed; toss until dressing and carrots are well blended. Cover and refrigerate until ready to serve.

TO SERVE: I like to present this appetizer in a pale green vegetable dish. A few fresh parsley sprigs here and there make an attractive garnish. Or, spoon carrots onto a crisp lettuce leaf on individual salad plates.

Escalopes de Veau Liégeoise

SAUTÉED VEAL CUTLETS GARNISHED WITH LEMON, CHOPPED EGG, PARSLEY, OLIVES, AND ANCHOVIES

When buying veal, look for light pink flesh. When the meat is red, you know that the animal was too old to be classified as veal when it was slaughtered. Recently, milk-fed veal has become easier to find. Meat producers have found that they can grow larger calves and still retain the tender, succulent meat by eliminating everything from their diet which contains blood-building iron, feeding them only on powdered milk and vitamins. This technique has helped make more high-quality veal available.

It takes only 5 minutes to sauté the veal. For best results this should be done immediately before serving. The preparation for the sautéing can be done a day ahead of time, if desired. If you plan to serve more than 4, you should make this veal in batches and serve it on two platters.

PREPARATION OF THE CUTLETS

INGREDIENTS

4 *veal cutlets, about 4 ounces apiece*
2 *to 4 tablespoons flour (1/2 to 1 tablespoon per cutlet)*
1/2 *cup bread crumbs*
1 *egg*
1 *teaspoon salad oil*
1/8 *teaspoon table salt*
1/8 *teaspoon freshly ground white pepper, fine grind*

USEFUL UTENSIL: *Goose-feather brush*

METHOD

On separate platters, pie tins, or waxed paper, have flour and bread crumbs ready for dipping.

In a small bowl, combine egg, oil, salt, and pepper. Mix well with a fork.

Being careful not to use more flour than is necessary to cover cutlets, dust them lightly; shake to remove excess.

Using a pastry brush, coat cutlets well on both sides with egg mixture; dip them in bread crumbs.

At this point, cutlets can be stored until you are ready to cook them. Seal in storage wrap and refrigerate.

FOR GARNISHING THE PLATTER

Since cutlets cook quickly, it is a good idea to have the serving platter garnished ahead of time.

INGREDIENTS

2 *hard-boiled eggs*
1 *parsley sprig, chopped finely*
2 *lemons*
4 *large black olives*
4 *flat anchovy fillets*

USEFUL UTENSIL: *Lemon stripper*

METHOD

TO HARD BOIL EGGS PROPERLY: Eggs will discolor an aluminum pan. Place them in a glass or enamel pan and cover with cold water.

1) *For Light-Colored, Firm, Dry Yolks:* Bring water to boiling point over high heat, then reduce heat and simmer gently for 12 minutes. This timing is right, no matter what size the egg (except for pullets, which cook in 8 minutes). Cool immediately under cold running water.

2) *For Deep Yellow, Moist Yolks:* Cover saucepan with lid. Bring water quickly to a boil over high heat. Remove pan from heat and let eggs steep in covered pan for 20 minutes. Cool immediately under cold running water.

When eggs have cooled, chop whites and yolks separately.

TO DECORATE PLATTER: Chop parsley. Wash lemons. Using lemon stripper, cut out parallel strips lengthwise to flute. Cut 4 slices. Save them to place atop each cutlet when done. Cut 5 or 6 more slices, then halve them. Arrange these around edge of platter.

Wrap anchovies around olives; set aside.

Next spread out chopped whites, parsley, and yolks, forming a narrow row of each along one side of the platter.

Platter is now ready to receive cutlets.

SAUTÉING THE CUTLETS AND FINISHING

INGREDIENTS

6 *to* 8 *tablespoons clarified butter*
2 *tablespoons unsalted butter (at room temperature)*
1 *tablespoon fresh lemon juice*

METHOD

Be sure frying pan is large enough so that meat is not crowded; about a 12-inch pan should do. If necessary, use two pans.

Heat clarified butter over fairly high heat until it sizzles. Sauté veal in butter, 3 minutes on one side, 2 minutes on the other. Since veal is a gelatinous meat with little fat, it is likely to stick to the pan unless you loosen it several times with a spatula while it is browning. When done, remove veal to warming pan and place in slow oven to keep hot.

Now to make *beurre noisette*, hazelnut butter (lightly browned butter which, in this recipe, has lemon juice added to it). Discard whatever remains of the sautéing butter. Using the same frying pan, melt the 2 tablespoons of butter until it is light brown. Add lemon juice and stir.

Quickly transfer cutlets to already garnished platter, and while the *beurre noisette* is still frothing, pour over cutlets. Place a round lemon slice on each cutlet. Top with an olive wrapped in an anchovy. Bring to the table immediately.

TO SERVE: Be sure a part of the garnish is served with each cutlet. Lemon slices are squeezed over the cutlets.

Céleri Braisé

CELERY BRAISED WITH STOCK AND VEGETABLES

Whenever I prepare braised celery for a class there never seems to be enough for the tasting session afterwards. My students find it delicious, as do my guests. I think it is a pity more people haven't discovered how good, appealing, and inexpensive celery can be!

All the preliminary preparation of the celery, *mirepoix*, and bouillon can be done ahead of time; the ingredients may be combined for baking when the rest of the meal is underway.

This recipe will serve 4.

PREPARING THE CELERY

INGREDIENTS

12 *cups boiling water*
3 *tablespoons coarse salt or* 1 1/2 *tablespoons table salt*
4 *whole celery hearts*

METHOD

Bring water and salt to a boil in a 6-quart pot.

Meanwhile, clean celery by gently separating stalks just enough to wash thoroughly under running water. Tie string around each heart to retain shape.

Drop hearts into boiling water. When water returns to a boil, continue boiling rapidly for about 15 minutes, uncovered. Then place celery immediately in colander and hold under running cold water to stop the cooking process.

When hearts are cool, remove strings, cut dark spots from root sections; set aside.

THE MIREPOIX

INGREDIENTS

4 *tablespoons unsalted butter*
1 *cup diced raw carrots*
1 *cup diced raw onions*
1 *garlic clove, peeled*
salt and pepper

METHOD

A *mirepoix* is a mixture of finely diced onions and carrots used in a dish solely for flavoring.*

Melt butter in a 1-quart saucepan and heat until it sings. Add carrots, onions, and garlic. Sauté gently for 5 minutes over medium heat, uncovered, shaking pan often. Then cover and cook for 5 minutes. Remove from heat; sprinkle lightly with salt and pepper. Stir.

THE BOUILLON

INGREDIENTS

2 *cups beef stock***
1 *teaspoon tomato paste*
2 *tablespoons unsalted butter (at room temperature)*
1 *butter pat*
bouquet garni (5 to 6 parsley sprigs and 1 large bay leaf tied together)

METHOD

Preheat oven to 400° F.

If you have no homemade beef stock, prepare bouillon as follows: Add cubes and salt to cold water. (If cubes you are using are very salty, you will not need any extra salt.) Bring to a boil and simmer 5 minutes, or until cubes dissolve. Stir in tomato paste and butter.

Coat an 8 × 10-inch baking dish with butter pat. Spread a bed of the *mirepoix* on the bottom of the dish. Rest celery on this bed. Lay *bouquet garni* among the hearts. Pour bouillon over all.

*A *mirepoix* is a mixture of several vegetables, all finely diced. It can also include diced ham and herbs.

**Use homemade stock (page 18) or 2 beef cubes dissolved in 2 cups of water, with 1 teaspoon table salt if needed.

Cut a piece of waxed paper large enough to cover baking dish and butter one side. Place buttered side down over celery. Bake 30 minutes, basting and turning celery at least twice.

When done, transfer celery to serving dish, cover with aluminum foil, and place in slow oven to keep hot.

TO COMPLETE SAUCE

INGREDIENTS

2 *teaspoons potato flour*
1 *teaspoon cold water*

chopped parsley

USEFUL UTENSIL: *Chinois (conical strainer)*

METHOD

Strain juices from baking dish into a saucepan through conical strainer, pressing the *mirepoix* with a whisk or fork to extract all the moisture. Reduce juices over high heat for 3 minutes.

In a small bowl, mix the potato flour with cold water until smooth. Add 2 to 3 tablespoons of the hot juice and blend briskly. Pour into remaining juice, stirring constantly with whisk until sauce thickens. (This takes from 3 to 5 minutes.) Mix well. Season to taste.

TO SERVE: Place celery in heated vegetable dish (a silver one if you arc fortunate enough to own one, because the celery looks so attractive in it and because silver retains heat longer). Pour sauce over celery. Sprinkle with chopped parsley. Bring to the table immediately.

Salade d'Escarole

ESCAROLE SALAD

Escarole, like chicory, is a member of the endive family; a more precise name for it is Batavian endive. It grows in a loose head of broad green leaves which wave lightly around the edges and are white toward their base. Mild and pleasant in flavor, it makes a refreshing salad green.

INGREDIENTS

1 *fresh escarole head**
1 *medium garlic clove, peeled and chopped or pressed*
1/8 *to* 1/4 *teaspoon freshly ground black pepper, medium
   grind*
1/2 *teaspoon table salt*
1 *tablespoon red wine vinegar*
2 *tablespoons salad oil*

USEFUL UTENSIL: *Salad basket*

METHOD

For a crisp, fresh-from-the-garden taste, wash escarole several hours ahead of time: Cut root section to free leaves, discard any imperfect ones, wash each leaf separately under running water. Wash once again in a large pan or bowl, changing the water several times. Be certain all dirt is removed.

Place greens in salad basket and shake out excess water. Dry leaves still further by patting gently in a clean linen towel. Place greens loosely in hydrator until just before serving.

As it takes only a minute to make a proper dressing, this should be done just before the salad is to be brought to the table.

The average 2-quart salad bowl is adequate for 4 ample servings of this salad. Place garlic, pepper, salt, vinegar, and oil in bowl in that order. Mix well.

Place salad fork and spoon in bowl; with fingers gently break leaves into bite-sized pieces, letting them rest on the utensils.

Bring to the table immediately.

TO SERVE: Toss thoroughly before serving.

Bananes Flambées au Rhum

BANANAS FLAMED IN RUM

This easy dessert should please friends and family alike. Although everything can be organized ahead of time, it should be

*A head weighing 1/2 pound will be more than enough for 4 generous servings. Washed, dried, and stored properly, it will remain crisp for several days.

made at the last minute and can be prepared right at the table in either a chafing dish or an electric frying pan. For unexpected company it is a quick showy surprise.

INGREDIENTS

4 *bananas (on the green side)*
3 *tablespoons rum*
4 *heaping tablespoons granulated sugar*
4 *heaping tablespoons flour (preferably granulated)*
7 *to 8 tablespoons clarified butter*
1/4 *to 1/3 cup rum*

USEFUL UTENSIL: *Chafing dish or electric frying pan*

METHOD

Peel and halve bananas lengthwise. Place in a shallow dish or pie plate. (If they are prepared much in advance, sprinkle with lemon juice to prevent them from turning black.) Sprinkle with rum. The best way to do this, I find, is to place your index finger into the neck of the bottle and shake out liquor. Bananas should be well saturated.

Sprinkle with sugar until bananas are coated on both sides, using about 1/2 tablespoon for each banana half.

Remove to another platter and coat bananas well with flour. Use about 1/2 tablespoon (heaping) for each half banana.

Bananas are now ready for sautéing.

Sautéing should be done over high heat. With a chafing dish or on a stove burner, turn flame up high. Set an electric frying pan at 400° F.

Heat butter until bubbling hot. Put in bananas, cut side down first, and sauté until browned—2 to 3 minutes. Turn and sauté other side 1 minute or so, until golden brown.

Lower heat. Add whatever rum–sugar mixture is left from the first step of preparation.

Meanwhile be heating the additional rum in a 1-cup saucepan until it begins to boil. Pour over bananas and ignite immediately, stepping aside to avoid sudden flame. Turn bananas to baste. When flame dies out, serve at once.

TO SERVE: Serve two halves per person, dividing the small amount of liquid which remains after sautéing. Sprinkle lightly with sugar.

Quel dessert!

Menu XIV

Même si l'on n'Aime pas le Poisson
EVEN IF YOU DON'T LIKE FISH

Chou Rouge en Salade
RED CABBAGE SALAD WITH SHALLOTS

Paupiettes de Carrelets à la Dugléré
POACHED ROLLED FILLETS OF FLOUNDER ON A BED OF TOMATOES AND HERBS, SERVED WITH A WHITE WINE SAUCE

Riz Sauté
RICE SAUTÉED WITH ONIONS AND HERBS

Salade Verte
GREEN SALAD

Mousse au Chocolat
CHOCOLATE MOUSSE

*Vouvray de Touraine
or Sainte-Croix-du-Mont*

I HOPE that you won't hesitate to prepare this menu even if your family is not fond of fish. The main course has converted many a fish avoider. Piquant shredded cabbage, sautéed rice, a green salad, and *Mousse au Chocolat,* round out the meal.

RECOMMENDED WINE: A white wine is usually suggested to accompany fish. When a white sauce is being served with the fish, as in this recipe, it is best if the wine is mellow to sweet. Try a still Vouvray de Touraine or a Sainte-Croix-du-Mont from the southern part of Bordeaux, which produces naturally sweet wines. Enjoy the wine with the main course and with dessert. Use it also in the preparation of the fish.

ORDER OF PREPARATION: The cabbage may be made several days ahead. The rice can also be prepared ahead and reheated. The mousse and the fish should be made on the day they are to be served, but the preparation of the fish, up to the baking point, may be done a few hours in advance.

Chou Rouge en Salade

RED CABBAGE SALAD WITH SHALLOTS

Red cabbage is a refreshing appetizer with an interesting, crunchy texture. It makes a nice contrast in color and taste when served as a prelude to fish. It can be prepared and mixed with the dressing up to a week ahead of time.

This recipe will serve 4 to 6.

INGREDIENTS

4 *cups shredded red cabbage (2 to 2 1/2 pounds)*
2 *teaspoons table salt*
1/4 *teaspoon freshly ground pepper, medium grind*
4 *tablespoons red wine vinegar*
2 *tablespoons salad oil*
2 *tablespoons chopped shallots*

METHOD

Red cabbages are usually fairly large. Cut the amount you need and store the remainder, well wrapped, in the refrigerator.

Remove any outer leaves which are wilted. Wash under running water, quarter, and grate, using a hand grater or food processor. Or slice in fine julienne.

Place shredded cabbage in 2-quart bowl. Add salt, pepper, vinegar, and oil. Add shallots if desired. Mix thoroughly.

TO SERVE: Place in vegetable dish.

Serve about 2 serving spoonfuls per person on small salad plates. This is an ample helping for an appetizer.

Paupiettes de Carrelets à la Dugléré

**POACHED ROLLED FILLETS OF FLOUNDER
ON A BED OF TOMATOES AND HERBS,
SERVED WITH A WHITE WINE SAUCE**

The reason I call this fish flounder instead of fillet of sole is that in the United States all sole is really flounder. Frozen Dover sole can be bought here, but fresh fish is always better. Try to buy grey sole, a variety of flounder; its texture is close to that of Dover sole. Most fish markets will order it for you.

Don't be frightened by the number of steps in this recipe—the divisions are just for convenience. There is no complication here, only an impressive list of ingredients.

This is fish prepared with imagination. There is but one thing to remember: *Never overcook fish,* for it will become dry and cottony.

The recipe is ample for 4 to 6 servings. The amount of fish may be increased to 2 1/2 pounds; the recipe will then serve 6 to 8.

POACHING THE FISH

INGREDIENTS

1 *pat unsalted butter*
1 *pound fresh tomatoes (1 to 4 tomatoes, depending on size)*
5 *sprigs parsley, chopped*
1/2 *teaspoon thyme*
1/2 *teaspoon tarragon*
1/2 *teaspoon chervil*
1/2 *teaspoon chopped chives*
4 *tablespoons chopped shallots or red onions*
white pepper
salt
2 *pounds fillet of grey sole or other variety of flounder*
1 *cup mellow to sweet white wine*

METHOD

Preheat oven to 400° F.

Prepare a 2-quart Dutch oven, or any fireproof dish which can be used both in the oven and directly over a stove burner, by coating with butter pat.

Drop tomatoes into 2 quarts of boiling water for 1 minute so that skins will peel off easily. Skin tomatoes and chill, if you have time, for easier handling. Then slice in half and gently squeeze to remove juice and seeds. Cut remaining pulp into thin strips. It is important to do this carefully because this sauce will not be strained.

Place tomatoes in your prepared dish along with parsley, thyme, tarragon, chervil, chives, and shallots. Sprinkle lightly with salt and pepper.

Salt and pepper fillets lightly on each side. Roll, preferably with side which has been next to the skin on the inside. Fillets roll better that way and will hold without toothpicks.

Place rolled fish on top of tomatoes and herbs. Add wine. Poach in oven 10 minutes, uncovered, turning once so that both sides of fish steep in liquid.

Turn off heat; leave in oven with door ajar to keep warm.

WHITE WINE SAUCE

INGREDIENTS

2 *tablespoons clarified butter*
2 *tablespoons flour*
1 *cup mellow to sweet white wine*
4 *tablespoons heavy cream*
1/2 *teaspoon table salt*
1/8 *teaspoon white pepper, medium grind*

METHOD

Heat clarified butter in a 4-cup saucepan. Gradually add flour and stir with wire whisk until well mixed. Cook over medium heat for 1 minute in order to allow *roux* to moisten and swell. Add wine, stirring with whisk. When sauce comes to a boil, cook for 5 minutes over medium heat, stirring occasionally. Stir in cream 1 tablespoon at a time; add salt and pepper. Remove from heat.

FINISHING SAUCE AND BAKING

INGREDIENTS

2 *tablespoons unsalted butter*
5 *to 6 tablespoons grated Swiss cheese*
4 *tablespoons clarified butter*
4 *tablespoons bread crumbs*

METHOD

Remove fish from poaching pan and continue to keep warm either in the oven or in a covered dish on top of the stove.

Place poaching pan with its contents over high heat on stove burner for 3 minutes, uncovered, to reduce liquid. Add unsalted butter, stirring until melted. Add this liquid to the wine sauce; stir.

Turn oven up to preheat at 450° F.

Place fish in a 10 × 10 or 10 × 12-inch baking dish suitable for carrying to the table. Pour sauce over fish. Sprinkle with grated cheese. Return to oven for 5 minutes, or until cheese melts.

Heat clarified butter. Add crumbs, 1 tablespoon at a time; stir. When crumbs are uniformly coated, sprinkle over fish, which is now ready to serve.

TO SERVE: Both for looks and practicality, carry the sizzling hot fish to table in its baking dish. The only accompaniment needed is the sautéed rice and the chilled wine.

Riz Sauté

RICE SAUTÉED WITH ONIONS AND HERBS

There are over 20 different ways I can think of that I have prepared rice, but when it is served as a vegetable, this is the way I like best.

The one secret of light fluffy rice is not to touch it any more than is necessary. A fork can be used, but I merely shake the pan over the heat to stir.

Use long-grained rice, follow these simple instructions, and there is no way to fail.* Have your serving platter hot to receive rice when it is done.

The recipe will serve 4 to 6.

INGREDIENTS

3 *tablespoons clarified butter*
1/2 *cup chopped white onion*
1 1/2 *cups rice*
2 *tablespoons unsalted butter*
3 *cups chicken bouillon**
bouquet garni (5 sprigs parsley and 2 bay leaves tied together with string)

METHOD

Heat clarified butter in a 1 1/2-quart saucepan or frying pan. Add onions and shake pan until onions are glossy—about a minute over high heat.

Add rice and 1 tablespoon of butter and shake pan until rice is coated and glossy. Shake pan enough so that rice does not stick.

When rice is glossy, add hot bouillon and *bouquet garni*. Cover and boil gently 20 minutes over medium heat. All liquid should be absorbed.

*Do not use minute rice for this recipe.
**Use homemade stock (p. 19) or 3 chicken cubes dissolved in 3 1/2 cups water. When packaged cubes are used, taste before adding salt.

When rice is done, add remaining butter, distributing it lightly with a two-pronged fork. Remove *bouquet garni.* Taste and correct seasoning if necessary.

TO SERVE: Serve at once or keep up to 3 hours, covered with buttered waxed paper and a lid, in a warm oven. Check periodically; add tablespoons of bouillon if rice is drying.

Mousse au Chocolat

CHOCOLATE MOUSSE

This recipe is a true mousse, light and airy egg whites without any egg yolks or whipped cream.

As a child this was my favorite dessert. I looked forward to going to the home of my best friend on the outskirts of Paris because her mother always made this mousse *pour la petite amie—* for her little friend.

This recipe will serve 4. However, 6 egg whites may be used with the same amount of chocolate if you wish to serve 6.

INGREDIENTS

6 *ounces semi-sweet chocolate*
4 *egg whites**
1 *to 2 tablespoons liqueur or brandy (optional)*

USEFUL UTENSIL: *Electric mixer*

METHOD

Melt chocolate just before beating egg whites.** Add liqueur or brandy, if desired, to the chocolate 1 tablespoon at a time and stir in quickly.

*Because eggs separate easier when they are cold, this operation should be performed when they are first taken from refrigerator. Whites will rise better, however, when warm, so allow them to reach room temperature before beating.

A FRENCH CHEF'S TRICK FOR MELTING CHOCOLATE QUICKLY AND EASILY: If using morsel chocolate, pour into a 3- to 4-cup bowl and cover with about 2 cups of very hot tap water or boiling water. When chocolate changes color, pour off water and stir with a wooden spoon until smooth. (This will take no longer than a minute.)

Place whites in mixing bowl. Beat with electric mixer at low speed for 30 seconds, then beat at high speed until stiff—about 2 minutes.

Pour melted chocolate quickly into stiffened egg whites and beat at high speed just until well blended (about 10 seconds), using rubber spatula to scrape sides of bowl. The mixture will liquify. Transfer into dessert dishes or sherbet glasses and chill in refrigerator for at least 1 hour before serving.*

TO SERVE: No whipped cream, please! It is rich enough. A plain homemade cookie or plain wafer may be inserted upright on the top to decorate your mousse.

*If your mousse stands too long, it may become watery at the bottom. If this happens, simply stir it with a spatula.

Un Pur Délice
AMBROSIA

Champignons Marcelle
**MUSHROOM SALAD WITH MUSTARD
AND HERBS**

Caneton à l'Orange
DUCKLING WITH ORANGE SAUCE

Pommes de Terre Dauphine
PUFFED POTATO FRITTERS

Salade Verte
GREEN SALAD

Crème Renversée au Caramel
**MOLDED VANILLA CUSTARD WITH
CARAMEL**

La Romanée or Mercurey

THE recipes that follow are truly fit for the gods: An appetizer of marinated mushrooms with a very special flavor; duckling with a tangy sauce; potato fritters, light and golden; and a finely textured caramel custard. A watercress salad (see page 178) may be served as an additional course.

RECOMMENDED WINE: This menu is worthy of La Romanée, a prince of Burgundy wines. A Mercurey from the Côte Chalonnaise or another full-bodied red Burgundy will serve almost as well.

ORDER OF PREPARATION: The appetizer and dessert can be made a day or two in advance. The first step in the preparation of the potatoes and the duckling may be done ahead of time, if desired. Thus, only the frying of the potato puffs and the final tossing of the salad need to be done at the last minute.

Champignons Marcelle

MUSHROOM SALAD WITH MUSTARD AND HERBS

This appetizer was a specialty of my childhood friend, Marcelle, at whose home I often enjoyed its piquant flavor. Marcelle had an instinct for proportion, but her instructions consisted of "chop a little bit of this and combine it with a little bit of that." After considerable trial and error, I have found the proportions that give her special flavor.

The recipe will provide 4 servings.

INGREDIENTS

1/2 *pound fresh, firm white mushrooms (enough to make about 3 cups, sliced)*
1 *teaspoon Dijon mustard*
1 *teaspoon salt*
5 *turns of black pepper mill, medium grind*
3 *tablespoons fresh lemon juice*
4 *tablespoons salad oil*

1 *teaspoon fresh chopped parsley, tossed with*
2 *teaspoons fresh chopped chives*

METHOD

Cut tips from mushroom stems to make a clean surface. Wipe mushrooms with clean damp sponge.

Spoon mustard into a 4- to 6-cup mixing bowl; stir in salt, pepper, lemon juice, and oil. Blend well.

Slice half the mushrooms into this mixture. Toss well. Slice in remaining mushrooms; toss again.

Sprinkle on parsley–chive mixture; toss.

These mushrooms have a fresh taste if eaten at once, but they are equally delicious if allowed to marinate a day or two in the refrigerator. If you marinate them, add an extra teaspoon of parsley and chives just before serving and toss.

TO SERVE: Spoon onto small salad plates.

Caneton à l'Orange

DUCKLING WITH ORANGE SAUCE

There are many ways to prepare duck with orange sauce, but I think this recipe produces a truly unimprovable flavor. The duck is roasted slowly to remove every trace of grease, and the addition of caramel to the sauce gives it extra pungency and color.

Unfortunately, fresh ducks are found only occasionally in American markets, because duck is not as popular here as other meats. However, this recipe can be prepared with frozen duck quite successfully.

Ready to cook ducks usually weigh 4 to 6 pounds. Since they have larger carcasses and less meat than chicken, one this size will serve no more than 4 or at the most 5. Each side of the breast will yield 2 to 3 slices.

THE BOUILLON

INGREDIENTS

4 *cups cold water*
1 *heaping teaspoon coarse salt or* 1/2 *teaspoon table salt*
1 *medium-sized yellow onion, unpeeled*
bouquet garni (4 parsley sprigs, 2 celery stalks tied together)
neck, gizzard, and heart of duck

METHOD

If your duck is frozen, defrost it completely by allowing it to remain at room temperature overnight. If not preparing it by noon, return it to the refrigerator until ready to roast.

Remove the neck, gizzard, heart, and liver usually found in the cavity.*

If you are planning to use duck bouillon in your sauce, prepare it first:** Combine all ingredients in a 6- to 8-cup saucepan; cover and bring to roaring boil; reduce heat and simmer 1 hour. Discard onion and *bouquet garni;* remove duck parts. (These, of course, are edible, but will not be used further in this recipe.)

Remove fat from surface. An easy way to do this before it has had time to coagulate is to swish a piece of tissue paper across the surface. It is better, however, if you can make the stock a day ahead so that the fat can solidify.

PREPARING AND ROASTING THE DUCK

INGREDIENTS

1 4- to 6-*pound duck*
4 *teaspoons table salt*
1 *orange, quartered, with peel*
4 *sprigs of parsley tied together*
1 *teaspoon shortening*

USEFUL UTENSIL: *Trussing needle and string or poultry lacers*

METHOD

Preheat oven to 300° F. Remove as much fat as possible from inside of neck and body cavity. Dry duck inside and out with a paper towel. Rub 1 teaspoon of salt inside neck area; rub 1 teaspoon of salt inside body cavity.

Place 3/4 of the orange and the parsley inside body cavity. Close the opening with poultry lacer or by sewing it up with a large needle and double thickness of white thread.

Insert remaining quarter orange in the neck cavity. Close by folding neck skin over opening and securing with poultry lacer; or secure neck skin with string which will be used to hold wings tightly against body in trussing.

*The liver may be chopped raw, sprinkled with salt, and added to the sauce just before completion; or it may be roasted with the duck for the last 5 minutes and eaten separately.

**Bouillon can also be made by combining 1 chicken cube with 3/4 cup cold water in a small saucepan and simmering 5 minutes, or until the cube has thoroughly dissolved.

TO TRUSS: The purpose of trussing is to have the bird hold its shape during and after cooking. Legs and wings are bound tightly against the body with string. The string is passed through parts of the body with the aid of a trussing needle which is from 10 to 12 inches long.

Cut a double length of string about 2 feet long; tie a knot about 3 inches from the ends, leaving enough to tie when finishing off.

Place bird on its back with tail section toward your left—if you are right handed. (If you are left handed, reverse these directions.) Pick up legs with left hand and push them into an upright position.

Insert needle through body from just above thigh joint nearest you. Needle should come out at the same point on the opposite side and not hit any bones if it is placed properly. Pull string through as far as knot.

Push legs back down; pass string over far leg; insert needle down through the tail section of bird. Then bring it back up through tail again, pass string over second leg, and tie securely with knotted end.

Turn bird onto breast with hind part toward your left hand. Rethread needle, again with about 2 feet of string, doubled. Knot about 3 inches from end. Insert needle through back just above hip joint and pull string through as far as knot.

Turn duck so that the head section is now toward your left hand. Pass needle out through near wing at its tip; bring it out again through webbed skin at the wing joint. Reinsert needle again about an inch away through wing skin, passing it through left-hand side of body and coming out at the base of the neck. Pick up neck skin in two places (if you have not laced it), and pull it back tightly over body. Thrust needle down through body, coming out through webbed skin at second wing joint. Pull string through. Keeping wing close to body, pass string over wing bone, then, from the top downwards, plunge needle in and out of body to catch wing tip. Pull tightly and tie with knotted end.

TO ROAST: Rub duck with remaining 2 teaspoons of salt. Grease bottom of heavy roasting pan with the shortening; place duck in pan; place pan in preheated 300° F. oven.

The purpose of the first hour of roasting is to remove as much fat as possible. Every 10 to 15 minutes, turn duck and prick skin with a roasting fork in as many places as possible to let the fat out. At the end of the hour, lift duck from pan and discard all fat.

Duck may be cooled and refrigerated at this point if you wish. Wash pan or place duck in another roasting pan. Raise oven temperature to 350° F.

Return duck to oven for 1 more hour, turning occasionally so that it will brown evenly.

When done, transfer duck to heated platter and return to a slow oven to keep hot.

THE SAUCE

INGREDIENTS

1 *cup dry white wine*
1/2 *cup duck (or chicken) bouillon*

2 *tablespoons white vinegar*
2 *sugar lumps*

juice of 1 *orange*
juice of 1/2 *lemon*
peel of 1 *orange and* 1/2 *lemon, cut in fine strips and blanched**
4 *tablespoons Grand Marnier or Cointreau***

extra orange slices to decorate platter
maraschino cherries

USEFUL UTENSIL: *Lemon stripper*

METHOD

Again discard all fat from roasting pan, leaving the brown particles. Add wine and bring to a boil over high heat, scraping bottom and sides of pan with wooden spoon or wooden spatula to loosen drippings. If the chopped liver is being used, add it at this point.

Add bouillon and bring to a boil.

While this mixture is coming to a boil, the caramel can be made: it takes only 2 to 3 minutes. It is the caramel that gives the sauce its pungent taste and deep color. Combine vinegar and sugar in a small saucepan; place over high heat. Bring to a boil and allow to bubble. Watch carefully until one spot turns brown. Remove immediately from heat. Give pan a swirl and your caramel is ready.

Add caramel immediately to wine–bouillon mixture, which

---

*If a lemon stripper is used, these can be peeled rapidly. **TO BLANCH:** Drop peels into 1 cup boiling water in a small saucepan. Wait until water returns to boiling, then time for 3 minutes. Immediately pour into strainer or colander and hold under cold running water to refresh peels.

**Any liqueur with an orange base may be used.

should be just about reaching its boiling point. Allow combination to boil about 3 minutes.

Then add orange and lemon juices and boil for another 5 minutes. For the last minute add blanched peels. Add the liqueur for the last half minute. Sauce is done.

Remove duck from oven; untruss; discard orange sections and parsley.

TO SERVE: Decorate duck with two or three orange slices on either side of the breastbone; top each slice with a maraschino cherry secured with a toothpick. Slip paper frills on legs. (See page 59 for directions on making frills.) Surround platter with half slices of orange.

Serve sauce in gravy boat.

In the French home when duck is decorated in this way, it is brought to the table for everyone to admire, then returned to the kitchen or sideboard to be carved. The sliced portions from the breast and legs are then returned to the platter, with the orange slices, for serving.

The duck may also be quartered and served with the sauce poured over each quarter, the orange slices decorating each individual portion.

Pommes de Terre Dauphine

PUFFED POTATO FRITTERS

Potato fritters make a marvelous accompaniment for many kinds of roasts served either with the entrée or in the Continental way as a third course. They are fascinating to prepare and impressive to bring to the table. Many of my novice students have overcome their nervousness and made them with great success, much to my delight.

This recipe makes about 14 fritters, enough for 4 generous servings.

BOILING THE POTATOES

INGREDIENTS

2 cups cubed potatoes (about 3/4 pound)
3/4 tablespoon coarse salt or 1/2 tablespoon table salt
3 cups cold water

METHOD

Place cubed potatoes in a 2-quart saucepan; add salt; cover with cold water. Bring to a boil, cover, and boil gently for 15 to 20 minutes, or until soft enough so that cubes can be broken easily with a fork. Pour off water, return potatoes to low heat, and mash with a potato masher. (This is done over heat so that the potatoes will be as dry as possible.) Remove from heat.

PREPARING PÂTE À CHOU (CREAM PUFF PASTE)

INGREDIENTS

1/2 *cup milk*
2 1/2 *tablespoons butter*
4 *turns of black pepper mill, medium grind*
1/2 *cup flour*
2 *jumbo eggs (or 3 smaller ones)*

USEFUL UTENSIL: *Wooden spoon*

METHOD

In a 2-quart saucepan combine milk, butter, and pepper. Bring to boiling point; stir to be sure butter is melted. Add flour all at one time, stirring vigorously with a wooden spoon. *A wooden spoon is the only implement with which a proper cream puff paste can be made!* It becomes particularly important when you add the eggs.

When mixture forms a cohesive mass and comes away from the sides of the pan, remove from heat and add eggs, one at a time. Stir vigorously after each egg until it is thoroughly blended into the mixture.

Batter should now resemble thick mayonnaise.

Add the mashed potatoes a little at a time, mixing well with wooden spoon. Allow to cool.

Preparation up to this point may be done as much as a day ahead of time. Cover and refrigerate.

FRYING THE DAUPHINES

INGREDIENTS

4 *cups salad oil (preferably peanut) or shortening*
salt

USEFUL UTENSIL: *Frying vessel or Dutch oven*

METHOD

Choose a frying vessel or Dutch oven with at least a 4-quart capacity; be sure oil does not more than half fill it.* Heat oil for 10 minutes over medium heat. This should bring it to just the right temperature for frying. It should not be too hot, as puffs will brown too quickly. If you have a frying thermometer, it should read between 360° F. and 380° F.

Drop potato batter a tablespoonful at a time into hot oil, being sure that you do not crowd the puffs. Fry from 5 to 12 minutes. (Time depends upon the type of vessel: In a metal one the heat is more intense than in an enamel one.) Puffs should be a light even brown when done.

When they are cooked, remove puffs with any utensil that will allow excess oil to drip off, such as a skimmer, batter beater, or slotted spoon. Sprinkle with salt. If you have a frying basket, allow them to drain a few minutes in it. Then place them on a cookie sheet on a bed of crumpled paper toweling to absorb fat. Place the cookie sheet in slow oven to keep puffs hot while others are frying.

Fried foods are best when eaten hot from the fryer. One-half hour is the maximum time they should be prepared ahead. Considering the short time it takes to cook these fritters, I suggest that the cook make family or guests wait at the table.

TO SERVE: Place *Les Pommes de Terre Dauphine* in a vegetable dish or shallow bowl lined with a linen napkin to absorb any grease. (Instructions for folding the napkin are given on page 122.) They should be served as a separate course after the duck.

Crème Renversée au Caramel

MOLDED VANILLA CUSTARD WITH CARAMEL

Ah, *la Crème au Caramel* and the childhood memories it evokes! This silken custard is to French children what ice cream is to American youngsters (or, perhaps I should say, what ice cream was to American youngsters before it became such an everyday commodity).

*Use enough oil to cover the pan to a depth of at least 1 inch. Leftover oil may be strained through a cheesecloth after it has cooled off, and stored in a cool, dry place (not the refrigerator).

When I was growing up there was no school on Thursdays. The Thursday *goûter* (afternoon snack) was always a much anticipated treat. When *Crème au Caramel* was served, the day became a special one.

Crème au Caramel reminds me especially of the *Buttes-Chaumont*,

a beautiful park in the nineteenth *Arrondissement* of Paris. This paradise of bluffs, grottos, lakes, and flowers contained swings and see-saws, a puppet theatre, a merry-go-round, and a waffle stand; some days an outdoor concert filled the air with music. A Thursday stroll in the park with a good friend, and an extra special *goûter—Crème au Caramel*—when we returned home, made Thursday a day to remember.

This recipe will make 6 or 8 servings. Invite some friends in for dessert and coffee if you have any left over.

THE CUSTARD

INGREDIENTS

4 *cups milk*
1 *vanilla bean or* 1 *teaspoon vanilla extract*
4 *egg yolks*
2/3 *cup granulated sugar*
2 *whole eggs*

USEFUL UTENSIL: *A* 6-*cup mold**

METHOD

Place milk and vanilla bean (or extract) in a 4- to 6-cup sauce-pan and heat to boiling point.

Meanwhile, in a 2-quart bowl, stir egg yolks with a rubber spatula for about 2 minutes, or until they turn light yellow. Add sugar gradually, stirring constantly. Add whole eggs one at a time, continuing to stir. Then stir 1 minute longer.

Pour heated milk over eggs and combine well with a whisk. Set mixture aside to allow bubbles to rise to the surface. While waiting for this to happen, preheat oven to 325° F. and coat mold with caramel.

THE CARAMEL

INGREDIENTS

14 *lumps of sugar*** *or* 1/2 *cup granulated sugar*
1/4 *cup cold water*

*This recipe requires a 6-cup mold made of metal or some other material which can be used on top of the stove as well as in the oven. *Never use a Teflon-lined pan for this recipe, as it does not accept the caramel.* It may have fluted or straight sides.
**Use 28 if they are the smaller hostess lumps.

METHOD

Put sugar and cold water in mold, without stirring. Place mold on burner over high heat. In about 5 minutes the sugar will begin to form big bubbles; watch it closely. In another minute one side is going to start to turn brown. At this point, using two potholders, remove mold from heat and swirl sugar mixture around to coat bottom and sides as much as possible. (It will coat 1/3 to 1/2 of mold.)

The color of the caramel should be a rich amber. If it seems too pale, return mold to high heat for another 1/2 minute. Repeat swirling process.

BAKING THE CUSTARD

Set mold in a pan half filled with lukewarm water (I use a 6-quart Dutch oven).

Now skim off bubbles and foam which have risen to the surface of the egg and milk mixture. This little step prevents the top of the custard from turning dark or burning while it is baking.

Remove vanilla bean, if used. Strain custard into coated mold. Again skim off any foam.

Adjust shelf so that custard will bake in the center of the oven. Bake custard for 2 hours, checking occasionally. Turn custard if necessary to prevent too much darkening on any one side.

When testing needle or knife comes out dry and custard feels firm to the touch, it is done. Remove from oven, but leave mold in its *bain-marie* until it can be lifted out without burning your fingers (about 1/2 hour).

After custard has cooled completely, refrigerate and thoroughly chill before unmolding. (This will take several hours.) Custard may be kept for several days. Do not unmold until shortly before serving.

UNMOLDING: Loosen custard from mold with a knife blade. Place shallow serving platter on top of mold and turn mold, giving a slight shake. Custard and caramel should come out easily. If it does not, turn right side up and loosen again with the knife.

Do *not* immerse mold in water!

TO SERVE: For each serving, cut a wedge and spoon caramel over the top.

One of my guests once said, "It's like eating a dream!"

Menu XVI

Un Régal
WHAT A TREAT

Les Hors-d'Oeuvre Variés
A SELECTION OF APPETIZERS

Blanquette de Veau à l'Ancienne
VEAL TENDERLOIN IN A DELICATE
CREAM SAUCE GARNISHED WITH
TINY ONIONS, CARROTS, AND
MUSHROOMS

Salade de Cresson
WATERCRESS SALAD

Ananas au Kirsch
PINEAPPLE IN KIRSCH

Auxey-Duresses or Graves de Vayres

T HE French often begin a meal with a variety of appetizers served in small portions. I like to start this menu with two: tasty fried cheese bits and dressed avocado. The entrée is veal tenderloin in a delicate sauce, the salad, fresh watercress. Pineapple slices in Kirsch provide a refreshing finish to this delicious meal.

RECOMMENDED WINE: For this menu a white wine is preferable. Try an Auxey-Duresses, a dry–mellow paradox from the Côte de Beaune. Some of this wine comes from vineyards bequeathed to the Charitable Hospital of Beaune (*Hospice de Beaune*). Or, try another white wine, Graves de Vayres, a product of the gravelly soil of Bordeaux.

ORDER OF PREPARATION: The pineapple is best when it is made a day or more in advance. The first steps for the cheese bits, the avocado salad, and the meat may be done ahead if you wish. The salad should be prepared at the last minute.

Les Hors-d'Oeuvre Variés

A SELECTION OF APPETIZERS

Hors-d'Oeuvre Variés provide an interesting contrast of textures and flavors to open a meal. Both can be presented simultaneously at the table, and guests may help themselves onto small salad plates.

Friands au Fromage

DEEP-FRIED CHEESE TRIANGLES

Serve these tasty cheese morsels as an appetizer or as an hors-d'oeuvre; either way they will awaken your appetite delightfully.

They are made with triangles of Gruyère cheese, which can be found in most supermarkets. Gruyère is packaged in round boxes which contain 6, 8, or 12 individually wrapped triangles. Those which come 6 to a box are the largest.

To serve them as an appetizer, use the large triangles whole, planning 1 or 2 per person. To serve as an hors-d'oeuvre, slice the larger ones in half or use the smaller triangles, allowing 3 to 5 per person.

INGREDIENTS

2 *whole eggs*
about 5 *tablespoons bread crumbs*
1 *box processed Gruyère cheese*
1 *to* 1 1/2 *quarts salad oil or vegetable shortening**

USEFUL UTENSIL: *A frying vessel or electric frying pan*

METHOD

Break eggs into a small bowl and mix briskly with a fork. Spread bread crumbs in a shallow dish.

Dip each triangle of cheese first into the egg, then into the bread crumbs; coat well. Repeat dipping process once more.

To make the cheese bits easier to handle when frying, refrigerate for at least 1 hour (overnight if possible). Place on a cookie sheet or any adequate plate, stick toothpicks in each so that wrap will not adhere, cover with storage paper. Up to this point they can be prepared a day or two in advance.

Just before you are ready to serve, heat oil over medium heat for 10 minutes. If you are using an electric frying pan, 350° F. should be the right temperature. If you use a frying thermometer, it should read between 360° F. and 380° F.

Carefully drop cheese bits into oil and fry, 3 minutes on one side, 2 minutes on the other; or until golden brown. Don't crowd your pan; it's better to fry a few at a time.

Lift from oil and drain on crumpled paper towels on a cookie sheet.

To keep them warm, place them on a cookie sheet in a very slow oven until ready to serve. Unlike most fried foods, these delicacies will keep crisp for about 2 hours in a slow oven. Make sure the oven is at its lowest temperature.

TO SERVE: Place a small linen towel or napkin in a serving dish; arrange cheese bits on the dish; decorate with sprigs of fresh parsley.**

*Use enough to cover the bottom of your pan about 1 inch deep.
**Instructions for folding napkin for presenting fried foods are given on page 122.

As an hors-d'oeuvre, cheese bits can be picked up with toothpicks. As an appetizer, they should be eaten from small salad plates, using knives and forks.

Salade d'Avocat

AVOCADO WITH LEMON JUICE AND PEPPER

Avocados are found year round in America, but they are not as plentiful in France, and therefore are considered a special treat.

If you are buying avocados for immediate use, the skin should yield slightly to pressure; a toothpick should flow easily in and out near the stem end. Although the skin will vary in texture, thickness, and shade, this does not indicate the quality of the fruit. Avocados may be ripened at home; a drawer or other dark place is best. If your avocados are too ripe, use the alternate method of preparation given below.*

This simple yet delicious appetizer may be made in advance and refrigerated. The recipe will serve 4.

INGREDIENTS

2 *avocados of about 1/2 pound each or 1 1/2 to 2 pounds cocktail avocados*
1/4 *teaspoon table salt*
3 *turns of black pepper mill, medium grind*
1 *tablespoon lemon juice*

METHOD

Strip away avocado skins. Slice into rings about 1/8 inch thick, carefully severing pulp from stone. (If you are using cocktail avocados, simply cut them in half.)

Place rings of one avocado in serving dish; sprinkle with half of dressing ingredients; slice in second avocado; sprinkle with remaining ingredients. Toss well.

TO SERVE: Serve 2 or 3 slices per person on salad plates.

*ALTERNATE METHOD: If your avocado is too ripe to provide attractive rings, separate pulp from pit and mash into a purée with a fork. Mix well with the dressing. Use the mixture either as a spread on crackers or as a filling for hard-boiled eggs. (The latter can be prepared simply by adding cooked yolks to avocado mixture.)

Blanquette de Veau à l'Ancienne

VEAL TENDERLOIN IN A DELICATE CREAM SAUCE
GARNISHED WITH TINY ONIONS, CARROTS,
AND MUSHROOMS

Blanquette de Veau—an attractive, sophisticated stew of veal, prepared in a white sauce and garnished with onions, carrots, and mushrooms—is completed with a *liaison*, a binding of raw egg yolks and sour cream. Because veal lacks fat, it is at its most succulent when cooked in liquid and served in a sauce.

This recipe is not difficult if you organize your materials and ingredients beforehand. Two pounds of meat will serve 4; to serve 6, use 3 pounds.

SIMMERING THE MEAT

INGREDIENTS

2 *to* 3 *pounds veal tenderloin, cut into* 2*-inch cubes*
5 1/2 *cups cold water*
1 1/2 *teaspoons table salt*
1 *large yellow onion, peeled*
bouquet garni (8 sprigs of parsley, 4 celery stalks with leaves,
tied together)
1/2 *to* 1 *pound carrots, cleaned and cut into* 2*-inch chunks*
or shaped with potato peeler to resemble baby carrots

METHOD

In a pot of at least 2-quart capacity, bring veal, 4 cups of cold water, and salt slowly to a boil, covered. (This will take about 1/2 hour over medium heat.) It is important that boiling point be reached slowly. Each time liquid begins to boil, remove surface froth and add 1/2 cup of cold water. Repeat this process three times, stirring from time to time with a wooden spoon to encourage the rising of the foam.

Add onion and *bouquet garni,* set lid ajar, and simmer 1/2 hour.

Add carrots and simmer 1/2 hour longer, or until carrots are done. Meat should be tender but firm.

Remove meat and carrots to another pan; place a piece of buttered waxed paper over them to prevent drying; cover pan with lid; put in slow oven to keep hot.

Discard *bouquet garni;* strain meat broth into another saucepan and keep hot to use in sauce.

While meat is simmering for the hour, prepare the other vegetables.

THE ONIONS

INGREDIENTS

1 *dozen small white onions*
2 *tablespoons butter*
4 *tablespoons veal broth (reserved from simmering the veal)*

METHOD

TO PEEL ONIONS: Place in strainer or colander and plunge into a pan of boiling water for 1 minute, no more. Cut off root sections. Skin will slide off easily. Cut a cross in the stem end to prevent bursting during cooking.

Place onions, butter, and strained veal broth in a 2-cup saucepan; bring slowly to the boiling point, reduce heat, and simmer gently for 35 minutes, covered, shaking pan often. When a knife blade glides easily through the onions, they are done.

THE MUSHROOMS

INGREDIENTS

1/2 *to* 1 *pound fresh white mushrooms*
1/3 *cup cold water*
1/4 *teaspoon table salt*
1 *tablespoon fresh lemon juice*

METHOD

Wipe mushrooms with clean damp sponge; cut tips from stems. Flute if desired: With a lemon stripper, cut a radial groove from top center of cap to edge, twisting the mushrooms slightly clockwise under the pressure of the stripper to curve the groove. Reserve the peels. (See the drawing on page 88.)

Place mushrooms, water, salt, and lemon juice in a 2- to 4-cup saucepan. Cover, bring to a boil and time for 4 minutes. Remove mushrooms to a small bowl, cover with buttered waxed paper, and place in a slow oven to keep hot. Preserve the juice, as it is a precious ingredient for the sauce.

THE SAUCE

INGREDIENTS

5 *tablespoons clarified butter*
3 *tablespoons all-purpose flour*
2 2/3 *cups hot veal broth (reserved from simmering the meat)*
reserved mushroom liquor
1 *teaspoon grated nutmeg*
1/8 *teaspoon white pepper or 6 turns white pepper mill, fine*
   grind
mushroom peels (the shavings from fluting, if any)

METHOD

Heat clarified butter in a 4-cup saucepan. When butter crackles, add flour gradually, stirring constantly with wire whisk. Let this *roux* swell for 1/2 minute over medium heat.

Gradually add hot veal broth, whisking constantly; add liquid from mushrooms, nutmeg, and pepper. Add mushroom shavings, if any.

Bring to boiling point. Move pan so that only half of it rests on the burner, and simmer gently for 20 minutes. Do not stir, but allow skin to form on surface. After the 20 minutes, carefully remove this skin.

THE LIAISON

INGREDIENTS

2 *egg yolks*
1/3 *cup sour cream*
1 *tablespoon fresh lemon juice (optional)*

chopped fresh parsley

METHOD

To make the *liaison,* place egg yolks in a small bowl, beat together with a fork; beat in sour cream gradually.

Add about 1/4 cup of the hot sauce to this *liaison;* stir well. Now add *liaison* to the sauce, whisking vigorously.

Taste and correct seasoning if necessary. If mushroom liquor has not given enough tartness, the juice of another half lemon may be added.

If sauce is to stand before serving, keep it in a double boiler. Dot surface with butter, cover with a circle of buttered waxed paper to prevent drying, cover with lid.

TO SERVE: Warm a deep platter or shallow serving dish large enough to hold *Blanquette* without spilling. Pour a small portion of the sauce into dish; stir. Arrange meat, onions, carrots, and mushrooms attractively in sauce. Pour on remaining sauce. Sprinkle with parsley.

Serve crusty French bread with which to soak up the sauce.

If an extra vegetable is desired, serve steamed potatoes (page 88) or sautéed rice (page 156).

This whole dish may be prepared ahead of time. To reheat: Preheat oven to 250° F.; place in double boiler or in a Dutch oven set in a pan of water. Cut a circle of waxed paper for the top; cover with lid. Heat in oven for 1 hour.

Salade de Cresson

WATERCRESS SALAD

Watercress is a lovely and refreshing salad green. One bunch usually makes enough salad for 4 people. If you buy it in advance, place it in a jar of water as you would place flowers in a vase. Stored in this way, it will keep fresh in the refrigerator for several days.

INGREDIENTS

1 *bunch watercress (2 to 3 ounces)*
1/4 *teaspoon chopped garlic*
1/4 *teaspoon table salt*
5 *turns of the black pepper mill, medium grind*
1 *tablespoon red wine vinegar*
2 *tablespoons salad oil*

METHOD

Snip off almost half of each watercress stem. Wash in several changes of cold water; drain well. Place in salad basket or colander and shake. Spread greens on a linen towel and pat gently to dry. Watercress may be washed in advance and stored in the refrigerator.

Place all dressing ingredients in a salad bowl in the order listed. A 4- to 6-cup bowl will be adequate for 4 servings. Stir well.

Add watercress just before serving time and toss. If greens are placed in the bowl before serving time, rest them on the serving utensils, not in the dressing.

TO SERVE: Toss salad well. If you are dining informally, each diner may use a piece of crusty French bread to clean his plate well; salad can then be served on the dinner plates. Otherwise, remove them and use salad plates.

Ananas au Kirsch

PINEAPPLE IN KIRSCH

Pineapple is a rare delicacy in France. It is always a treat to serve this tropical fruit, especially when its flavor is combined with Kirsch.

Be sure that the pineapple you buy will be fully ripe when you use it. For the best flavor, it should be slightly soft to the touch. Beware of signs of decay, particularly at the base. If I want perfect rings, I buy several pineapples to be sure that there are enough good slices.

The recipe will serve 4.

INGREDIENTS

8 *to* 10 *slices fresh pineapple**
1 *tablespoon sugar per slice*
1 *tablespoon Kirsch per slice*

*angelica steeped in Kirsch, fresh mint leaves, or candied
  cherries soaked in Kirsch*

USEFUL UTENSIL: *Pineapple corer*

*A 3-pound fruit will yield about 10 slices.

METHOD

Using a good sharp knife, cut off the top of the pineapple. Cut slices 1/4 to 1/2 inch thick. Peel each slice by placing it on a wooden board and trimming off the rind. Remove core with the tip of a small knife, or use one of the pineapple corers made especially for the purpose.

Fill the bottom of a shallow bowl with pineapple slices; sprinkle with sugar, then Kirsch. Add another layer of slices and sprinkle again. Repeat until all slices have been used. (To effectively sprinkle the Kirsch, place your forefinger in neck of bottle, turn it upside down, and shake.)

Refrigerate at least 1 hour before serving. This dessert may be made several days in advance. However, if you do make it ahead, remove it from the refrigerator and stir from time to time.

TO SERVE: Two slices of pineapple are sufficient for a serving. Spoon the sugar–Kirsch mixture, which will look like a light syrup, over the fruit. Arrange slivers of angelica around the pineapple slices or place fresh mint leaves or candied cherries in the center of each slice as an attractive garnish. The garnish is an important part of the presentation of this dessert.

MENU XVII

Quelques Plats Fins
A FINE MEAL

Potage Crème de Laitue
CREAM OF LETTUCE SOUP

Homard à l'Américaine
LOBSTER SIMMERED IN WINE,
SHALLOTS, AND HERBS

Salade de Riz aux Piments
RICE SALAD WITH SWEET GREEN
PEPPER

Biscuit Roulé aux Amandes
ou aux Noisettes
ROLLED ALMOND OR HAZELNUT CAKE

Champagne Brut or Sylvaner

THIS menu includes some of my husband's favorite dishes: a creamy lettuce soup, lobster in a wine and herb sauce, a rice and green pepper salad, and a delicate almond cake. I often choose it for his birthday or our anniversary. Each course has its own distinctive, subtle flavor. Crusty French bread may be added if you wish; it will allow you to garner every drop of the elegant sauce.

RECOMMENDED WINE: Champagne Brut (extra dry) served from start to finish is particularly festive. Another enjoyable wine to complement the meal might be a white *vin d'Alsace*, a light, fresh Sylvaner, always excellent with seafood. Serve either wine chilled.

ORDER OF PREPARATION: The cake may be baked and stored well wrapped up to 2 days in advance. The soup can be prepared ahead up to the last step, which will take only a moment. The rice salad, too, can be stored for several days. The lobster should of course be eaten the day it is purchased.

Potage Crème de Laitue

CREAM OF LETTUCE SOUP

One of my students, who had visited France, was searching for a particular taste and texture in a soup that she had enjoyed there. When the *Crème de Laitue* was presented in one of my classes, she tasted it and exclaimed, "That's it! That's it!" *Enfin,* this was the soup she had been unable to describe to me.

The thickening agent here is *crème de riz* (rice cream), which is used instead of flour to make the *roux*. It contributes to the distinctive texture of this soup. All-purpose flour may be used instead, but the special texture will be lost. Rice cream is sold in supermarkets as a breakfast cereal called Cream of Rice. However, it does not have the flavor or character of the rice cream found in shops which specialize in Chinese or health foods. The latter is made from toasted, short-grain brown rice and feels like grainy flour.

These ingredients will yield 4 to 6 servings. *Crème de Laitue* can be prepared several days ahead of time and reheated or served cold. Freeze it before the last step, if you like, and finish it according to directions.

BLANCHING

INGREDIENTS

1 *pound lettuce (about* 2 *good-sized heads)**
3 *quarts cold water*
2 *tablespoons coarse salt*

METHOD

Wash the lettuce under running water, keeping the heads whole.

Bring water and salt to a boil in a 6- to 8-quart pot. Drop in lettuce. When water returns to boil, boil rapidly, uncovered, 5 minutes. Drain lettuce heads immediately under cold running water in colander to stop cooking process.

Trim off vestiges of roots and any brown spots.

SIMMERING

INGREDIENTS

5 *tablespoons clarified butter*
5 *tablespoons rice cream (or* 4 *tablespoons all-purpose flour)*
4 *cups hot chicken or veal stock***

1/2 *cup warm milk*
2 *tablespoons unsalted butter*

METHOD

For roux: Heat clarified butter in a 6- to 8-cup pot. When butter crackles, add *crème de riz* gradually, stirring constantly with a wire whisk. Let the *roux* swell for 1 minute over medium heat.

Gradually add hot broth, stirring constantly. Drop in lettuce and push down so that it is covered with broth. Cover pot, return to boiling, reduce heat, and simmer 30 minutes.

*Use Boston or Bibb lettuce if available. Do *not* use Iceberg, as it lacks flavor.
**Preferably, use homemade stock (page 19). If you are using cubes, dissolve 4 cubes in 4 1/2 cups boiling water, stirring frequently. Do not add salt without tasting, as chicken cubes can be quite salty. Keep hot.

Process broth and lettuce through a food mill, using a medium disc, or through a ricer, colander, or whatever utensil you use to mash vegetables. (A food processor will not give the same texture.)

Up to this point, soup may be made up to a week in advance; cool and store in refrigerator until needed.

When you are ready to finish the soup, bring it again to a simmer. Stir in the warm milk, then the butter, 1 tablespoon at a time.

THE LIAISON AND GARNISH

INGREDIENTS

2 *egg yolks*
4 *tablespoons heavy cream*
salt
freshly ground white pepper (medium grind)

croûtons

METHOD

Just before serving, prepare the *liaison*—a mixture of egg yolks and cream to which the hot soup is added. Stir the yolks in a 1-cup bowl, briefly, with a fork or whisk. Then add the cream, a little at a time, stirring constantly. Stir about 1/2 cup of the hot soup into the *liaison;* stir well.

Now pour the *liaison* into a tureen, add the remainder of the soup, and stir. Taste and correct seasoning. Keep hot in a warm oven or on a hot plate while making croûtons.

Croûtons may be sautéed, but I prefer to roast them: Preheat oven to 450° F. Cut slices of bread with a cookie cutter into the desired shapes. Butter one side. Place butter side up on a pie pan or cookie sheet and brown in oven for about a minute. Turn and brown the other side, watching closely.

Croûtons are tastier if made just before serving. They can be shaped and buttered in advance, and roasted just before mealtime.

TO SERVE: Ladle the soup into individual dishes or bowls and top each serving with a croûton.

Homard à l'Américaine

LOBSTER SIMMERED IN WINE, SHALLOTS, AND HERBS

Homard à l'Américaine is a well-known French dish with many variations. This version is my own. Even persons not particularly fond of lobster will find themselves soaking up the last bit of the sauce with pieces of French bread!

The recipe calls for killing the lobster by plunging a knife into the center of the body. This will kill it as instantly as boiling water. But if you are hesitant, ask the person at the fish market or the fish counter at your supermarket to do it for you, saving any juice which might escape. Bring a container with you to the market to recover the juice.

When purchasing lobsters, make sure that they are fresh: Their feelers should be moving, they should attempt to crawl, and their tails should snap back when pulled out. Buy them weighing between 1 and 2 pounds apiece.

The number of ingredients in this recipe may disguise the simplicity of its preparation: The key is to have them all laid out at your fingertips in advance.

The proportions given will serve 4 to 6 people.

COOKING THE LOBSTER

INGREDIENTS

7 *pounds live lobster*
6 *tablespoons whipped sweet butter*
5 *or 6 tomatoes (about 1 1/2 pounds)*
12 *tablespoons olive oil*
12 *tablespoons clarified butter*
salt and pepper
1/2 *cup Cognac*
3 *cups white wine*
lobster juice
3 *garlic cloves, pressed*
12 *teaspoons chopped shallots or red onion*
9 *level tablespoons tomato paste*
1 *teaspoon saffron, mixed with 2 tablespoons hot water*

METHOD

Place live lobsters on their stomachs with a tray underneath to catch any juices. Thrust a large French knife into the part where the tail and body meet to kill them instantly. Break claws into two segments and crack shells. Cut the tail crosswise into three sections. Split body in half, remove and discard sac near the eyes. Reserve all juices.

Remove the liver and coral, if any. Using the fingers, blend these with the butter and refrigerate until ready to use.

Plunge tomatoes into boiling water for 1 minute. Skins will slip off once slit with a paring knife. Refrigerate to cool; then cut in half and squeeze them gently to remove seeds and juice. Set aside.

In a heavy skillet or roasting pan, heat oil and clarified butter over high heat until it begins to smoke. Add only the amount of lobster that fits comfortably into the pan, and sauté, turning often, until shells are red. Set sautéed lobster aside and repeat the process until all lobster has been done. Return all the lobster to the skillet.

Sprinkle with salt and pepper; pour on Cognac, reduce heat, and ignite. Shake pan until flames have died away, pour in wine and lobster juice; stir.

Add garlic, shallots, tomatoes, and tomato paste; blend well. Taste and correct seasoning if necessary. Mix saffron and water and stir into the sauce. Cover and simmer gently for 20 minutes.

Transfer lobster from sauce to a chafing dish or to a heated platter in a warm oven; cover.

FINISHING THE SAUCE

INGREDIENTS

5 *teaspoons chopped fresh parsley*
5 *teaspoons dried tarragon or 8 teaspoons chopped fresh*
tarragon
4 *bay leaves*
1 *teaspoon dried thyme or 1 fresh sprig*
2 *to 4 tablespoons meat glaze (optional)**
6 *tablespoons whipped sweet butter mixed with lobster*
liver and coral (reserved from first part of recipe)

chopped fresh parsley

METHOD

Return pan to high heat. Add herbs, meat glaze, and liver–butter mixture. Reduce over high heat for 4 minutes, stirring with wooden spoon. If tomatoes have rendered a lot of juice, leave over heat a few minutes longer. Remove bay leaf; stir well. Sauce should be a rich carmine red.

TO SERVE: If lobster is already in a chafing dish or serving platter, pour on sauce; sprinkle with parsley; serve at once.

Provide nut crackers and picks, large dinner napkins, and plenty of crusty French bread.

Pour everyone a fresh glass of Champagne or light wine . . . *oh là là!*

*Glaze may be either the jellied juices from a roast or 4 cups of strong beef stock, reduced to about 5 tablespoons.

Salade de Riz aux Piments

RICE SALAD WITH SWEET GREEN PEPPER

Salade de Riz is good and refreshing served either hot or cold. It may be made several days in advance. When serving it cold, take it from the refrigerator a half hour ahead of time.

Proportions given are for 4 to 6 servings.

INGREDIENTS

1 *cup raw long-grained rice*
3 *cups cold water*
1 *teaspoon table salt*
1 *tablespoon salad oil*
1/2 *cup hot water*

1 *cup sliced sweet green pepper*
2 *to 3 turns black pepper mill, medium grind*
1 1/2 *tablespoons red wine vinegar*
2 *tablespoons salad oil*

METHOD

Combine rice and cold water in a 6- to 8-cup saucepan; cover and bring to boiling point over medium heat. (This will take about 3 minutes.) Pour off water.

Add salt and oil, cover, and cook over medium heat for 20 minutes, adding the additional hot water after 10 minutes cooking time. Towards the end of cooking time, check to make sure rice is not sticking; loosen with a roasting fork.

Meanwhile prepare green pepper. Wash under cold running water, dry, cut in half lengthwise, remove seeds. Slice into strips.

When rice is done, transfer to salad bowl. Add remaining ingredients in the order listed; toss well. If you are storing salad for more than a few hours, add an extra teaspoon of vinegar and toss again just before serving.

TO SERVE: Spoon onto a leaf of Boston lettuce on individual salad plates. Eat after the main course.

Biscuit Roulé aux Amandes ou aux Noisettes

ROLLED ALMOND OR HAZELNUT CAKE

This delicate pastry is a marvel of lightness and flavor. My youngest daughter always requests it for her birthday. It is baked on a cookie sheet like a jelly roll cake, then filled with whipped cream and rolled. It always surprises those who taste it that it contains no flour, only ground almonds or hazelnuts.

The recipe yields 14 to 16 slices. The cake can be baked, rolled, and refrigerated a few days before serving.

INGREDIENTS

salad oil
8 egg yolks
3/4 cup granulated sugar
1 1/2 cups ground almonds or hazelnuts*
8 egg whites

1 cup heavy cream
1 tablespoon confectioners' sugar, sifted
whole almonds or hazelnuts

USEFUL UTENSIL: *Cookie sheet*

METHOD

Saturate a piece of paper towel with oil and coat a Teflon or other cookie sheet that measures roughly 11 × 15 inches. Be sure the bottom, corners, and sides are all well coated. Line with waxed paper, being careful to fit it up the sides, too. Snip corners with scissors so that the paper will fit well into the corners. Oil again on top of waxed paper.

Preheat oven to 350° F.

Using a large wire whisk, beat egg yolks in a large bowl for

---

*A 6-ounce cellophane bag will yield 1 2/3 cups of nuts when ground. Place 3/4 cup at a time in an electric blender and whirl at high speed while you count to 10. Or use a food processor.

1 minute; then gradually beat in sugar. This will take another 4 minutes.

Next, gradually blend in ground nuts with a wooden spoon.

In a large bowl, beat egg whites with electric mixer at high speed for 2 minutes, cleaning sides of bowl several times with a rubber spatula. Then, slowly fold egg whites carefully into almond batter, a small portion at a time. Do not stir.

Pour this batter onto prepared cookie sheet, spread out evenly with a spatula; bake on middle rack of oven for 18 minutes. When done, pastry should feel firm to the touch; it will be a light golden brown.

Remove from oven, cool completely, then cover with a damp linen towel and refrigerate for a minimum of 2 hours. Up to this point cake may be made as much as 2 days ahead of time. If keeping more than 2 hours, be sure towel stays damp, wetting it again if necessary.

Chill bowl and beaters in freezer; then whip cream for 3 minutes at high speed, using rubber spatula to clean bowl. Using a large wire whisk, fold in confectioners' sugar.

Cover a pastry board with two sheets of waxed paper, making them large enough to overlap the board at least 4 inches all the way around. Turn cake onto the board so that its underside is on top. Peel off original waxed paper.

Working with a long edge of cake near you, spread about 2/3 of the cream in a narrow line about 1 inch in from front edge, leaving an inch at both ends also, so that cream will not be squeezed out when the cake is rolled.

Starting with the front edge, roll cake, folding cream within it. It helps to roll the waxed paper with it until the cake begins to overlap. Decorate the outside with remaining cream, using a rubber spatula or pastry bag. Fill in both ends and cracks, if any.

Sprinkle the top with almonds or hazelnuts, depending upon which kind of cake was made.

TO SERVE: Slice cake into 1/2-inch pieces. It should be eaten with a fork.

Any leftover cake will keep well. To store it, insert toothpicks in it to prevent the storage wrap from sticking, cover, and refrigerate.

MENU XVIII

Venez Dîner Avec Nous
WON'T YOU COME FOR DINNER?

Potage Portugais
A CREAMY TOMATO SOUP

Poulet de Grain à la Crapaudine
CORNISH HEN OR SQUAB WITH
MUSTARD, BREAD CRUMBS, AND BROWN
SAUCE

Tiges de Blettes au Beurre
SAUTÉED SWISS CHARD

Salade Verte
GREEN SALAD

Riz Condé
RICE DESSERT WITH KIRSCH
AND CANDIED FRUIT, GARNISHED WITH
POACHED PEARS

*Givry, Juliénas, or Moulin à Vent
or Mousseux Brut Blanc de Blancs*

ONE of my students who moved to the Midwest 6 years ago telephoned me recently to tell me that she continues to use my recipes. In particular, she loves to prepare this menu, especially when she entertains, because each dish is so delectable and impressive. Moreover, all of the preliminaries may be done long before mealtime, a real advantage for a busy hostess.

The soup, *Potage Portugais,* a smooth-textured tomato soup, is followed by a succulent Cornish hen. The roasted and broiled hen is accompanied by a marvelous sauce and an easy and different vegetable, sautéed stems of Swiss chard. A spectacular dessert, *Riz Condé,* completes the menu. If you wish to serve a salad course, I would suggest lettuce salad (page 250) or escarole salad (page 148).

RECOMMENDED WINE: With the poultry, try a young and tender light red wine from the region of Châlon in southern Burgundy, a Givry, or a Beaujolais such as Juliénas or Moulin à Vent. Or, Mousseux (sparkling), Brut (very dry) Blanc de Blancs, a white wine made exclusively from naturally fermented white grapes, may be served chilled, as an *apéritif* and throughout the meal.

ORDER OF PREPARATION: The dessert may be made several days before serving. The major preparations for the soup, poultry, and vegetable can also be done in advance. The final step of each dish will take only a few minutes to complete.

Potage Portugais

A CREAMY TOMATO SOUP

In French culinary language, the designation *Portugais* refers to a blending of tomatoes, other vegetables, herbs, and tapioca or

rice. The *potage* is bound together with a *liaison* of egg yolks and cream, which gives it a smooth texture and a delicate taste.

The recipe will serve 4 to 6 people.

THE MIREPOIX

INGREDIENTS

8 *tablespoons clarified butter*
1 *cup finely diced yellow onions (about 1/4 pound)*
1 *cup finely diced carrots (about 1/2 pound)*
1 *pound tomatoes, peeled (about 4 medium tomatoes)**
salt

METHOD

Heat butter in a 2- to 4-cup pan. Add onions and sauté 1 minute, stirring with wooden spoon; add carrots and sauté 5 minutes, stirring occasionally. Add tomatoes. Cook uncovered over fairly high heat for another 5 minutes, stirring occasionally. Remove from heat; sprinkle with salt; stir.

ROUX AND PRELIMINARY SIMMERING

INGREDIENTS

5 *cups boiling water or hot veal or chicken stock*
6 *tablespoons clarified butter*
1/3 *cup flour*
1/2 *teaspoon table salt*
4 *turns of black pepper mill, medium grind*

1 *teaspoon table salt*
bouquet garni (5 celery stalks and 5 parsley sprigs tied together)

USEFUL UTENSIL: *Food mill*

*Blanch first by dipping for 1 minute in boiling water; skins will then peel off easily.

METHOD

Have the 5 cups of hot liquid ready.

PREPARE ROUX: Heat butter in a 2- to 4-quart pan—one large enough so that liquid can be added later. Slowly add flour, stirring with a whisk. When blended, allow *roux* to moisten and swell for half a minute over low heat. Add salt and pepper.

Now, slowly add hot water or stock to *roux*, whisking constantly. Bring to boiling point and boil 1 minute. Add *mirepoix* and 1 teaspoon salt; stir. Add *bouquet garni*.

Cover pan and simmer 1 hour, stirring occasionally. Make sure the boil is gentle.

Pour soup through food mill, using medium disc, or through a potato ricer, strainer, or colander—whatever you have to mash vegetables. (A food processor does not, in my opinion, give the proper consistency for this recipe.)

Up to this point, soup may be made in advance; cool and store in the refrigerator or freeze until needed.

ADDING TAPIOCA AND LIAISON

INGREDIENTS

3 *tablespoons tapioca* *

2 *egg yolks*
2 *tablespoons sour cream*
2 *tablespoons heavy cream*
1/2 *teaspoon table salt*

1 *teaspoon chopped fresh tarragon or parsley*

METHOD

To complete preparation of soup, bring it to boiling point, then add tapioca. To ensure even distribution and no lumping, pour in tapioca from a height of 5 to 6 inches above pot, stirring constantly with a wire whisk. (The whisk will produce a smoother texture than a wooden spoon.) Boil gently for 5 to 20 minutes until thick.

PREPARE LIAISON: Just before serving, prepare the *liaison*, which is simply a mixture of egg yolks and cream to which the

---

*I prefer to use imported small pearl tapioca, available in some supermarkets. If you cannot find it, minute tapioca is an acceptable substitute, but you should use only 1 1/2 tablespoons.

liquid will be added. Stir yolks briefly; add sour cream and heavy cream a little at a time, stirring constantly. Add about 1/2 cup of the hot soup to the *liaison;* stir well.

Pour *liaison* mixture into tureen, add soup, and stir. Add salt. Taste and correct seasoning if desired.

TO SERVE: Bring to the table piping hot in tureen or bowl; ladle out at once. Sprinkle with chopped herbs.

Poulet de Grain à la Crapaudine

CORNISH HEN OR SQUAB WITH MUSTARD, BREAD CRUMBS, AND BROWN SAUCE

The traditional way to serve this delectable dish is to prepare a Cornish hen or squab for each diner. The breastbone of the bird is broken to give it the appearance of a *crapaud* (toad).

The sauce recipe is sufficient for up to 8 servings.

THE GASTRIQUE AND PRELIMINARY SAUCE PREPARATION

INGREDIENTS

1/4 *cup red wine vinegar*
1/4 *cup dry white wine*
1/2 *teaspoon tarragon*
2 *teaspoons chopped shallots*

2 *tablespoons salad oil*
2 *heaping tablespoons all-purpose flour*
1/4 *teaspoon salt*
1 1/2 *turns of black pepper mill, medium grind*
2 *teaspoons chopped shallots*
2 *cups hot beef stock**
1 1/2 *teaspoons tomato paste*
1 *medium-size ripe tomato, unpeeled*

USEFUL UTENSIL: *A chinois (conical strainer)*

*Use homemade stock (page 18), or 4 beef cubes dissolved in 2 1/2 cups boiling water, plus 1/4 teaspoon of salt if required. Bouillon should be prepared before starting the sauce.

METHOD

THE GASTRIQUE: In culinary language, the *gastrique* is a reduction of vinegar, white wine, and herbs which gives the sauce a pungent flavor. It is easily made, but must be watched carefully.

Combine wine vinegar, white wine, tarragon, and chopped shallots in a 1- to 2-cup saucepan and stir well with a fork. (The pan should be heavy. Do not use aluminum, which is discolored by vinegar.) Bring to the boiling point over high heat and let it boil for about 7 minutes until not more than 1 tablespoon is left. Remove from heat.

Heat oil in a heavy 1-quart saucepan until faint smoke appears. Using a whisk, gradually stir in flour, then let it swell for about 1 minute to ensure that the flour is well cooked. Add salt, pepper, shallots, the *gastrique,* hot bouillon, and tomato paste, continuing to heat and stir during the additions. Cut the tomato in half and squeeze out and discard the juice. When the sauce starts to boil, add the tomato, and lower the heat to maintain a simmer for at least 2 hours.

Once all the ingredients are added, do not stir the sauce. If your burner is at its lowest setting, and the simmer is not gentle enough, push the pan to the side of the burner. In a short time a skin will form on the surface. *Do not remove it.* If gentle bubbles are noticeable under the skin, the temperature is perfect. At no time should the sauce boil rapidly or come to a standstill.

Remove and discard the skin. Pour the sauce through a *chinois* or other strainer into the top of a double boiler, pressing the solids to extract all the juice.

Up to this point sauce may be prepared ahead of time. It can be reheated in a double boiler.

ROASTING AND BROILING THE BIRDS

INGREDIENTS

4 3/4- to 1-pound Cornish hens or squabs
8 heaping tablespoons clarified butter
table salt
freshly ground black pepper

3 teaspoons Dijon mustard
6 tablespoons juices from roasting pan
plain bread crumbs
unsalted butter

USEFUL UTENSIL: *Goose-feather brush*

METHOD

Remove fat from bird and store for rendering if you like (see page 20). Place the wings on the back of the bird with the tips meeting. Rest the bird on its breast. Using the heel of your fist, punch it in the middle of the back to break the breastbone, making it look like a toad. Wipe bird inside and out with a paper towel; sprinkle the cavity with salt.

ROASTING: Preheat oven to 325° F.

Coat a heatproof pan or dish and one side of the birds with clarified butter. Roast for 15 minutes; sprinkle with salt and pepper. Turn birds over and brush the other side with clarified butter. Sprinkle again with salt and pepper and roast 10 minutes more. Turn again, baste with butter, roast for another 10 minutes. Repeat basting every 10 minutes until birds are done. (They should take about 50 minutes.) Remove from pan, and reserve pan and juices for finishing the sauce.

Birds can be roasted ahead of time and warmed up before the next step.

BROILING: In a small bowl, mix mustard with about 6 tablespoons of the juice from the roasting pan. Using a pastry brush, spread this mixture on the breast side of the birds. Sprinkle with bread crumbs and dot with butter.

Adjust your broiler rack to be about 8 inches from the heat source and broil for about 3 minutes, until dark brown. Turn the birds over carefully, coat the other side with the mustard mixture, bread crumbs, and butter, broil for 3 minutes, and turn off heat.

ALTERNATE RECIPE: Quartered broilers can also be used. Proportions given here are sufficient for 3 pounds of poultry, which will serve 4 to 6 people. The method for chicken is the same, although roasting will require only 35–45 minutes.

Transfer birds to heated dinner plates, back side up, and keep warm in the oven with door ajar while finishing the sauce.

COMPLETION OF SAUCE AND GARNISHING

INGREDIENTS

4 *tablespoons dry white wine*
1 *teaspoon tarragon*

lemons
*petits cornichons**
watercress (optional)
*paper frills***

METHOD

DEGLAZING ROASTING PAN: Add white wine and tarragon to the juices that remain in the roasting pan. (If you haven't already mixed some of the juice with the mustard for broiling, be sure to reserve 6 tablespoons for this purpose.) Bring to boiling over high heat, stirring constantly with a wooden spoon for about 1/2 minute.

Strain a tablespoon at a time of this mixture into the brown sauce. Keep warm in the double boiler until ready to serve.

GARNISHING: Make grooves in the lemons using a lemon stripper or sharp knife. Slice lemons and cut slices in half. Cut enough to fit all around the edge of each dinner plate.

Make fan shapes out of the *cornichons* by making several cuts at one end and pressing them between your fingers.

TO SERVE: Arrange the half slices of lemon around the edge of your dinner plates. Between the lemon slices place the fan-shaped *cornichons*.

Flank each side of the bird with watercress, tucking the stems underneath.

*These are small French gherkins preserved in vinegar.
**For instructions in making paper frills, see page 59.
ALTERNATE PRESENTATION: If you are preparing the dish using broilers, place all the pieces on a heated serving platter as follows: Arrange the breasts in the center with the sides touching. Place the leg pieces upright alongside the breasts, and fit them with paper frills. Garnish the platter with lemon slices and *cornichons* as described above.

Cover the drumsticks with paper frills. Pass the brown sauce in a gravy boat. Only a couple of tablespoons should be ladled over each bird. The lemon slices may be squeezed over them, and the pickles eaten as an accompaniment.

Tiges de Blettes au Beurre

SAUTÉED SWISS CHARD

Swiss chard is a member of the beet family. It is a pity that this vegetable is not served more often in the United States, since it is so plentiful and inexpensive.

The leaves or the whole stalks of Swiss chard may be cooked like spinach (see page 264). However, with this menu, I prefer to serve only the stems. They should be served after the main dish as a separate course.

This recipe yields 4 to 6 servings. For more, blanch in batches.

INGREDIENTS

3 *quarts water*
2 *tablespoons coarse salt or* 1 *tablespoon table salt*
3 *pounds Swiss chard*

8 *tablespoons clarified butter*
salt
freshly ground pepper

METHOD

Bring salted water to a boil in a 6-quart pot. While waiting for the water to boil, clean the Swiss chard by cutting off the root ends. Wash in several changes of cold water, drain, cut off leaves and set them aside for another use. (They will keep well in the refrigerator in the hydrator compartment.)

Cut the stems into 2- to 4-inch sticks and drop them in the boiling water. Continue boiling for 5 minutes, uncovered. Place them in a colander and run cold water over them to halt the cooking process. Drain well and pat dry with paper towels.

This vegetable may be prepared several days ahead of time, covered with storage wrap, and refrigerated at this point.

Shortly before mealtime, heat butter in a frying pan large enough so that *blettes* are not crowded. When butter sings, add them and sauté until just heated through. Season to taste with salt and pepper.

TO SERVE: Serve after the main course on a heated salad plate placed over a clean dinner plate.

Riz Condé

RICE DESSERT WITH KIRSCH AND CANDIED FRUIT, GARNISHED WITH POACHED PEARS

Riz Condé, or *Riz à l'Impérial* as it is sometimes called, is an elegant dessert to end almost any meal that does not include other dishes made with rice.

The origin of the dish is attributed to a Prince de Condé, for whom it may have been created. The Condé family played an influential role in French history. I do not know if my mother knew the legend of the dish. She never used a recipe; she cooked by instinct. This is her version of this dessert, which always impressed our family and friends.

Every step of *Riz Condé* can be accomplished in advance. However, on a humid day it is preferable to glaze the pears shortly before serving. Preparing the glaze, spreading it on the pears, and arranging them on top of the rice should take no more than a few minutes.

This recipe should serve 4 to 6.

PREPARING THE FRUITS

INGREDIENTS

1 *cup candied fruits*
7 *tablespoons Kirsch*

1 *cup plus 2 tablespoons granulated sugar*
4 *cups cold water*
1 *vanilla bean (or 1 teaspoon vanilla extract)*
3 *to 4 fresh pears (preferably Bosc)*
fresh lemon juice

METHOD

Soak candied fruits in Kirsch in a small bowl, covered, for at least 2 hours—the longer, the better, up to several days.

PREPARE SYRUP: Combine the sugar, water, and vanilla bean in a large cooking vessel. Bring to a rolling boil, uncovered. Reduce heat and simmer 20 minutes, stirring occasionally with a wooden spoon. (If vanilla extract is used, add it 5 minutes before cooking time is over.) Continue to simmer over low heat.

While syrup is cooking, prepare pears: Peel, but do not remove stems. Rub lemon juice over each pear to prevent discoloring.

Poach the pears, whole, in the syrup. The liquid should be just trembling, with only an occasional bubble appearing. Timing depends on the ripeness of the fruit. It could take from 5 to 30 minutes. Turn and baste pears occasionally. They are done when the tip of a knife slides easily into the fruit.

Remove pears from the liquid with a slotted spoon and drain on a cake rack. When cool, slice them in half lengthwise all the way through the stem, leaving the stem attached. Discard cores and seeds.

PREPARING THE RICE

INGREDIENTS

3/4 *cup uncooked rice*
4 *cups water*

2 *cups milk*
1 *vanilla bean (or 1 teaspoon vanilla extract)*
2/3 *cup granulated sugar*
4 *egg yolks*

METHOD

In a 1 1/2-quart saucepan, blanch rice in boiling water, uncovered, over medium to high heat for 8 minutes. Drain rice in colander. Immerse colander in a bowl of very hot water. Drain again and pour hot water over rice. Allow to drain a third time.

Combine milk and vanilla bean in a 1- or 2-quart saucepan. Bring to boiling point over low to medium heat and mix in the rice. Cover, bring to the boiling point again over medium heat, and simmer 15 minutes. Mix in sugar carefully with a fork and cook

5 minutes longer. (At this point the milk should be absorbed by the rice.)

Remove from heat and take out vanilla bean. (Bean may be washed well under running water, dried thoroughly, and stored for future use.) Stir in egg yolks, one at a time, with a wooden spoon. Return saucepan to medium heat* and cook for about 3 minutes, stirring lightly with wooden spoon.

Remove pan from heat. Mix in half the candied fruit and transfer the mixture to a shallow serving bowl. Smooth the surface and sprinkle the remaining candied fruit over it.

This step may be done up to a week ahead of time. The mixture can be refrigerated, covered with storage wrap.

GLAZING

INGREDIENTS

*red food coloring (optional)***
10 *to* 12 *tablespoons apricot preserves*

USEFUL UTENSIL: *Goose-feather pastry brush*

METHOD

In a small saucepan, heat the apricot preserves over medium heat. Let the preserves come to boiling and boil for 5 minutes, stirring occasionally with a wire whisk. Remove from heat and let them cool for a minute.

TO SERVE: Put a drop of food coloring on your finger, if desired, and rub it on the convex side of the pea s. Then coat them with the apricot glaze, using a pastry brush. Arrange the pears, cut side down, in a circle on top of the rice, with the stems facing the edge of the dish.

Serve at room temperature or, if you prefer, chilled.

*If vanilla extract is used instead of vanilla bean, add it at this point.
**If you prefer not to use food coloring, beet juice is an acceptable substitute.

MENU XIX

Nous Serons Huit
DINNER FOR EIGHT

Velouté de Concombres
CUCUMBER SOUP WITH CREAM

Oiseaux Sans-Tête
VEAL BIRDS WITH SAUSAGE AND HERBS

Purée Saint-Germain
PURÉE OF SPLIT PEAS, CARROTS,
AND ONIONS, GARNISHED WITH
CROÛTONS

Salade Verte
GREEN SALAD

Croquantes à la Crème Ganache
CRISP, ROLLED PETITS FOURS
DIPPED IN CHOCOLATE CREAM

Saint-Péray or Entre-Deux-Mers

A WISE Greek host of old once proclaimed that to entertain properly, the guests should number no less than the Graces (3), no more than the Muses (9). To make an occasion festive and lively, yet intimate, 8 is a good round number. It is, also, the maximum number for which I enjoy preparing an intricate menu like the one that follows.

This dinner consists of a delicate cucumber soup, rolled veal cutlets, split pea purée, and a delightfully crunchy, cream-filled cookie. For a salad course, watercress salad (page 178) would be appropriate.

RECOMMENDED WINE: Serve a Saint-Péray, a light, sparkling white wine from vineyards mid-way along the Rhône Valley; or a dry white Bordeaux from the Entre-Deux-Mers, that tableland between the area's two great rivers, the Garonne and the Dordogne.

ORDER OF PREPARATION: The *petits fours* can be made and stored in a tight tin days in advance. Fill them just a few hours before serving. The soup and purée can both be prepared up to the final step and completed just before mealtime. The veal birds, too, can be cooked ahead, and the sauce made at the last minute.

Velouté de Concombres

CUCUMBER SOUP WITH CREAM

This soup is pure ambrosia; its texture silken, its taste delicate. The recipe will provide 8 servings.

INGREDIENTS

8 *cups hot chicken bouillon**
8 *cups water*
2 *teaspoons coarse salt or* 1 *teaspoon table salt*
4 *cups diced cucumbers (about* 2 *pounds)*

4 *tablespoons clarified butter*
1/2 *teaspoon table salt*

1 *cup heavy cream (2 tablespoons per serving)*
chopped fresh tarragon when available, or chopped fresh parsley

*Use homemade stock (page 19), or 8 chicken cubes dissolved in 8 cups water.

METHOD

Have hot broth or bouillon ready. If using cubes, combine water and cubes in a 4-quart pot; bring to a boil and simmer 5 minutes.

Bring water and salt to boiling point in a covered, 4-quart pot.

Meanwhile, peel cucumbers; cut in half lengthwise. Using a teaspoon, remove all seeds; slice into thin strips; then dice these strips. Cut at an angle for a more attractive shape.

Drop diced cucumber into boiling water to blanch. Bring water again to a gentle boil and time for 5 minutes. Pour vegetable into colander or strainer, and pass under cold running water. Such a pretty sight—the pieces look like precious stones!

Drain well and pat with paper towel to remove most of the moisture. Dry pot in which the cucumbers were blanched and heat clarified butter in it. Butter is hot enough when it begins to crackle. Test by dropping in a cucumber piece. If the butter sings, it is hot enough. It should not brown. Add cucumbers and toss for several minutes, until they are glossy and impregnated with butter.

Add hot chicken stock and stir well with wooden spoon; cover and simmer for 20 minutes. Taste and add 1/2 teaspoon of salt if necessary. Remove all traces of grease by swishing a piece of tissue paper over surface.

If soup is being made in advance, it may now be cooled, poured into a storage container, and kept in the refrigerator up to 3 days. It may also be frozen.

TO SERVE: Shake cream well. Measure 2 tablespoons of cream into each bowl. Using a small whisk or fork, stir soup in gradually. Sprinkle with tarragon or parsley. Serve at once.

If soup is to be presented in a tureen, pour 1 cup of cream into the tureen and gradually stir in soup. Sprinkle with chopped herb.

Oiseaux Sans-Tête

VEAL BIRDS WITH SAUSAGE AND HERBS

Oiseaux Sans-Tête, "birds without a head," are rolled veal cutlets, stuffed with sausage and herbs, and served with a deglazed pan gravy. An alternate stuffing is also given for those who do not eat pork.

The recipe serves 8.

THE STUFFING

INGREDIENTS

1 *cup cold water*
3 *slices white sandwich bread, preferably stale*
1 *pound sweet Italian sausage*
1 *whole egg (jumbo)*
2 *tablespoons clarified butter*
5 *teaspoons chopped fresh parsley*
5 *teaspoons chopped shallots or red onion*
2 *tablespoons Cognac*

METHOD

Cut crusts from bread and soak in water; when soft, squeeze out water.

Remove sausage from casing; place in large mixing bowl. Crumble in softened bread; add egg; mix together thoroughly with hands or pastry blender.

In a medium-sized frying pan, heat the clarified butter. Sauté stuffing until meat has lost its raw appearance. Cover and simmer 10 minutes, stirring occasionally. Remove lid and cook 5 minutes more.

Transfer stuffing back into mixing bowl; add parsley, shallots, and Cognac; mix thoroughly.

If stuffing is not to be used immediately, it should be cooled completely, covered, and refrigerated. It may also be frozen.

THE CUTLETS

INGREDIENTS

8 *veal cutlets weighing 1/4 to 1/2 pound each, pounded to*
  1/8" thickness*
8 *tablespoons clarified butter*
salt

USEFUL UTENSIL: *Butcher's twine*

*If cutlets weigh less than 1/4 pound each, plan 2 per person.

METHOD

Pat cutlets with a paper towel to soak up any moisture. Lay them out on a board or table. Distribute stuffing evenly on cutlets. Then roll meat around stuffing and tie with a piece of twine, making a neat little bundle.

Heat butter in a heavy 12-inch frying pan until it sings. The cutlets should have room to brown without crowding. (If you do not have a pan large enough, brown a few at a time.)

Brown meat on all sides over medium to high heat. Sprinkle with salt; cover and simmer gently from 30 to 45 minutes, turning and basting from time to time. When cutlets are tender, they are done; slice off a sliver to taste.

When done, place birds on a board to remove strings; transfer to heated serving platter and keep hot in a slow oven. *Save the sautéing pan and its contents, as they are crucial to the preparation of the sauce.* (If desired, birds may be cooled completely, covered, and refrigerated at this point.)

THE SAUCE

INGREDIENTS

1/2 cup hot chicken or beef bouillon*
2 teaspoons tomato paste
3 tablespoons hot water or hot bouillon
2 teaspoons potato flour
5 teaspoons cold water

chopped fresh parsley

METHOD

If using packaged bouillon, combine 1 cup water and 1 bouillon cube in a small saucepan and simmer 5 minutes.

DEGLAZE PAN: Return pan in which *Oiseaux* were simmered to high heat. Add hot bouillon and, using a wooden spoon, scrape all particles from the bottom of the pan. Continue to boil for about a minute.

In a small bowl, dilute the tomato paste with the hot water or bouillon. In another small bowl, mix the potato flour with cold water.

* Use homemade stock (pages 18–20) or 1 cube dissolved in 1 cup boiling water.

Stir the diluted tomato paste quickly into the deglazed pan. Add the potato flour mixture quickly, stirring vigorously for 1/2 minute. (If sauce remains over heat for more than a minute, it will separate.)*

As soon as sauce has a little body, remove from heat. There will be just enough to coat the birds. Taste and correct seasoning if necessary.

TO SERVE: Spoon sauce over birds and sprinkle with chopped parsley. Savor *les Oiseaux Sans-Tête* with only crusty French bread or with the *Purée Saint-Germain* that follows.

* If your sauce should separate, don't panic. It can be repaired by whisking in 1 1/2 tablespoons very hot water.

ALTERNATE STUFFING: An alternate stuffing is offered here for those who do not eat pork.

INGREDIENTS

1 *cup cold water*
3 *slices white sandwich bread*
1 *pound ground veal (If you buy a piece to grind yourself, get* 1/4 *pound extra as there is always a little waste.)*
1 *egg (jumbo)*
1/2 *teaspoon allspice*
1/2 *teaspoon basil*
1/2 *teaspoon sage*
1 *teaspoon thyme*
1 *teaspoon table salt*
4 *tablespoons clarified butter*
5 *teaspoons chopped shallots*
5 *teaspoons chopped fresh parsley*
2 *tablespoons Cognac*

METHOD

Cut crusts from bread and soak in cold water; when soft, squeeze out moisture. Crumble into mixing bowl with veal, egg, spices, and salt; blend well with fingers or pastry blender.

Heat butter in a medium-sized frying pan and sauté bread and veal mixture over medium heat, turning with a wooden spoon to be sure it does not stick to the pan. Veal has a tendency to stick, so it has to be watched carefully.

When meat has lost its raw appearance, cover and simmer 5 minutes. Return to mixing bowl; add shallots, parsley, and Cognac. Blend thoroughly.

If stuffing is not to be used at once, cool completely, cover, and refrigerate or freeze.

Purée Saint-Germain

PURÉE OF SPLIT PEAS, CARROTS, AND ONIONS, GARNISHED WITH CROÛTONS

Delicious, attractive, and so inexpensive, this purée makes a wonderful accompaniment for the *Oiseaux Sans-Tête*. The recipe will provide 8 servings.

PREPARING THE PEAS

INGREDIENTS

2 *cups dried split green peas*
2 *cups lukewarm water*
2 *more cups lukewarm water*
1 *teaspoon table salt*

METHOD

Sort peas to remove any foreign matter. Wash in several changes of warm water. Then soak in 2 cups warm water for 2 hours. (If soaked only 1 hour, peas will require at least 1 cup more water when cooking.)

Discard soaking water and transfer peas to a 4-quart pan or Dutch oven. Add 2 cups warm water, salt, and cover. Bring slowly to boiling point. (This will take about 10 minutes.) When foam appears on surface, skim off as much as possible.

ADDING THE MIREPOIX AND PURÉEING

INGREDIENTS

3/4 *cup diced carrots (about 1/4 pound)*
3/4 *cup diced yellow onion (1 medium onion)*
2 *ounces boiled ham (2 slices)*
4 *tablespoons unsalted butter*
1 *bay leaf*
bouquet garni (3 to 6 parsley sprigs plus 3 celery stalks tied together)

USEFUL UTENSIL: *Food mill or ricer*

METHOD

Dice carrots, onions, and ham into 1/8-inch cubes. Slowly melt butter in a small frying pan. Do not brown. Add carrots, onions, ham, and bay leaf; simmer 5 minutes, uncovered.

When peas reach the boiling point add *mirepoix* and *bouquet garni;* stir well with wooden spoon; cover and simmer gently until peas are very soft. This will take from 50 minutes to 1 hour and 15 minutes, depending upon the peas and their soaking time. Check every 10 to 15 minutes to make certain that there is enough liquid; if necessary, add a few tablespoons of hot water during cooking. When peas are done there should be no liquid left.

Remove *bouquet garni* and purée peas in a food mill, using disc with the finest holes if you have an adjustable one; or use a potato ricer or a strainer, pressing vegetables through with a wooden spoon. *Do not use a blender or a food processor.* They will make the texture heavy, rather than light and delicate as it should be.

At this point, purée can be cooled, covered, and refrigerated for a day or two, or frozen.

FINISHING THE PURÉE

INGREDIENTS

4 *tablespoons unsalted butter*
salt and pepper
3 *tablespoons heavy cream*
croûtons

METHOD

Return purée to cooking pan, place over low heat, and stir with wooden spoon for about a minute to remove any moisture. Melt in butter, a little at a time. Taste and adjust seasoning.

Remove from heat and stir in cream, 1 tablespoon at a time. Keep hot in slow oven while making croûtons.* Once the butter

*TO MAKE CROÛTONS: With a 2- to 4-inch round cookie cutter, cut circles from slices of white bread. Cut these in half. They may be sautéed in clarified butter, but I prefer to roast them: Preheat oven to 450° F. Butter one side of the cut bread, place buttered side up on a cookie sheet and roast for about 2 minutes. Turn and brown second side for 1 minute. Croûtons are tastier when made just before serving.

and cream have been added, make sure the purée does not boil. It may be reheated in a double boiler.

TO SERVE: Spoon purée into heated serving dish; twirl with a fork into an attractive design, building it up like a pyramid. Arrange croûtons at peak and around base. Serve either with or after the main course.

Croquantes à la Crème Ganache

CRISP, ROLLED PETITS FOURS
DIPPED IN CHOCOLATE CREAM

There are many kinds of *petits fours*. Those best known in the United States are the tiny cakes covered with various shades and flavors of fondant.

These *Croquantes* are small drop cookies which are rolled into a slender cylinder while still warm, filled with a delicious chocolate cream at both ends, then dipped in chocolate shot. They are appropriate to serve after any meal or at tea time.

This recipe will make about 20 *petits fours*. For more, prepare several batches.

THE COOKIES

INGREDIENTS

1 *jumbo egg*
1/4 *cup granulated sugar*
1/4 *cup granulated flour or sifted all-purpose flour*
butter

METHOD

Preheat oven to 400° F.

Break egg into small mixing bowl. Add sugar gradually, mixing with a spatula. Stir vigorously for about 2 minutes, or until egg becomes lighter in color. Add flour gradually, stirring continuously.

With the butter, grease 3 or 4 large circles on a cookie sheet. Drop 1/2 to 3/4 of a teaspoonful of the batter onto these circles, flatten with a fork, and bake 3 to 4 minutes, until edges are medium to dark brown. (If they are too light, they will not be crisp enough when cold.)

Make no more than this at a time, for they must be rolled rapidly as they come from the oven before they cool.

Remove one at a time with a metal spatula, leaving the others in the oven with door open. Quickly roll biscuits around your finger or a buttered pencil. Place on wire rack, seam side down.

Stir the batter each time it is to be spooned out. Repeat this process until batter is used up.

The *Croquantes* may be stored in an air-tight tin for several weeks.

CRÈME GANACHE (CREAM FILLING)

INGREDIENTS

2/3 cup semi-sweet chocolate bits
1 tablespoon cold water
2 tablespoons sour cream
1 bottle chocolate shot

METHOD

Melt chocolate with water in a double boiler over medium heat without stirring. (This will take about 15 minutes.)

Remove from heat and add sour cream. Now stir with rubber spatula.

Spread this chocolate cream into and around both ends of the *Croquantes,* using a round-tipped knife. Roll ends in chocolate shot.

TO SERVE: Place individual *petits fours* in tiny paper cups.

When the *Croquantes* are served for dessert, their best accompaniment is a *demi-tasse* of strong black coffee *avec la goutte* (a teardrop of brandy) or *un canard* (a sugar lump dipped in brandy), if you wish.

MENU XX

Une Envie de Fruits de Mer
IN THE MOOD FOR SEAFOOD

Crêpes aux Champignons
CRÊPES WITH MUSHROOMS

Coquilles Saint-Jacques
à la Parisienne
SCALLOPS POACHED IN WINE, SERVED
IN THE SHELLS WITH CREAM SAUCE,
CAPERS, AND SWISS CHEESE

Petits Pois à la Française
FRESH PEAS SIMMERED WITH BUTTER
AND SHREDDED LETTUCE

Salade Verte
GREEN SALAD

Babas au Rhum
DELICATE RUM CAKES WITH RAISINS

Riesling or Loupiac

THE main course of this menu is scallops prepared in their shells, one of the tastiest fruits of the sea. Here they are introduced by mushroom crêpes and accompanied by green peas prepared in the French manner. An escarole salad (page 148) could be served as an additional course. Rum *Babas* give a proper finishing touch.

RECOMMENDED WINE: To go with the scallops, try a Riesling, king of Alsatian wines. Powerful yet Spartan because of its northern origin, it is a perfect match for any seafood. Or, if you prefer a sweeter wine with your cream sauce, try a Loupiac from the Sauternes district of Bordeaux. Use either one in the preparation as well as throughout the meal.

ORDER OF PREPARATION: Although this is a fairly complex menu, a great deal of it can be prepared ahead of time. The *Crêpes* may be cooked and filled and reheated a few minutes before mealtime. The *Petits Pois* also may be cooked ahead if necessary. The *Babas* may be baked, frozen, and warmed up for the final preparation, which should be done on the day they are to be served. The *Coquilles* should be purchased and prepared on the day they are to be eaten, but all the preparations except the final baking may be done several hours before dinner.

Crêpes aux Champignons.

CRÊPES WITH MUSHROOMS

Savory crêpes—mushroom, cheese, and herbs—and sweet crêpes—raspberry, strawberry, currant, and sweet cream—are specialties of little shops, *les Crêperies*, which abound in Paris, especially in Montparnasse. In this area many of the owners are Bretons, for *crêpes* are a specialty of Brittany. They are also sold wrapped in napkins, from little stands along the boulevards.

The recipe that follows is an unusual savory crêpe, filled simply with briefly sautéed mushrooms, rather than the more common creamed filling. It provides a light and interesting introduction to the *Coquilles*. I plan 1 *crêpe* per person when serving them as an appetizer; 3 or 4 when they are to be a main dish.

The recipe will serve 4 as an appetizer.

PÂTE À CRÊPES

INGREDIENTS

3/4 *cup all-purpose flour*
1 *jumbo egg*
1/4 *teaspoon table salt*
1 *cup cold milk*
1 1/2 *tablespoons unsalted butter, measured solid then melted*
1 *stick of butter wrapped in cheesecloth*

USEFUL UTENSIL: *8-inch iron or stainless steel skillet**

METHOD

There are three keys to success for *crêpes:* 1) Use a heavy cast-iron or stainless steel skillet and get it very hot. 2) Rub the pan with butter before each *crêpe* is made. 3) Stir the batter thoroughly each time before spooning out.

For the *crêpes* needed in this recipe an 8-inch pan is best. If you are using a stainless steel pan, be sure that it is extremely hot so that the first *crêpes* will be perfect.

Measure flour into a 2-quart mixing bowl. Make a well in center of flour; add egg, salt, and milk. Beat with whisk until well blended and any lumps disappear. Stir in melted butter.

Cover bowl with a clean linen towel and let the batter rest at room temperature at least 2 hours, or overnight in the refrigerator. A longer period of rest, up to 8 hours, is all to the good. Stir from time to time. Batter will thicken; *crêpes* will be lighter and thinner.

When you are ready to begin, heat frying pan over high heat for a minute or so. Rub pan with butter stick. Stir batter well, then spoon 3 tablespoons into the 8-inch pan. (If another size pan is used, vary the amount accordingly; batter should cover bottom of pan.) Tilt pan quickly to spread batter evenly. When batter has set, loosen edges with a metal spatula. Shake pan to be sure *crêpe* is not sticking on underside. When bubbles appear, flip *crêpe* over.

TO FLIP: Be sure *crêpe* is not sticking to pan. Shake pan briskly from side to side; *crêpe* should slide slightly. Then, with one quick movement, push pan forward and draw it back toward you. *Crêpe* should flip over nicely and land again in pan. (If this technique

*An 8-inch pan measures 6 1/2 inches across the cooking surface.

scares you, turn it with a metal spatula.) Cook about half a minute on second side, or until light golden brown.

Crêpes should be soft and pliable for rolling; to keep warm and moist, place them between two damp towels on a cookie sheet in a warm oven.

Crêpes may also be made in advance and stored in the refrigerator. Reheat them slowly in a warm oven, a covered double boiler, or a covered electric frying pan set at 150° F.

FILLING THE CRÊPES

INGREDIENTS

1/2 *pound fresh white mushrooms (almost 3 cups sliced)*
6 *tablespoons clarified butter*

chopped fresh parsley

METHOD

Cut tips off mushroom stems and wipe with a clean damp sponge. Slice enough of the largest ones in half to decorate each *crêpe*. Slice small and medium ones in half; quarter remaining large ones.

In a 12-inch frying pan, heat butter over high heat until it sings. Sauté large halves first, shaking pan constantly, for 1 minute. Remove with a slotted spoon from pan into a fire-proof dish; sprinkle with salt and pepper and set in a warm oven. Sauté remaining slices.

ASSEMBLING THE CRÊPES

Place 2 tablespoons of sautéed mushrooms on each *crêpe* and roll. Crêpes can be covered and refrigerated at this point if desired. When ready to serve, place in chafing dish or electric frying pan to warm. (Set electric pan at 150° F.) Warm up perfect mushroom slices separately and arrange on crêpes just before serving.

TO SERVE: Sprinkle with parsley. Dish onto salad plates. Eat with a knife and fork.

Coquilles Saint-Jacques à la Parisienne

SCALLOPS POACHED IN WINE, SERVED IN THE SHELLS
WITH CREAM SAUCE, CAPERS, AND SWISS CHEESE

To me, scallops are at their best served in their shells with this delectable sauce. Since in France scallops are always bought whole, it is natural that this recipe utilizes the shell. I have prepared this recipe in a casserole, but for some reason it does not taste the same. Perhaps it is the proportion of sauce to scallops that is so appealing; perhaps it is the attractiveness of the shell.

If you cannot find shells at your fish market, you can purchase them in fancy food stores or in the specialty sections of some department stores. You can use them again and again; simply clean them thoroughly before putting them away.

Scallops are considered a great delicacy in France. The French eat the whole scallop, not just the fleshy, sweet nugget of meat that is available in America. The roe, coral-colored in the female and white in the male scallop, is considered a special treat.

Many New Englanders prefer the smaller, sweeter bay scallop when it is in season, but the larger sea scallops are available year round throughout the country and are more economical. One may be cut into several slices. A rich source of protein and minerals, scallops are also low in calories.

This recipe will serve 4.

POACHING THE SCALLOPS

INGREDIENTS

1 *pound bay or sea scallops**
1 *tablespoon chopped shallots or red onion*
1 *teaspoon table salt*
1/2 *cup mellow white wine*

METHOD

Preheat over to 400 ° F.
In a 1-quart oven-proof dish, combine scallops and shallots;

*If sea scallops are used, cut each into 3 or 4 round slices.

sprinkle with salt; add wine. Place dish in oven, uncovered. After 5 minutes, turn scallops and baste. Bake another 5 minutes, then remove from oven. Set aside, reserving liquid.

MAKING THE WHITE SAUCE

INGREDIENTS

2 *tablespoons clarified butter*
2 *tablespoons all-purpose flour*
2 *cups warm milk*
3/4 *teaspoon table salt*
1/4 *teaspoon white pepper* (12 *turns of pepper mill, fine grind*)
2 *tablespoons unsalted butter, at room temperature*
2 *tablespoons poaching liquid from scallops*
1/4 *cup capers, drained*
1/4 *cup grated Swiss cheese*

METHOD

Begin with a *roux:* In a 4-cup saucepan melt butter over medium heat. Gradually add flour, stirring briskly with whisk. Cook 30 to 60 seconds, allowing *roux* to moisten and swell. Slowly add warm milk, stirring constantly until mixture comes to a boil. Add salt and pepper; let mixture simmer 20 to 30 minutes, stirring occasionally.

Press sauce with whisk through strainer into a 3- to 4-cup mixing bowl. Blend in unsalted butter.

Measure 4 tablespoons of this sauce into a cup and set aside.

Into the remaining white sauce, stir 2 tablespoons of the poaching liquid from the scallops.* Add capers and cheese. Drain scallops and add them; mix well into the sauce.

*The rest of the liquid remaining from the scallops may be saved to use for poaching other fish or to add to other fish sauces. It may be frozen.

BAKING

INGREDIENTS

4 *tablespoons reserved white sauce*
1/2 *cup grated Swiss cheese*
4 *heaping tablespoons bread crumbs*
4 *tablespoons butter*

METHOD

Preheat oven to 400° F.

Fill shells with scallop mixture, being sure to distribute scallops evenly. Over each shell spread 1 tablespoon of the white sauce previously set aside. Sprinkle on cheese, then bread crumbs. Dot with butter.

At this point, scallops may be refrigerated, covered with storage wrap. Insert toothpicks into scallops so that wrap does not touch them. Remember, however, that seafood is at its best when it is eaten very fresh.

Bake scallops on middle rack of oven for 15 to 25 minutes, until nicely browned.

TO SERVE: Place doilies on dinner plates. Place scallops piping hot in their shells on the doilies. Decorate plates with a few sprigs of fresh parsley. As with all seafood, fish knives and fish forks are appropriate to use with scallops.

With some crusty French bread and a glass of chilled white wine, the same wine used in the poaching liquid . . . *quelle euphorie!*

Petits Pois à la Française

FRESH PEAS SIMMERED WITH BUTTER
AND SHREDDED LETTUCE

A special variety of tiny sweet pea, the *petits pois,* is grown throughout the rolling farmlands southwest of Paris. It is smaller and sweeter than any I have been able to find in the American market. When you are buying fresh peas for this recipe, pick the tiniest ones possible.

Since good fresh peas are not available year round in the markets, I have included a modified recipe using frozen peas.

Again, choose them as small as possible. I like to buy those that come in plastic bags rather than cartons, so that I can see what size I'm getting.

See if you don't feel a breath of spring at the sight of this dish when it is ready for the table!

The recipe will provide 4 servings.

INGREDIENTS

2 1/4 *pounds fresh green peas in the pod (enough to make 2*
  to 2 1/2 cups when shelled)
8 *to 12 tiny white onions, preferably pearl onions**
6 *parsley sprigs tied together*
1 *heaping teaspoon table salt*
1 *heaping teaspoon sugar*
2 *tablespoons unsalted butter*
1 *cup cold water*

1 *small head of Boston lettuce*

2 *tablespoons whipped sweet butter***
1 1/2 *tablespoons granulated flour*
table salt

METHOD

Shell peas.

Prepare onions. To peel off the paper-thin outer skin, place them in a colander or strainer and plunge them into a pan of boiling water for no more than a minute. Cut off root section and skin will slide off easily. Cut a cross in the stem end to prevent bursting during cooking.

In a 6-cup saucepan combine peas, onions, parsley, salt, sugar, butter, and water. Cover and bring to boiling point over medium heat. Simmer gently, shaking pan from time to time, for 30 to 45 minutes, depending upon size and tenderness of peas. Keep checking; they should be firm but soft when done.

Test onions after 15 minutes of cooking time. When a small knife blade glides easily in and out, they are done. Pearl onions usually take from 10 to 20 minutes; larger ones from 25 to 35 minutes. Remove them when they are done so they will not be overcooked; keep hot.

Meanwhile, prepare the lettuce: Cut out core; discard any imperfect outer leaves; separate off about 10 large leaves and wash

---

* If your onions are larger than Ping-Pong balls, 4 to 8 are enough.
**Taken from refrigerator 1/2 hour before using.

them in several changes of cold water; shred them 1/4 to 1/2 inch wide and set aside. Keep the lettuce heart intact to use as a decoration for the serving dish.

After the peas have been simmering for about 25 minutes, add the shredded lettuce. It may look like too much, but it will cook down considerably.

Prepare a *beurre manié:* With your fingers, knead together the butter and flour until it forms a paste.

When peas are almost done, add *beurre manié,* shaking pan until butter has melted. Simmer for 5 more minutes.

Return onions to pan to heat thoroughly. Remove parsley. Taste and sprinkle lightly with salt if necessary.

PETITS POIS À LA FRANÇAISE (with Frozen Peas): If fresh peas are not available, the following recipe is an acceptable substitute.

INGREDIENTS

8 to 10 *tiny white onions, preferably pearl onions*
1/4 *cup cold water*
1 *teaspoon sugar*
2 *tablespoons unsalted butter*
1/2 *teaspoon salt*
1 *small head Boston lettuce*
2 *tablespoons whipped sweet butter*
1 1/2 *tablespoons granulated flour*

2 *cups frozen peas*
1 *teaspoon sugar*
6 *parsley sprigs tied together*
1/2 *cup cold water*
table salt

METHOD

Peel and incise onions as described above. Combine water, sugar, butter, and salt with the onions in a 2-cup saucepan. Bring liquid to a vigorous boil, uncovered; reduce heat and simmer gently 15 to 20 minutes, shaking pan from time to time to prevent sticking and give an even glaze to the onions. They are done when a small knife blade glides easily in and out. Liquid will be mostly evaporated. Reserve and add to the peas when called for. Shred lettuce and reserve.

Knead together butter and flour until it forms a *beurre manié.*

Now, in a 6-cup saucepan, combine peas, sugar, parsley, and water, and bring to boiling point over medium heat. Immediately stir in *beurre manié.* When butter has melted, add lettuce and simmer for 5 minutes. If, after 2 or 3 minutes, there is very little liquid, stir in 1/4 to 1/2 cup hot water slowly.

Add onions and heat through. Taste and salt lightly if necessary. Remove parsley.

TO SERVE: Transfer to a heated vegetable dish, preferably one with a cover. Arrange onions attractively around edge; place small lettuce heart in center. Bring to the table piping hot.

If you plan to accompany the *Coquilles Saint-Jacques* with the peas, present them after the main course. Remove scallop shells and doilies from the dinner plates; pass the vegetable dish so everyone may help themselves.

Babas au Rhum

DELICATE RUM CAKES WITH RAISINS

First christened Ali Baba by a romantic-minded royal *gastronome,* this is a cake of leavened dough strewn with raisins and steeped in rum syrup after baking.

To be a *Baba,* this dough must be baked in small round molds about 2 1/2 inches in diameter by 2 1/2 inches high. The same recipe, baked in a ring mold, is called a *Savarin,* named after the noted *gastronome,* Brillat-Savarin.

This recipe will fill 12 traditional *Baba* molds, which may be purchased in the housewares section of most department stores or in pot shops, or 12 muffin tins. It will also fill a 1 1/2-quart ring mold, 9 inches in diameter.

Plan ahead when making *Babas:* The raisins should be put to soak at least a day ahead. As with all yeast dough, the various risings will take several hours.

Like the students in my classes, you will probably become impatient for a taste before you complete the final step. Hold off! The finished product is guaranteed to give you a feeling of accomplishment.

To enjoy their fresh yeasty texture, these confections should be eaten the day they are made. However, if this is not practical

for you, you can make them ahead and freeze them before soaking them in rum. It will take about an hour for them to defrost. When you are ready to eat them, heat syrup and proceed to soak and glaze as described below.

STEEPING THE RAISINS

INGREDIENTS

1 *cup lukewarm water*
3 *tablespoons granulated sugar*
1/2 *cup raisins*
1/4 *cup good dark rum*

METHOD

There are two keys for success in making yeast dough: 1) Be sure the liquid with which it is mixed is only lukewarm, never hot. 2) Let the dough rise slowly in a warm oven, never a hot one.

Prepare raisins at least a day ahead, if possible, so that they will be well impregnated with rum: Combine water, sugar, and raisins in a 2-cup saucepan and bring to boiling point, uncovered, over medium heat. Simmer 20 minutes.

Drain and pat raisins dry with paper towel.

Pour rum into a 2-cup bowl; add raisins; cover and soak 24 hours.

PREPARING THE MOLDS

INGREDIENTS

12 *tablespoons unsalted butter*

USEFUL UTENSILS: *Baba molds, goose-feather brush*

METHOD

Melt butter over low heat. Using a pastry brush, coat molds thoroughly; tip and pour out excess butter; set aside to use in dough.

Drain enough raisins from the rum to place several in the bottom of each mold and to press a few around the sides of each mold. Some of those pressed to the sides will fall to the bottom, but no matter. Set aside until ready to fill with dough.

MAKING THE SPONGE

INGREDIENTS

1/2 *cup all-purpose flour*
1 *yeast cake*
3 1/2 *tablespoons tepid milk*

3 *cups tepid water*

METHOD

Turn oven to lowest possible heat (usually indicated by "warm").
Place flour in a 2-cup mixing bowl. Make a well in center of flour and crumble in yeast cake. Add milk and, using the tips of your fingers, combine ingredients thoroughly. Form into a ball. Using a knife, cut a cross in the top of the ball. (This will help sponge to rise.)

Pour the 3 cups of tepid water into a 1-quart saucepan and drop ball into it with the cross side up. Place in warm oven to rise for 20 to 25 minutes.

COMPLETING THE DOUGH AND RISING

INGREDIENTS

1 1/2 *cups all-purpose flour*
1 *tablespoon granulated sugar*
1 *teaspoon table salt*
4 *jumbo eggs**
3 *tablespoons tepid milk*
melted butter left over from preparing the molds

METHOD

After sponge has risen for the appropriate time, rinse a 2 1/2-quart bowl with hot water to heat. Lift sponge from water, using a metal spatula, and place on a paper towel to remove some of the excess moisture; transfer to the heated mixing bowl.

Add flour, sugar, salt, eggs, and milk. Work dough vigorously with the hands for 4 minutes, slapping and pulling it for about 200 slaps, cleaning the sides of bowl often with fingers.

*Remove from refrigerator at least 1 hour before using.

Add butter and work again for another 2 minutes, or about 100 slaps.

Drain remaining raisins from their rum bath and work into dough with fingers. Reserve the rum to use in making the syrup.

Cover bowl with clean dishtowel; place in warm oven and allow to rise 1 1/2 hours. After about 45 minutes, stick your finger into the middle of dough and stir briefly. Dough may be left 2 hours, but no longer.

After this length of time, the dough will look more like batter. Fold batter over with your hands several times until deflated.

Using your fingers as a scoop, fill the prepared molds 1/3 to 1/2 full.* Set all the molds on a cookie sheet; place in warm oven, uncovered, and allow to rise another 20 to 30 minutes, until almost to rim. (It may take as long as 45 minutes.) During last 10 minutes, remove tray of *Babas* to top of stove and preheat oven to 425° F.**

MAKING THE SYRUP

INGREDIENTS

2 *cups cold water*
2 *cups granulated sugar*
1/2 *cup rum (use that in which the raisins have soaked plus enough to make the 1/2 cup)*

METHOD

During the first or second rising of the dough, make the syrup: In a saucepan large enough to be used for dipping afterwards (one of at least 5-quart capacity), bring water and sugar to boiling and simmer 20 minutes, stirring from time to time with wooden spoon. Cool to lukewarm and add rum. Set aside and keep lukewarm to await baked *Babas*.

BAKING AND GLAZING

INGREDIENTS

12-*ounce jar apricot preserves*
rum

*If you are uncomfortable about this, you can use a spoon.
**If you have two ovens, preheat second to 425° F. and allow *Babas* to remain in first oven.

USEFUL UTENSIL: *Goose-feather pastry brush*

METHOD

Bake on the cookie sheet on middle rack of the preheated oven for 15 minutes.

Remove from oven and set molds on cooling racks. When you can handle them comfortably, unmold. *Babas* should still be warm.

TO UNMOLD: Insert the blade of a small dull knife between cake and mold and work gently along rim. If the molds have been well greased and *Babas* baked sufficiently, they should slip out without trouble. If they don't, return to oven for a few minutes or loosen with a knife.

Prick all sides of the *Babas* with a pastry needle or toothpick so that liquid will soak in better, and drop immediately into the warm syrup. Allow to soak in syrup as long as possible, turning from time to time.

MAKE GLAZE: Heat up preserves in a 2-cup saucepan and simmer 5 minutes, stirring with whisk. Remove from heat and stir. Use glaze at once so that it won't solidify.

Place wire rack over cookie sheet. Remove *Babas* from syrup; place on rack to drain for several minutes.

Using a pastry brush, coat *Babas* with preserve. (Any left over may be returned to the jar for normal use.)

TO SERVE: Sprinkle with rum: Place your second finger in mouth of bottle and shake over *Babas*.

Put confections in paper cups. Arrange attractively on a cake plate or on individual dessert dishes. The *Babas* should be eaten with dessert forks.

Menu XXI

Allons Manger Sur la Terrasse
LET'S EAT ON THE TERRACE

*Pâté de Foie
à la Mode de Pradeix*
PORK LIVER PÂTÉ

*Filets de Maquereaux
Marinés au Vin Blanc*
MACKEREL FILLETS COOKED
AND MARINATED IN WHITE WINE

Enchaud
BRAISED PORK WITH GREEN
PEPPERCORNS, GARLIC, AND HERBS

Salade Estivale
FRESH GREEN AND WAX BEAN SALAD

Coeurs à la Crème
A CREAMY, HEART-SHAPED DESSERT

Muscadet or Chinon

HERE is an assortment of cold dishes which will make entertaining a pleasure. Since they can all be prepared and arranged
ahead of time, they make an ideal meal for a summer get-together
on the terrace. Appropriate as well for an indoor buffet, the menu
offers two appetizers—a pork liver pâté with a fine texture and
tangy cold marinated mackerel. These are followed by a braised
pork loin, which can be served hot or cold, a colorful vegetable
salad, and *Petits Coeurs à la Crème,* a dessert which melts in your
mouth. The recipes provide 8 generous servings.

RECOMMENDED WINES: A young white wine from the banks of
the Loire, a chilled Muscadet, would be suitable to accompany all
dishes. As a refreshing alternative, a Chinon, a fruity, light red
wine from Touraine, could be served with the pork. (This wine
should be served slightly chilled. Like any *rubis* from the Loire
region, it will not lose its charm when cool.)

ORDER OF PREPARATION: All these dishes can be made days in
advance. The pâté and the *Coeur à la Crème* can be unmolded, the
mackerel marinated in its serving dish, and the cooked roast sliced
and arranged on its serving platter ahead of time. Even the salad
can be prepared in advance.

Pâté à la Mode de Pradeix

PORK LIVER PÂTÉ

Pradeix is a mountainous hamlet in central France. When the
Germans invaded Paris in June of 1940, it became our refuge. We
were 13 people living in a barn, but fortunately it was summer, and
the mountain scenery was breathtaking. We became friends with
the few farmers of the area, and I learned a great deal about pork.
When the pigs were slaughtered, there was great excitement. One
whole day was devoted to making pâté. This is my version of that
regional specialty.

This pâté should be made 2 or 3 days before serving, so that
the flavor will have time to develop. It will keep up to 2 weeks in
the refrigerator, and may be frozen. The seasoning is enough for
2 cups of chopped pork liver and 1 cup of chopped fatback. This
amount of meat will be enough to fill a 4-cup *terrine* or bread pan.

PREPARING THE MOLD

INGREDIENTS

1/2 *to* 1 *pound fatback or bacon* (10 *to* 12 *strips,* 1 1/2 *to* 2 *inches long)**

USEFUL UTENSIL: *A 4-cup terrine** or bread pan*

METHOD

To line the mold, put fatback in the freezer for 1/2 hour to make cutting the strips easier. Using a large, very sharp knife, cut long thin sheets and divide them into 1 1/2- to 2-inch strips, making enough to line the mold. Pound the strips between sheets of waxed paper to make them thinner and wider. (Even if bacon is used, the strips should be pounded.)

Line the mold by placing the strips side by side, *not overlapping*. Push them together so that they are tightly fused. The strips should hang over the sides of the mold about 2 inches all around. (If they are not long enough, use two or more strips.) They should be long enough to enclose the pâté mixture completely.

The mold can be lined ahead of time and refrigerated. When ready to fill it, leave at room temperature for 1/2 hour, so that the strips of fatback will be soft enough to fold over, enclosing the pâté.

*Fresh fatback (*gras dur*) has the advantage of not dissolving when it is cooked. It is inexpensive and can be kept frozen indefinitely. Buy it in long sheets to make the strips for lining the mold. Salted fatback can be found in many supermarkets, usually in short chunks. Try to get the longest piece available. To remove salt, soak in very hot or boiling water several times, for 15 minutes each time, changing the water after each soaking. If bacon is used, it should be blanched in the same way.

**A *terrine* is a glazed earthenware mold with a lid which is sold in pot shops.

MARINATING THE PORK LIVER

INGREDIENTS

1 *pound pork liver*
1 *teaspoon table salt*
1/4 *teaspoon freshly ground white pepper*
1/4 *teaspoon thyme*
4 *teaspoons chopped garlic*
4 *teaspoons chopped shallots*
1/8 *teaspoon allspice*
2 *tablespoons Cognac*

METHOD

Combine all ingredients in a 3- to 4-cup bowl or shallow dish. Cover with storage wrap and keep in a cool place or in the refrigerator for a minimum of 2 hours (up to 48 hours).

MARINATING THE FATBACK

INGREDIENTS

1/4 *pound fatback (enough to make 1 cup, in thin strips or small cubes)*
1/2 *teaspoon table salt*
1/8 *teaspoon freshly ground white pepper*
1/8 *teaspoon thyme*
2 *teaspoons chopped garlic*
2 *teaspoons chopped shallots*
a sprinkling of allspice
1 *tablespoon Cognac*

METHOD

In a 2-cup bowl, combine all the ingredients. Cover and refrigerate or keep in a cool place for 2 to 48 hours.

ASSEMBLING AND BAKING

INGREDIENTS

2 *jumbo eggs, slightly beaten*
2 *to 4 bay leaves*
1/3 *cup all-purpose flour (optional)*
2 *to 3 tablespoons cold water (optional)*

METHOD

Combine marinated liver and fatback. Chop or grind a small quantity at a time using a meat grinder, a food processor with a steel blade, or a blender. Reserve the liquid. Put the meat mixture and reserved marinades in a 4- to 6-cup bowl and blend well.

This step can be accomplished ahead of time. Covered and refrigerated, the mixture will keep 2 to 3 days.

When ready to bake, preheat oven to 325° F. Stir eggs into meat mixture. Fill the lined mold with the mixture, pack well, and fold the hanging strips of fat over the pâté. (If your mold is rectangular, fold the shorter sides first.) Trim any overlapping edges. Place 2 to 4 bay leaves on top along the length of the pâté.

If you are using a mold without a lid, make one by covering it with a double thickness of aluminum foil, folding it tightly around the pan to seal. If a *terrine* is used, it should be sealed with a *lut* (flour paste). To make it, combine the flour with the cold water, mix quickly with your fingers or a fork, and apply all around the edge of the *terrine* lid to seal it. Set the mold in a pan of lukewarm water (*bain-marie*). The water should reach half-way up the container.

Bake on the middle shelf of the preheated oven for 2 hours. Pâté can be tested by inserting a pastry needle in the center of the loaf. If it comes out very hot, the pâté is done. Turn off heat, leave door ajar, and let the pâté cool 1 or 2 hours.

When it is cool, remove the pâté from the oven and *bain-marie*. Place on a cookie sheet for easier handling. Put a weight, such as a small board weighted with canned goods, on it. Weighting it will make the texture more compact. When it is completely cold, store it, still under the weight, in the refrigerator for 2 or 3 days.

TO SERVE: If you are using a mold without a lid, remove the aluminum foil cover. Remove the bay leaves and set aside. Turn the pâté upside down on a platter. (If it sticks, dip the mold briefly in hot water or, when the pan is upside down, cover it with a hot moist towel for a few seconds.)

If the pâté is made in a *terrine,* there is no need to unmold it.

Arrange the reserved bay leaves on top of the pâté. Surround the platter with *petits cornichons* (small French pickles). To give a professional touch, shape them into fans by making several cuts at one end and pressing them between your fingers.

Provide a sharp knife and a spatula, cut a few slices of pâté, and let the guests serve themselves.

Besides the *cornichons,* ideal accompaniments are, of course, crusty French bread and a glass of chilled dry white wine.

Filets de Maquereaux Marinés au Vin Blanc

MACKEREL FILLETS COOKED
AND MARINATED IN WHITE WINE

This is an uncomplicated appetizer, which can also be served as a main course for a light meal. Bluefish may be used for this dish, but I prefer the flavor of mackerel.

The ingredients will serve 4. If the mackerel is to be served with another appetizer, as in this menu, the fillets may be halved after cooking to make 8 portions. For more servings, make in batches.

INGREDIENTS

pat of butter (scant 1/2 tablespoon)
4 mackerel fillets, 8 inches long or smaller
salt and pepper
5 tablespoons fresh lemon juice
2 large bay leaves
1 teaspoon dried thyme or 4 sprigs fresh thyme
12 sprigs parsley tied together
1 cup dry white wine

3 heaping tablespoons chopped white onion
lemons

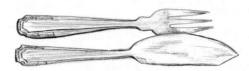

METHOD

Coat bottom and sides of large frying pan (about 12 inches) with butter. Wipe fillets with paper towel and score them on each side to prevent curling while cooking. Sprinkle both sides with salt and pepper and arrange skin side down in prepared pan.

Sprinkle lemon juice evenly over fish. Add bay leaves, thyme, parsley, and wine. Cover pan, place over medium heat, and bring to boiling. (This will take 5 to 8 minutes.) Simmer for 4 minutes, basting several times. Remove pan from heat and let it rest, covered, for 15 minutes. (Resting will help keep the fish supple.)

Carefully transfer the fillets to a shallow platter, using flexible spatulas. Put bay leaves on top of fish and pour liquid over them. Discard parsley. Sprinkle mackerel with chopped onion.

When the dish is cold, cover with storage wrap and refrigerate. Sauce will gel in a few hours.

TO SERVE: Arrange on a platter on a bed of watercress or lettuce. Serve each guest 1/2 fillet and add some of the sauce. Serve a wedge of lemon with each portion.

Enchaud

BRAISED PORK WITH GREEN PEPPERCORNS, GARLIC, AND HERBS

Enchaud, a roasted and braised pork loin, is a specialty of Périgord. During our exodus from Paris just before the German occupation of the city, I visited with friends in Sarlat, a small town in Périgord. The region is famous for its food, and the *Enchaud* was one of the most delectable dishes that I tasted there. In spite of the fact that *enchaud* means "hot," traditionally the roast is served cold. This is my way of making it.

The amount of meat and seasoning is quite sufficient for 8 people. The roast can also be served hot. It can be cooked up to 4 or 5 days ahead of time.

INGREDIENTS

4 1/4- to 4 1/2-*pound eye of the loin pork roast*
lots of garlic (at least 7 large cloves)
1 *heaping teaspoon green peppercorns**
table salt
1 *cup lukewarm water*

8 *tablespoons fresh chopped parsley*
8 *tablespoons fresh (or freeze-dried) chopped chives*
8 *tablespoons fresh (or freeze-dried) chopped chervil*

METHOD

Preheat oven to 400° F. Trim off and reserve excess fat from the roast. Pat with paper towels to absorb surface moisture. Peel and cut garlic into slivers. Starting at one end, cut three or four short slits across the width of the roast and insert garlic in them. Repeat procedure about every inch along the length of the meat. Turn and cut short slits down the length of the roast. Insert green peppercorns, about two or three every inch. Before inserting the green peppercorns, crush them lightly to release their flavor.

With a piece of fat from the roast, coat the bottom of a large roasting pan. Place pork in it, uncovered. Reduce oven temperature to 350° F. and brown on all sides. (This should take about 45 minutes.) Sprinkle salt on each side of roast, add water, cover, and braise for 1 hour and 15 minutes. (If the cover is fitted with a vent, make sure it is closed.) Baste the meat with the pan gravy every 20 minutes, turning it so that it browns evenly.

While the roast is cooking, mix the parsley, chives, and chervil together. When the roast is done, transfer it to a platter and pour some of the pan gravy over it. Spread half the herb mixture down the length of the roast and carefully pour on more of the gravy to set the herb mixture. Turn roast on the other side and repeat with remaining gravy and herb mixture. Let the roast cool completely, for about 2 hours. Place toothpicks in the roast so the herbs won't be disturbed, cover with storage wrap, and refrigerate. When serving, leave at room temperature for 1/2 hour.

TO SERVE: Remove toothpicks and present the whole roast before slicing it. The slices should be no thicker than 1/2 inch.

*If you buy green peppercorns in a can, transfer the unused ones to a jar and cover with lightly salted water (1/4 teaspoon table salt to 2/3 cup cold water). If you buy them in a jar, just remove what you need; the rest will keep in the remaining liquid.

Maybe you would like to try to eat the *Enchaud* the *vendangeurs'* (grape pickers') way. During *les vendanges* (grape-gathering season), it is customary to spread congealed fat and pan gravy on a slice of bread and eat it with grapes, along with the meat.

Salade Estivale

FRESH GREEN AND WAX BEAN SALAD
WITH HAM, HARD-BOILED EGGS, TOMATOES,
AND HOMEMADE MAYONNAISE

This salad is a fine dish to serve for a light meal. It can be made at any time of the year, but it is particularly tempting when native vegetables are in season.

The mayonnaise can be made several days in advance. The vegetables and eggs can also be cooked ahead. It takes only a few minutes to assemble them for a lovely presentation.

These ingredients will provide 8 generous servings.

THE MAYONNAISE

INGREDIENTS

2 *egg yolks**
1/4 *teaspoon table salt*
4 *turns of black pepper mill, medium grind*
1 *teaspoon Dijon mustard*
2 *cups salad oil*
3/4 *to* 1 *teaspoon red wine vinegar*
3/4 *teaspoon fresh lemon juice*
1 *tablespoon hot water*

METHOD

Place the egg yolks, salt, pepper, and mustard in a 1-quart bowl and beat half a minute with a wire whisk. Begin adding oil, drop by drop, whisking vigorously. When more than 1/4 cup has been added, you can pour more generously until 1 cup has been mixed in well. Now stir in the vinegar. Add the second cup of oil

*Take from refrigerator at least 2 hours before using.

gradually, again whisking vigorously. Beat in lemon juice and hot water.

Mayonnaise will keep over a week, refrigerated. Beat again just before using.

BOILING THE EGGS

INGREDIENTS

8 *pullet eggs (the smallest you can find)*
2 *jumbo eggs*
water

METHOD

Eggs will discolor an aluminum pan. Place them in a glass or enamel pan and cover with cold water.

FOR LIGHT-COLORED, FIRM, DRY YOLKS: Bring water to boiling point over high heat, then reduce heat and simmer gently. Pullet eggs will require only 8 minutes, any other size will require 12. Cool immediately under running cold water.

FOR DEEP YELLOW, MOIST YOLKS: Cover saucepan with lid. Bring water rapidly to a boil over high heat. Remove pan from heat and let eggs steep in covered pan for 20 minutes. Cool immediately under cold running water.

Do not shell eggs if you are storing them for any length of time. Otherwise, shell them and refrigerate until thoroughly cold before slicing. To make slicing easier, dip knife in hot water between cuts.

COOKING THE BEANS

INGREDIENTS

6 *quarts cold water*
3 *tablespoons coarse salt or* 1 1/2 *tablespoons table salt*
1 1/4 *to* 1 1/2 *pounds green beans*

6 *quarts cold water*
3 *tablespoons coarse salt or* 1 1/2 *tablespoons table salt*
1 1/4 *to* 1 1/2 *pounds wax beans*

METHOD

Remove tips and strings from green beans and wash under cold running water. Bring salted water to a vigorous boil. Drop in beans and boil, uncovered. Test after 6 minutes. Beans should be firm but not hard. They should not take longer than 8 minutes to cook. When done, remove from water and place in colander to drain, then place in large bowl.

Repeat the procedure for the wax beans. (Although both beans will be mixed when you assemble the salad, there is better control if they are cooked and dressed separately.)

DRESSING THE BEANS

INGREDIENTS

(make two batches)
1/2 *teaspoon salt*
a *few turns of the black pepper mill (medium grind)*
1/2 *teaspoon chopped garlic*
1 *tablespoon red wine vinegar*
2 *tablespoons peanut or other salad oil*

METHOD

Mix dressing ingredients and add to the green beans. Repeat for the wax beans. Toss thoroughly, then mix the beans together.

ASSEMBLING THE SALAD

INGREDIENTS

4 *perfect slices of boiled ham*
8 *small tomatoes (about 2 inches in diameter)*

METHOD

Wash the tomatoes, slice off the tops, and scoop out a bit of the inside.

Cut the ham slices in half to make rectangles.

Make a bed with the mixed beans on a large round platter.

Cut the 2 hard-boiled jumbo eggs lengthwise into 8 wedges. Wrap each section with a half-slice of ham, so that part of the white and yolk is visible. Arrange wrapped eggs, with the ends of ham down, around the outer edges of the beans.

Place small eggs on top of the beans in a circle. Top each egg with an inverted tomato, so that it looks like a mushroom. Using a fork, make dots of mayonnaise on the tomatoes.

TO SERVE: Give each guest a helping of beans, a wrapped egg, and a tomato–egg mushroom. Serve additional mayonnaise as an accompaniment.

Coeurs à la Crème

A NORMANDY CLASSIC:
A CREAMY, HEART-SHAPED DESSERT

"Coeurs à la Crème . . . Voyez mes beaux coeurs! Qui prendra mes beaux coeurs? . . ." I still hear the voice of that *Normande* with the missing front tooth. Summer after summer, during my vacation in Bernières, a small resort on the Normandy coast, the same *marchande de fromage* appeared with her *petite voiture* (pushcart) selling only *Coeurs à la Crème* made on her farm. As soon as I heard her cry, whoever was taking care of me had to rush out and buy me a *Coeur*.

Who would have thought at that time that Bernières would

become part of the battleground of the American invasion on D-Day in World War II?

Like many good things, the texture of the *Coeur* changes if it is made in a big mold. Ideally, it should be made in a simple heart-shaped porcelain or wicker basket measuring about 3 inches in diameter and 1 inch deep. These can be purchased in most pot shops.

Although *Coeurs* can be prepared many days before serving, I do not like to make them more than 2 days in advance. They must be refrigerated or placed in a cool place for 24 hours so that they can drain and be firm enough to unmold.

The amount of ingredients given will provide 8 servings if made in the small molds described. The ingredients may be reduced by half, but if you wish to double the recipe, it is preferable to make two batches.

THE CHEESE AND CREAM MIXTURE

INGREDIENTS

1 *pound cottage cheese (small curd is preferable)**
1 *pound whipped cream cheese**
1/4 *teaspoon table salt*
2 *tablespoons sugar*
1/2 *cup heavy cream (1/4 pint, chilled)***

USEFUL UTENSILS: *Heart-shaped molds of porcelain or wicker; a food mill*

METHOD

Chill a 1- to 2-cup mixing bowl and beaters. Have ready 8 pieces of cheesecloth (single thickness) about 8 inches square.

Put cottage cheese and cream cheese a little at a time through a food mill with very small holes, placed over a 2- to 3-quart bowl. (A ricer may also be used. A food processor is adequate, but it will not give the smoothest texture.) Using a wire whisk, stir the mixture well and beat in salt and sugar.

Whip the heavy cream for about 2 minutes with an electric mixer at high speed. Then add it to the mixture, continuing to beat

*Take out of the refrigerator at least 2 hours before using.
**If you are fortunate enough to find *crème fraîche* in your market, you can substitute it for the heavy cream.

at high speed for no more than 30 seconds so that everything is well blended.

Wet the cheesecloth and line the interior of each mold with a piece. Fill the molds with the cheese and cream mixture, making sure they are well packed. Cover each one with the overlapping ends of the cheesecloth and put them on a wire rack to drain. Refrigerate for 24 hours to drain moisture and firm up the texture. (The amount of moisture will vary according to the amount of liquid in the cottage cheese.)

THE SAUCE

INGREDIENTS

2 *tablespoons granulated sugar*
1 *cup heavy cream*

METHOD

Prepare sauce by mixing the sugar with the heavy cream (chilled or at room temperature).

TO SERVE: Open the cheesecloth and unmold the *Coeurs* on dessert dishes. Spoon over each heart about 2 tablespoons of the sweetened cream.

A small pitcher of heavy cream and additional sugar can be kept on hand for those who prefer sweeter desserts. All sorts of garnishing may also be added, such as fresh strawberries, colored sugar, or even a candied violet. However, *pour déguster un Coeur à la Crème,* I don't recommend all that scenery!

MENU XXII

Pour les Becs Fins
FOR CULTIVATED PALATES

Escargots
SNAILS IN GARLIC AND PARSLEY
BUTTER

Ris de Veau Denise
BRAISED SWEETBREADS SURROUNDED
WITH GREEN PEAS AND SAUTÉED
MUSHROOMS

Salade de Laitue
aux Fines Herbes
BOSTON OR BIBB LETTUCE
WITH EGG YOLK AND HERB DRESSING

Paris-Brest
CREAM PUFF PASTE RING FILLED
WITH PASTRY CREAM AND PRALINE

*Sancerre, Médoc, and Château Rayne-
Vigneau or Château Climens*

241

THIS bill of fare is one to share with friends who appreciate the finer things of life and who can recognize an elegant repast. The offerings are especially choice: Snails in garlic butter, braised sweetbreads accompanied by fresh mushrooms and little green peas, a lettuce salad to be served after the main dish, and a Paris-Brest, an impressive pastry made of a ring of cream puff paste, filled with a praline pastry cream.

An assortment of cheeses would be served before the pastry in a more formal French meal. Such an assortment might contain Camembert, Brie, Fromage de Chèvre, Gruyère, Reblochon, and Roquefort. Among my friends it was considered poor taste in the *art de recevoir* to present only one kind of cheese. Crusty French bread and unsalted butter would be served with the cheeses.

RECOMMENDED WINES: The fresh white Sancerre from the Loire is a fitting companion to the enjoyment of *Escargots,* and may be drunk throughout the meal. If you favor red wine, a delicate and fragrant nectar from the Médoc district of Bordeaux would be suitable for the *Ris de Veau* and the cheeses. If you are in a celebrating mood, try a noble perfumed Sauternes—a Château Rayne-Vigneau or a Barsac Château Climens—to sip with the pastry. The wines can make a memorable occasion.

ORDER OF PREPARATION: The snails can be prepared well ahead of time. The preliminary blanching of the sweetbreads can also be done in advance. The pastry is at its best made the day it will be served.

Escargots

SNAILS WITH GARLIC AND PARSLEY BUTTER

In Paris, *escargots* are sold from sidewalk stalls, just like oysters and chestnuts. They are sealed with snail butter and need only 5 minutes baking in a hot oven. Seldom does a Parisian housewife start her preparation from scratch. I never understood why snails were so expensive until I did the entire process myself.

Snails come in cans of 1 to 10 dozen. This is one food I prefer to buy in cans! The shells are sterilized and packaged separately. They are sold in most specialty food stores, and are beginning to appear on the import shelves of some supermarkets. The shells can

be used again and again; just wash them thoroughly after each use. Wash in hot soapy water, then rinse, making sure that all the soap and food particles are removed. Place in a saucepan, cover with lukewarm water, and bring to the boiling point, uncovered. Boil gently for 5 minutes. Drain and dry completely before storing.

Escargots are such a popular hors-d'oeuvre that they have their own special plate, called an *escargotière*. It is a small, round metal dish with handles and shallow indentations to contain the shells. The snails are baked and served in this dish. There are also special tongs, *pinces à escargots*, for holding the hot shells, as well as tiny, two-pronged snail forks, called *fourchettes à escargots*, for extracting the snails. In provinces where snails live on grape leaves, the grapevine is cut where it forms a T to produce an implement called a *sarment* (literally, a vine branch). The crossbar fits nicely into the hand, and the tail is sharpened to a point, making a most efficient tool for prying out an *escargot*.

The recipe is sufficient to serve 8 diners with 6 snails each.

MARINATING THE SNAILS

INGREDIENTS

4 *dozen canned snails**
4 *tablespoons Cognac*
4 *tablespoons Pernod*

*Do *not* attempt to prepare this recipe with fresh snails, as one of my students once did! Fresh snails must be cleaned, blanched, boiled, and sautéed before they are ready to use.

METHOD

Drain canned snails in a strainer. Place in a 2-cup bowl, pour on Cognac and Pernod, mix well. Cover bowl with storage wrap and let stand several hours or overnight in refrigerator. Stir occasionally.

MAKING BEURRE ESCARGOT

INGREDIENTS

12 *tablespoons unsalted butter**
6 *tablespoons chopped fresh parsley*
4 *tablespoons chopped shallots*
2 *teaspoons chopped garlic*
1 *teaspoon table salt*
1/4 *teaspoon white pepper*

METHOD

Blend all ingredients thoroughly with fingers. (Refrigerate if the butter is made more than a few hours in advance.)

FILLING SHELLS AND BAKING

INGREDIENTS

4 *dozen snail shells*

USEFUL UTENSIL: *Escargotière*

METHOD

It will take about 10 minutes to fill 2 dozen shells and ready them for baking. They may be filled several hours ahead of time, covered, and refrigerated.

To fill shells, place a full 1/4 teaspoon of the marinade in each shell. Insert snails. Place a dab of snail butter over each opening with a knife point. Push the butter into opening with your thumb, and spread it over the surface to seal.

*Remove from refrigerator 20 minutes before using.

Preheat oven to 450° F.

Bake the *Escargots* in *escargotières* or in small baking dishes for 5 minutes, or until butter is sizzling. Serve at once.

TO SERVE: Place *escargotière* or baking dish on a dinner plate. Holding the shell with a *pince à escargots*, extract the snail with a *fourchette à escargots*. Sip the juices from the shells. Accompany with crusty French bread.

Ris de Veau Denise

BRAISED SWEETBREADS SURROUNDED
WITH GREEN PEAS AND SAUTÉED MUSHROOMS

One of our friends, a globe-trotter who searches out new and superb restaurants, claims that his evaluation of the quality of an eating establishment is determined by its preparation of sweetbreads. He has not tasted mine yet, but I hope that he will give me a four-star rating when he does.

Ris de veau is a gland found in very young animals, such as veal or lamb, which disappears when the animal is several months old. If purchased fresh, it should be cooked without delay. It can also be frozen until ready for use. It is not difficult to handle. The flesh is very delicate, making it a nice change from everyday fare. It is also very nutritious.

The ingredients given are for 8 servings. All preliminary blanching of the sweetbreads can be done ahead of time. They should be braised and the sauce completed shortly before the dish is served.

BLANCHING THE SWEETBREADS

INGREDIENTS

4 *pounds sweetbreads*
cold water for soaking
4 *cups cold water*
2 *teaspoons table salt*
2 *tablespoons vinegar*

USEFUL UTENSIL: *Chinois (conical strainer)*

METHOD

Sweetbreads should be soaked in cold water for at least 2 hours before preparing. They can be soaked as long as 24 hours. Change water often.

After soaking, put sweetbreads in an 8-cup saucepan and cover with cold water. Add salt and vinegar. Cover pan and bring gently to boiling point over medium heat. Once the boiling is reached, reduce heat and simmer gently for 15 minutes. Remove from heat. Put sweetbreads into colander to drain. Run cold water over them.

Trim away any cartilage and connective tissues, making sure to leave the membrane that covers the flesh to hold it together. (Otherwise, you may end up with only little pieces.) Do *not* discard trimmings.

Place sweetbreads on a cookie sheet, cover with waxed paper, and put under a weight for a minimum of 2 hours. (I use a small board and weigh it down with canned goods.) If your sweetbreads are large enough, you will be able to slice small cutlets. Weighing them down after blanching will flatten them so that slicing will be easier. Sprinkle very lightly with salt.

This step can be done a day ahead. Cover sweetbreads with storage wrap and refrigerate until ready to use.

THE MIREPOIX

INGREDIENTS

8 *tablespoons unsalted butter*
1 *cup diced carrots*
1 *cup diced yellow onions*
2 *garlic cloves*
table salt
freshly ground black pepper (medium grind)

METHOD

A *mirepoix* is a mixture of finely diced onions and carrots used in recipes solely for flavoring.

Melt butter in a 3- to 4-quart saucepan or Dutch oven and heat until it sings. Add carrots, onions, and garlic. Sauté gently for 5 minutes over medium heat, uncovered, shaking pan often. Then cover and cook for 5 minutes. Remove from heat and sprinkle lightly with salt and pepper.

BRAISING THE SWEETBREADS

INGREDIENTS

2 1/2 *cups chicken or veal stock**
1 *cup dry white wine*
1 *teaspoon thyme*
bouquet garni (10 *parsley sprigs, 3 bay leaves tied together*)
2 *pats butter*

METHOD

Pour bouillon into saucepan with *mirepoix;* add white wine and thyme. Mix well, and add *bouquet garni* and the connective tissues and cartilage from the sweetbreads. Bring to the boiling point uncovered. Add the sliced sweetbreads.

Preheat oven to 350° F.

Cut a piece of waxed paper large enough to cover your pan or baking dish, and butter one side. Place buttered side down over the *Ris de Veau.* Braise 30 minutes, basting and turning at least once.

When sweetbreads are done, transfer to a shallow, oven-proof serving dish and cover with the waxed paper to prevent drying. Place in a slow oven to keep warm.

Bring braising liquid and vegetables to boiling point over high heat with pan uncovered. Reduce for 2 minutes. Strain pan juices into a 2- to 4-cup saucepan through a conical strainer, pressing the *mirepoix* with a whisk or fork to extract all the juices. Reduce the liquid again for 1 minute over high heat.

Put braising liquid aside while preparing the vegetables.

*Use homemade stock (page 19) or 3 chicken cubes dissolved in 3 cups water, with 1/2 teaspoon of salt. (If cubes are very salty, do not add salt.)

THE PEAS

INGREDIENTS

4 *tablespoons butter*
3 *pounds fresh green peas (enough to make 3 cups, shelled)*
2 *cups lukewarm water*
1 *teaspoon table salt*
2 *tablespoons sugar*

METHOD

Melt butter in a 4-cup saucepan, add peas, and shake them a bit. Add water, salt, and sugar. Bring to the boiling point, uncovered. Continue boiling uncovered until done (about 10 minutes, depending on size of peas). Shake pan and stir vegetables a few times while cooking. When done, they should be firm but not hard.*

*ALTERNATE RECIPE FOR FROZEN PEAS: If fresh peas are not available, you can use the following recipe for frozen peas.

INGREDIENTS

2 10-*ounce packages of frozen peas (2 1/2 to 3 cups)*
4 *tablespoons cold water*
1/2 *teaspoon salt*
3 *teaspoons sugar*
2 *tablespoons butter*

METHOD

Put frozen peas in a 4- to 6-cup saucepan and loosen with a fork. Add water, salt, and sugar. Cover and bring to boil over medium heat (this takes about 5 minutes). Mix in butter and simmer, still covered, about 6 minutes.

THE MUSHROOMS

INGREDIENTS

1 *pound fresh mushrooms*
8 *tablespoons clarified butter*
table salt
freshly ground black pepper (medium grind)

METHOD

Mushrooms should be prepared as close to serving time as possible. They should not be washed, peeled, or overcooked. They are spongy vegetables which soak up and retain moisture, so the less contact they have with water the better. To clean them, wipe with a damp sponge. Cut off the tips of the stems and slice.

In a 10- to 12-inch frying pan, heat the butter. When faint smoke appears, add sliced mushrooms and sauté over high heat, shaking pan and tossing mushrooms often, for about 1 minute. Sprinkle lightly with salt and pepper. Cover and keep warm until ready to serve.

COMPLETING THE SAUCE

INGREDIENTS

4 *teaspoons potato flour*
4 *teaspoons cold water*
4 *tablespoons Cognac*

chopped fresh parsley

METHOD

When ready to serve, reheat strained braising liquid. Mix potato flour with water in a small bowl, beating with a small whisk or fork until smooth. Add 2 to 3 tablespoons of hot braising juice. Blend briskly with whisk, and add the mixture to the remaining juice, stirring constantly with whisk over high heat until sauce thickens. When it comes back to a boil, sauce should have a smooth, velvety texture.*

Stir in Cognac, 1 tablespoon at a time, and let sauce come to a quick boil. Remove from heat and put in a double boiler to keep warm.

TO SERVE: Arrange sweetbreads in center of a shallow serving dish. Surround them with a circle of mushroom slices. (Use a slotted spoon to transfer the mushrooms to the serving platter, so the juice

---

*If your sauce should separate, it can be repaired by whisking in 1 1/2 tablespoons very hot water for every half-cup of sauce.

is left behind.) Put peas around the mushrooms, again draining off the juice.*

Spoon sauce over sweetbreads and sprinkle with chopped parsley. Serve at once.

Salade de Laitue aux Fines Herbes

BOSTON OR BIBB LETTUCE
WITH EGG YOLK AND HERB DRESSING

Although I am fond of any salad, *"Une petite salade de laitue aux fines herbes"* is one of my favorites. The world *laitue* (lettuce) comes from the Latin word *lactuca*. It has been cultivated since ancient times. The early Hebrews used it as one of their religious symbols for Passover.

I use only Boston or Bibb lettuce for this salad. I never purchase the Iceberg variety, which has very little taste or character.

Fines herbes are usually a combination of fresh parsley, fresh chives, fresh chervil, and sometimes fresh tarragon. If all these herbs are not available in their fresh state, just use the ones that are available. I never use dry herbs for a green salad.

Two large heads of lettuce (weighing 1/2 pound apiece) should be sufficient for 8 servings.

INGREDIENTS

2 *large heads Boston or Bibb lettuce*
2 *egg yolks (any size)*
1 *teaspoon table salt*
1/4 *teaspoon fresh ground black pepper, medium grind*
2 *tablespoons red wine vinegar*
4 *tablespoons salad oil*
2 *heaping teaspoons each of fresh chopped parsley, chopped chives, and chopped chervil*

USEFUL UTENSIL: *Salad basket*

*Do not throw away the liquid from the mushrooms and peas. Refrigerate it to use for soup or gravy.

METHOD

Cut off root, separate leaves, remove imperfect leaves. Wash each leaf under running cold water, then place in bowl or pan and continue washing, changing water several times. Drain in colander or salad basket and continue draining in refrigerator until ready to use. Shake basket or colander to remove excess water, if any, and dry between paper or linen towels.

In a salad bowl of 2 1/2- to 3-quart capacity, mix the egg yolks, salt, pepper, and vinegar in the order listed. Then whisk in oil and add the *fines herbes*.

When ready to serve, gently break lettuce leaves into bite-sized pieces. Put them in bowl and toss well.

TO SERVE: Divide portions on small salad plates.

Paris-Brest

CREAM PUFF PASTE RING FILLED
WITH PASTRY CREAM AND PRALINE

The elegant climax to this dinner is *Paris-Brest,* a cream puff crown filled with praline and smooth *Crème Saint-Honoré.* It will serve 8.

MAKING PRALINE

INGREDIENTS

1 *cup granulated sugar*
1 *cup unblanched whole almonds*

USEFUL UTENSIL: 1-*quart copper or other heavy saucepan*

METHOD

Combine sugar and almonds in a quart saucepan, a copper one, if possible. Stir constantly with wooden spoon over medium heat until sugar turns a rich amber. (This will take about 20 minutes.)

Pour into buttered pie pan or plate. When praline has hardened, break into small pieces and powder in electric blender or food processor; or place in a plastic bag and pulverize by running a rolling pin over it.

MAKING CREAM PUFF RING

INGREDIENTS

1 *cup cold water*
1/2 *teaspoon table salt*
1 *tablespoon granulated sugar*
1/4 *pound unsalted butter, cut in small pieces*
1 *cup plus 1 tablespoon all-purpose flour*
4 *jumbo eggs*

USEFUL UTENSIL: *Wooden spoon*

METHOD

Butter a 10 × 15-inch cookie sheet, sprinkle with flour, and shake off excess. Using an 8-inch pie or cake pan, trace a circle in the center of floured surface with your finger. (If you have a lazy-Susan, place the cookie sheet on it and turn as you trace. It makes it easier!)

Preheat oven to 425° F.

Combine water, salt, sugar, and butter in a 2-quart saucepan; bring to a rolling boil. When butter is melted, add flour all at once and stir vigorously with a wooden spoon. *The wooden spoon is indispensable for making successful cream puff paste!* Continue stirring until mixture forms a compact mass that leaves the sides of the pan. This will take just about 1/2 minute.

Remove saucepan from heat. Add eggs, one at a time, stirring each one vigorously until it is well blended in before adding the next. Work rapidly. Batter should be smooth and shiny and have the consistency of thick mayonnaise.

Form a 1 1/2- to 2-inch thick ring on the floured cookie sheet by dropping the paste, 1 tablespoon at a time, around circle. Wet your fingers with water and smooth out paste. (You can also form the ring using a pastry bag fitted with a 1/2- to 3/4-inch tip. Use a fluted tip if possible, as it controls the paste better. Squeeze out two rings, one on top of the other.)

Drop small amounts of paste the size of silver dollars around edges of cookie sheet and in center of ring, making sure they do not touch. You can wait and bake these small puffs separately, if you prefer. You should have about a dozen puffs. (The extra ones can be frozen and used later to make cream puffs.)

GLAZING AND BAKING

INGREDIENTS

1 *egg yolk*
1 *teaspoon water*
1/8 *teaspoon table salt*
3 *ounces blanched, slivered almonds*

USEFUL UTENSIL: *Goose-feather pastry brush*

METHOD

Combine eggs, water, and salt; blend well with fork. Using a goose-feather or other pastry brush, cover the ring and puffs with this *dorure* (glaze). Be careful not to drip any glaze onto sheet around pastry, as this will prevent it from puffing fully. Sprinkle ring with slivered almonds.

Bake 25 minutes on middle rack of oven. If you are baking the smaller puffs separately, bake them only 20 minutes.

Turn oven off; prick ring and puffs with pastry needle or knife so that steam can escape. Return to oven for 5 to 10 minutes, leaving door ajar.

Loosen from sheet with wide metal spatula and place on wire rack to cool completely.

CRÈME SAINT-HONORÉ

INGREDIENTS

1 2/3 *cups milk*
1 *vanilla bean or* 1 *teaspoon vanilla extract*
4 *jumbo egg yolks*
1/2 *cup granulated sugar*
1/3 *cup all-purpose flour*
4 *tablespoons praline**
2 *egg whites*

*Leftover praline may be stored for future use in a tightly sealed container in a dry cool place. It will last indefinitely, and may be sprinkled over ice cream or other desserts.

METHOD

The base of this filling is French pastry cream; it becomes *Crème Saint-Honoré* when beaten egg whites are added. Usually the number of whites equals the number of yolks, but for this recipe, I prefer the consistency given by 2 egg whites.

The cream can be made while the ring is baking.

Scald milk with vanilla bean or extract in a quart pan over medium heat.

Meanwhile, in a 4-cup bowl, stir egg yolks with a rubber spatula; gradually add sugar and continue to beat until mixture becomes light yellow (about 2 minutes). Gradually blend in flour. Add scalded milk slowly, whisking thoroughly.

Pour back into saucepan and slowly bring to a boil over medium heat, stirring constantly so that cream will not stick to bottom and curdle. Surface foam will disappear and cream will thicken just before boiling point is reached.

Return cream to mixing bowl. Fold in praline.

Beat egg whites for 1 1/2 minutes at high speed with an electric mixer. Fold carefully into cream.

ASSEMBLING THE PARIS-BREST

INGREDIÉNTS

Confectioners' sugar

USEFUL UTENSIL: *Pastry bag*

METHOD

Stick 2 toothpicks into the side of ring, one above the other, so that you can later match halves. Carefully split ring in half horizontally with a bread knife.

Fill the bottom half of ring with cream. (A pastry bag fitted with a fluted tip is helpful here.)

Cut 4 of the small puffs in half and place the halves at regular intervals around ring on top of cream, allowing one half for each serving. Fill them with cream.

Being sure the toothpick markers coincide, replace top half of ring. Fill gaps between the half puffs with the remaining cream.

Sprinkle top of ring with confectioners' sugar.

TO SERVE: With a bread knife, slice portions between puffs. Serve with forks.

Menu XXIII

Essayons de la Haute Cuisine
TRYING HAUTE CUISINE

Topinambours
MARINATED JERUSALEM ARTICHOKES

Côtelettes en Cuirasse
RIB LAMB CHOPS BAKED IN A CRUST
WITH HAM AND MUSHROOMS

Épinards à la Crème
SAUTÉED SPINACH WITH CREAM

Salade Verte
GREEN SALAD

Crêpes Suzette
FLAMING CRÊPES FILLED WITH
TANGERINE-FLAVORED BUTTER,
SAUCED WITH ORANGE JUICE AND
LIQUEURS

Champagne Brut, Fleurie, or Margaux and Sauternes

THE main dish of this menu for 4 classifies as *haute cuisine,* the higher echelon in classic French cookery. It is accompanied by an unusual appetizer, Jerusalem artichokes, and by spinach sautéed in cream. An appropriate salad course would be escarole salad (page 148), or chicory salad (page 44). The whole is climaxed with that flaming star of Continental desserts, *Crêpes Suzette.* All who partake will leave the table in sheer euphoria!

RECOMMENDED WINES: A worthy companion is Champagne Brut, well chilled in ice, served from beginning to end. If not Champagne, choose that most versatile of red Burgundies, a fresh light Beaujolais, such as a Fleurie; or a red Bordeaux, like a delicate, fragrant Margaux from Médoc. If you serve a red wine, consider serving a dessert wine with the *crêpes.* Try a Sauternes, such as Château d'Yquem or Château Lafaurie Peyraguey.

ORDER OF PREPARATION: *Les Topinambours* may be prepared up to a week in advance. The lamb chops can wait, wrapped in dough and ready to be glazed and baked, until just before mealtime. The spinach can be cooked ahead of time, and the final sautéeing and addition of the cream done at the last minute. The *crêpes* also can be cooked ahead of time, and the sauce organized. The final flaming of the *crêpes* is, of course, best done at the table.

Topinambours

MARINATED JERUSALEM ARTICHOKES

Jerusalem artichokes resemble common artichokes in flavor only, for they actually belong to the sunflower family. They are edible roots which look like miniature potatoes with bulging instead of receding eyes; they have the same thin brown skin, the same earthy smell. They are usually available in supermarkets during the winter months.

The recipe will serve 4.

BOILING THE ARTICHOKES

INGREDIENTS

6 *cups cold water*
4 *tablespoons white vinegar*
4 *tablespoons coarse salt or 2 tablespoons table salt*
1 1/2 *pounds Jerusalem artichokes**

METHOD

In a saucepan of at least 2-quart capacity, combine water, vinegar, and salt.

Wash and peel artichokes. (A potato peeler is better for this than a knife.) Drop them immediately into the vinegar water to prevent discoloration.

When all are peeled, cover pan and bring to a roaring boil over high heat. Reduce heat and boil gently for 7 to 10 minutes. (If you have particularly large artichokes, they may take longer than 10 minutes.) When tip of paring knife glides easily through them, they are done: cooked, but firm.

Remove from water at once and allow to cool before adding dressing.

DRESSING

INGREDIENTS

1/2 *teaspoon table salt*
5 *turns of black pepper mill, medium grind*
1/4 *teaspoon chopped garlic*
1 *tablespoon plus 1 teaspoon red wine vinegar*
2 *tablespoons salad oil*

1 *tablespoon chopped fresh parsley*

METHOD

Place artichokes in a 3- to 4-cup vegetable dish; sprinkle with dressing ingredients in the order listed; toss well. Artichokes may be made ahead of time to marinate in the dressing. They will keep over a week if refrigerated.

*Try to purchase artichokes of uniform size to make timing easier.

TO SERVE: Toss; sprinkle with chopped parsley. Spoon onto salad plates.

Côtelettes en Cuirasse

LAMB CHOPS BAKED IN A CRUST
WITH HAM AND MUSHROOMS

Usually one *Côtelette en Cuirasse* is ample for a serving. But beware! I once served them to a professional chef who ate three of them, much to the quiet anger of my children, who ended up in the kitchen eating scrambled eggs for dinner.

Complete success is easy if you read the recipe over, know what is called for, and have all ingredients ready at your fingertips. All steps except the final baking may be done as much as 2 days ahead of time.

Wait until you bring *Côtelettes en Cuirasse* to the table: You will be so proud of yourself!

This recipe will make 4 *Côtelettes en Cuirasse*. For more, make them in batches.

MAKE THE CRUST

INGREDIENTS

1 2/3 *cups pastry or all-purpose flour**
1 *whole egg (jumbo or extra large)*
1 *teaspoon table salt*
6 *tablespoons butter at room temperature***
1/4 *cup cold water*

METHOD

Place flour in a 4- to 6-cup mixing bowl. Make a well in center of flour and put in the egg, salt, and butter, cut into small pieces for better distribution. Add water a little at a time, mixing lightly with fingertips until dough is sufficiently moist to hold together. It should adhere well into a firm ball; the mixing bowl should be

*Pastry flour is a little easier for beginners to handle.
**Take out of refrigerator at least 1/2 hour before using.

almost clean when dough is removed. (If you are making dough on a humid day, you may find that it is too soft and sticky to handle; add a little more flour to stiffen it.) Form into a loose ball.

Remove ball from bowl and place it on a lightly floured board or table top. With the heel of your hand press dough against surface and away from you a little at a time. Repeat until every portion has been treated in this manner. This process is called *fraiser,* and is done to press butter evenly and thoroughly throughout the dough.

Scrape dough again into a ball using a large-bladed knife or a *coupe-pâte.* Divide ball in half. Dust each half lightly with flour and roll into a ball. Cover with waxed paper and refrigerate for at least 45 minutes.

The crust can be made as much as 3 days in advance and stored in the refrigerator, or frozen if it is to be kept for a longer period. If it is prepared in advance, remove it from refrigerator at least 1/2 hour before rolling out.

SAUTÉ THE CHOPS

INGREDIENTS

4 *rib lamb chops,* 2 *to* 4 *ounces each (about* 3/4 *of an inch thick)**
8 *tablespoons clarified butter*
1/2 *teaspoon table salt*
1/8 *teaspoon black pepper or* 4 *turns of the pepper mill, medium grind*

METHOD

While dough is resting, prepare chops: Trim off excess fat and flatten them with a mallet or meat cleaver if your butcher has not done so already.

In a 12-inch skillet, heat butter until it sings. Sauté chops 3 minutes on each side over medium heat. They should be nicely browned. Remove from heat. Lift out chops, shaking them over skillet to remove excess juice; set aside to cool. Sprinkle with salt and pepper. Set skillet with sautéing butter aside until *duxelles* is ready.

*This recipe will produce a medium-rare chop. If you prefer your lamb rare, buy 1- to 1 1/2-inch chops and sauté only 1/2 to 1 minute on each side.

PREPARE THE DUXELLES

INGREDIENTS

1/3 *cup chopped white onions (about 2 small white onions)*
1/2 *pound fresh mushrooms*
1/2 *teaspoon table salt*
1/8 *teaspoon black pepper or 4 turns of pepper mill, medium grind*

METHOD

Chop onions.

Cut ends off mushroom stems; wipe mushrooms with clean damp sponge. Slice and chop into small pieces using a chopping bowl or a sharp knife. Turn mushrooms onto a linen towel and gently squeeze out water. Discard the water.

Return sautéing skillet to medium heat. Wait until butter again sings, then sauté onion for 1 minute, shaking pan continually. Add mushrooms and sauté another minute, shaking pan to ensure uniform cooking. Sprinkle with salt and pepper; toss with rubber spatula.

With a slotted spoon, transfer mixture to a strainer. Holding strainer over the sautéing skillet, press mixture to remove excess liquid. Reserve pan and liquid for use in sauce. If chops are not going to be baked immediately, *duxelles* should be completely cooled before using.

ROLL OUT THE DOUGH

Remove one ball of dough from refrigerator and return it to floured surface. Roll out into a fan shape large enough to accommodate 4 chops (about 18 inches across at the center). (See step 1 in the illustration.) Be sure working surface is always lightly floured and that underside of dough is not sticking. To prevent sticking, turn dough over after every three or four rolls by flipping it over the rolling pin.

If a hole appears here and there in the dough, don't worry about it. Mend it by cutting a small slice off end of dough and rolling it into torn area.

The fan does not have to be perfect. The important thing is that it be a large enough surface on which to place the chops with about 1 1/2 inches between them.

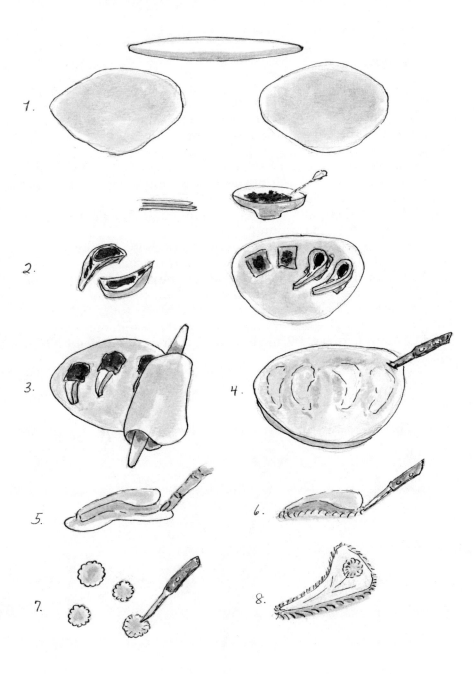

ASSEMBLE THE CÔTELETTES

INGREDIENTS

8 *slices boiled ham, cut into* 2 × 4-*inch pieces*

METHOD

Now, distribute 4 ham slices across the wide part of your fan-shaped dough. Place 1 tablespoon of the *duxelles* mixture on each slice. Lay chops on top of *duxelles;* cover each chop with another tablespoon of the *duxelles,* then top them with remaining ham slices (step 2).

Remove second ball of dough from refrigerator. On another lightly floured surface, roll out as before into a fan shape which will fully cover first fan and its filling (step 3).

When covered, allow to rest 5 minutes so that dough will be more supple when cut around chops.

With a sharp knife, cut around each chop, leaving enough margin so that edges may be rolled up and pinched together (step 4). To assure a good seal between layers, moisten edges of bottom dough with water; press layers together with fingers or fork, following outline of chops (step 5). Fold edge up for a tighter seal and, using the back edge of a knife blade, make indentations along edge of dough every 1/2 inch, a process known as *chiqueter* (step 6).

Incise one long line into top of each chop. Make several smaller branching cuts in a leaf-vein motif, to allow steam to escape while baking.

At this point chops may be covered and refrigerated up to 2 days before baking. Do not freeze.

Form leftover dough into a ball and roll out. Cut 4 circles, about 2 inches in diameter, with a cookie cutter. Incise a fan-shaped design into each circle by pressing flat knife tip into dough in a consecutive pattern (step 7). Set aside.

GLAZING AND BAKING

INGREDIENTS

2 *egg yolks*
1 *teaspoon water*
1/8 *teaspoon table salt*

METHOD

Preheat oven to 425° F. Mix egg yolks, water, and salt lightly with a fork to make the *dorure* (glaze). When ready to bake, coat dough with this mixture. Top each chop with the decorative circle previously cut (step 8); coat these also with the *dorure*. (Do not coat pastry with *dorure* until ready to bake, as it will dry out the dough.)

Place chops on a cookie sheet and bake 20 to 25 minutes until nicely brown.

MAKING THE SAUCE (OPTIONAL)

INGREDIENTS

3 *tablespoons dry white wine*

METHOD

To make a sauce for the chops, place skillet with remaining sautéing butter and liquid over high heat. Add wine; scrape sides and bottom with wooden spatula and boil for 2 minutes. Season to taste. Pour into gravy boat. (Chops may be served with or without this sauce.)

TO SERVE: Present chops attractively placed on a bed of watercress upon a silver platter.

Serve the sauce in a gravy boat. Tell your guests to remove a piece of the crust from the chop in order to ladle the sauce over the meat, rather than over the crust.

Épinards à la Crème

SAUTÉED SPINACH WITH CREAM

It is possible for spinach to be such a treat that it becomes your child's favorite vegetable! I'll never forget the day our daughter Susan ordered it in a restaurant. To her amazement (and my secret delight) she found it unpalatable, nothing like the spinach she was used to being served at home.

Although this recipe is for 4 servings, I am so fond of this dish I could eat the whole portion myself! If your diners like spinach, you may want to double or triple the amounts.

Spinach may be cooked in advance, then sautéed at the last minute.

INGREDIENTS

3 *quarts boiling water*
2 *tablespoons coarse salt or* 1 *tablespoon table salt*

1 1/2 *pounds fresh spinach*

4 *tablespoons clarified butter*
3/4 *cup heavy cream*
1/2 *teaspoon table salt*
1/8 *teaspoon freshly ground black pepper, medium grind*

METHOD

Bring salted water to roaring boil.

In the meantime, clean spinach: Snips ends from stems; wash in colander under cold running water or in a pan, changing water several times.

Drop washed spinach into boiling water. Let water come again to an active boil, uncovered. Reduce heat and boil gently for 5 minutes.

Drain spinach in a colander and run cold water over greens. Squeeze all moisture out of the spinach with your hand. Chop finely in chopping bowl or with chef's knife on a wooden board.

At this point, spinach can be stored until ready for final step.

Melt butter in an 8- to 10-inch frying pan. Add spinach and sauté, turning with a wooden spoon to coat evenly. After spinach has been thoroughly heated, reduce heat.

Add cream gradually, mixing with wooden spoon. Cook for

2 minutes. Take care mixture does not boil or it will curdle. Add salt and pepper; mix again.

TO SERVE: Place spinach in vegetable dish; swirl it with a fork to suit your fancy. Wipe any spatterings from dish edge with a paper towel. Spinach may be eaten with the *Côtelettes en Cuirasse* or, for a more formal meal, served as a separate course afterwards.

Let's hope you have prepared enough!

Crêpes Suzette

FLAMING CRÊPES FILLED WITH A TANGERINE-FLAVORED
BUTTER, SAUCED WITH ORANGE JUICE AND LIQUEURS

For many, this dessert is synonymous with French cuisine, and brings to mind flaming dishes and high-priced restaurants. For me, it brings back memories of the winter holidays, Mardi-Gras and Mi-Carême, when we would dress in costume and parade the streets. In the evening friends would join us for *Crêpes Suzette* or *Beignets Soufflés*, confections always associated with these celebrations. However, *Crêpes Suzette* don't need a special occasion; they make an appropriate dessert at any time.

Crêpes, a thin French pancake, take on the name *Suzette* only when filling and sauce are flavored with orange and brandy. Like so many French dishes, *Crêpes Suzette* has a legend surrounding its birth; in fact many legends. The story I like best, and one which no one can say for a fact is not true, is that told by Henri Charpentier, a renowned French chef:

As a boy of 14, back in 1895, he was assistant waiter at the *Café de Paris* in Monte-Carlo, a restaurant frequented by famous people, including Edward, Prince of Wales. One day when the proprietor was reprimanding Henri, the Prince stood up for the boy and asked him to serve him personally. As Henri was preparing the dessert in a chafing dish, impetuously he added an added touch of liqueurs to the sauce. Suddenly they ignited. Aghast, Henri waited for the flames which engulfed the dish to die out. Tentatively he tasted. What a happy surprise! When the Prince tried it, he was delighted. He asked what the dish was called. Henri quickly answered, "*Crêpes Princesse!*" But the prince pointed out that there was a young lady present and asked if the dish could be named for her. Thus was born and christened *Crêpes Suzette*. Henri Charpentier believed, and so do I, that one taste of this confection would change a cannibal into a civilized gentleman!

This recipe makes about 12 crêpes, enough for 3 per person.

MAKING THE CRÊPES

INGREDIENTS

1 *cup flour*
1 *teaspoon table salt*
1 *tablespoon sugar*
1 *whole egg*
2 *egg yolks*
1 1/4 *cups cold milk*
2 *tablespoons melted butter*
1 *tablespoon rum*

1 *butter stick wrapped in cheesecloth*

USEFUL UTENSIL: *Small iron skillet, 5 inches in diameter**

METHOD

There are three keys to successful *crêpes:* 1) Have your pan hot. A heavy iron skillet is best. A *crêpe* pan which measures 5 inches in diameter across the cooking surface is ideal for a dessert or hors-d'oeuvre *crêpe.* 2) Stir the batter each time before spooning out. 3) Butter the pan before making each *crêpe.*

MAKE BATTER: Place flour in a mixing bowl; make hole in center of flour; add salt, sugar, eggs, and milk. Mix well with wire whisk. Add melted butter, mix; add rum, whisk thoroughly.

Cover bowl with a linen towel and let batter rest at least 2 hours at room temperature, or overnight in refrigerator. Stir from time to time while resting. Resting will make the batter thicker and the pancakes thinner.

MAKE CRÊPES: Place skillet over high heat. In a minute or two it should be hot enough. Rub pan with butter stick.

Stir batter; measure 2 full tablespoons into skillet; tilt pan quickly to spread batter evenly. Add a little more batter if necessary to cover bottom.

*Measured across cooking surface.

When batter has set a little, loosen edges with a metal spatula. Shake pan to be sure *crêpe* is not sticking. Underside should turn a light golden brown. When bubbles appear, flip *crêpe* over.

Crêpes very early became the favorite recipe of my son Louis, who thoroughly enjoyed his mastery of flipping them. After one or two tries, I'm sure you will be enjoying it as he did. In France, it is said that one should hold a two-franc gold coin in the palm when handling the skillet. Why? For good luck!

TO FLIP: Be sure *crêpe* is loose and not sticking to pan. Shake pan briskly from side to side; *crêpe* should slide slightly. Then, with one quick movement, push pan forward and draw it back toward you. *Crêpe* should flip over nicely and land again in pan. At first they might miss the pan, but don't get discouraged. With a little practice, *crêpes* will be dutifully soaring at a flick of your wrist! (If all else fails, turn with spatula.)

Cook about half a minute on second side, or until light golden brown. Repeat process until batter is gone.

Crêpes should be soft and pliable for rolling. If they are to be used immediately, keep them warm and moist by placing them between two damp towels on a cookie sheet in a slow oven. If they are to be served later, place between layers of waxed paper and store at room temperature or in the refrigerator. (If refrigerated, bring them to room temperature before reheating.) Reheat in a covered double boiler or an electric frying pan with a low heat setting, for about 5 minutes.

THE FILLING

INGREDIENTS

8 *tablespoons unsalted butter at room temperature**
3 *tablespoons granulated sugar (vanilla sugar if possible)*
juice of 1 *tangerine (size does not matter as long as it is juicy).*
1 1/2 *tablespoons Cognac or Curaçao*

METHOD

The filling should be made at least 1 hour before using. Cream butter and sugar; add tangerine juice, mix well; add

*Remove from refrigerator at least 1/2 hour before using.

brandy and mix well again. Refrigerate for an hour so that butter will solidify again. Then spread onto center of each *crêpe* and roll.

THE SAUCE

INGREDIENTS

6 *sugar lumps*
1 *orange*
1 *lemon*
1/2 *cup orange juice*
8 *tablespoons unsalted butter (at room temperature)*
2 *tablespoons granulated sugar*
1/4 *cup Cointreau*
2 *tablespoons Curaçao or rum*
1/3 *cup Grand Marnier*

METHOD

Rub each sugar lump over skins of lemon and orange; dissolve lumps in orange juice.

Cream butter and sugar together.

Now, this final step may be done right at the table for all to watch: Melt creamed mixture in a chafing dish. (If an electric frying pan is used, set temperature at 350° F.; if frying pan is used, place over low to medium heat.) Add juice with dissolved sugar.

Placed filled, rolled *crêpes* in pan; baste them with sauce until heated through (about 5 minutes).

Add Cointreau, then the Curaçao or rum, and finally the Grand Marnier.

Reduce heat under pan to very low. Using a long-sticked match, step back and ignite sauce. Baste and turn *crêpes* until flame dies out.

TO SERVE: Dish onto dessert plates, allowing 3 *crêpes* per serving; spoon on sauce.

Refill Champagne glasses or bring on glasses for the dessert wine. Relax in the quiet glow of candlelight and know that you have dined like the gods!

MENU XXIV

Fêtons le Réveillon
CELEBRATING THE NEW YEAR

Coulibiac
BRIOCHE LOAF FILLED WITH CRÊPES,
MUSHROOMS, POACHED SALMON,
AND HARD-BOILED EGGS

Rôti de Dinde Farcie
ROAST TURKEY WITH A CHOICE OF
STUFFINGS

Chou Rouge à la Flamande
BRAISED RED CABBAGE WITH APPLES
AND CURRANT JELLY

Salade d'Épinards
SPINACH SALAD WITH
A MUSTARD–GARLIC DRESSING

Bûche aux Marrons
PURÉED CHESTNUT LOG FLAVORED
WITH SEMI-SWEET CHOCOLATE
AND RUM

*Chassagne-Montrachet, Puligny-
Montrachet, or white Hermitage
and Pomerol or Pauillac and
Champagne Demi-Sec or Muscat d'Alsace*

IN France, Christmas Eve and New Year's Eve are celebrated with a midnight supper, *le réveillon. Le réveillon du jour de l'an,* the New Year's Eve feast, was a major celebration in our family. My parents invited friends who truly appreciated Mother's culinary efforts; it seemed that each year the number increased.

Because the dining room in our Paris apartment could not accommodate all the guests, Mother would place a long table in my father's store. After working there all day, she would wait until closing time, about 8 o'clock at night, then clean the store and set the table. Only then could she begin all the last-minute preparations for a meal she had planned and worked on for over a week. After everyone else had collapsed, she was still clearing and doing dishes as the sun rose.

As an old friend, one privileged to have enjoyed many of these *réveillons,* recently reminisced: "It was Anna's pleasure to cook for people. She always seemed much happier to entertain than to be entertained. Her meals were occasions to remember."

The menu that follows would have her approval, I know. It serves 10 to 12 persons amply. It starts off with *Coulibiac,* a *brioche* loaf filled with salmon and mushrooms, crêpes, and hard-boiled eggs, followed by turkey browned *juste à point.* Colorful and tasty red cabbage is both a complement to the turkey and a comparatively inexpensive vegetable for a large gathering. A crisp salad of spinach smooths the way for the *Bûche aux Marrons,* a delicate chestnut confection which is traditional for winter holidays in France.

RECOMMENDED WINES: Such a gala celebration is the ideal time to serve a different wine with each course. For something very special with *Coulibiac,* serve a Chassagne-Montrachet or a Puligny-Montrachet, indisputably the greatest dry white wines of Burgundy; or a more modest white Hermitage from the Côtes du Rhône. With the turkey, serve a Pomerol or a Pauillac, both among the finest wines of Bordeaux, light-bodied and fragrant. With dessert savor a Champagne Demi-Sec, or a Muscat d'Alsace.

ORDER OF PREPARATION: The *Bûche aux Marrons* and the cabbage may be prepared 2 or 3 days ahead and stored in the refrigerator. The turkey may be stuffed and trussed the day before, providing the stuffing is cold. The *Coulibiac* may be baked in advance and reheated. The salad should, of course, be tossed at the last minute.

Coulibiac

BRIOCHE LOAF FILLED WITH CRÊPES, MUSHROOMS, POACHED SALMON, AND HARD-BOILED EGGS

Although Russian in origin, *Coulibiac** is very much a part of French *haute cuisine*. One of the traditional recipes calls for *vesiga*, the spinal marrow of sturgeon, which is not easily found in the United States, and rice, which makes the loaf difficult to slice neatly. My recipe eliminates both of these difficulties.

There are numerous steps to its preparation, but, since most of them can be done ahead of time, the assembly and baking of the *Coulibiac* is very simple. The secret is to organize each step separately and proceed calmly. Since the *brioche* dough must rise overnight, it should be started at least a day in advance.

This recipe will yield 8 to 10 good slices.

PÂTE À BRIOCHE COMMUNE (DOUGH)

INGREDIENTS

3 1/2 *cups all-purpose flour*
2 *yeast cakes*
2 *teaspoons table salt*
3 *jumbo eggs*
10 *tablespoons whipped sweet butter*

a pat of butter at room temperature (1/2 to 1 tablespoon)

METHOD

Begin the dough a day ahead, as it should rise overnight.

Measure flour into a 2-quart mixing bowl; make well in center of flour and crumble in yeast; add salt, eggs, and butter, softening it first for half a second with fingers. Work all ingredients together rapidly with the tips of the fingers until they form a compact ball.

Knead dough for 5 minutes on a lightly floured surface: Punch dough with your fists, push it out with your palms, bring it back into a ball and punch again. Then form dough again into a ball.

*Also spelled *Kulebiak*.

Place ball of dough on a lightly buttered plate, spread top with softened butter, cover with a clean linen towel, and let rise at room temperature for 2 hours.

Flatten dough again, form again into a ball, butter top lightly, cover with towel, and set in refrigerator to rise overnight.

PÂTE À CRÊPES

INGREDIENTS

3/4 *cup all-purpose flour*
1 *jumbo egg*
1/4 *teaspoon table salt*
1 *cup cold milk*
1 1/2 *tablespoons unsalted butter, melted*

1 *butter stick wrapped in cheesecloth*

USEFUL UTENSIL: *A cast iron skillet, 5 inches in diameter**

METHOD

Crêpes may be made a day ahead, if desired.

Measure flour into a quart mixing bowl; make well in center of flour and add egg, salt, and milk. Blend into a smooth batter with a whisk. Stir in melted butter.

Cover bowl with a clean linen towel and let rest at room temperature for at least 2 hours. Batter will thicken, making lighter, thinner *crêpes*.

TO FRY: A 5-inch frying pan is perfect for this recipe. Heat pan over high heat for 1 1/2 to 2 minutes. Coat bottom and sides with the butter stick. When butter sizzles, pan is hot enough. Reduce heat to medium.

Using a potholder if necessary, remove pan from heat and measure in 2 tablespoons of batter. Swirl pan around to spread batter evenly over bottom.

Return to heat. After a few seconds, begin shaking pan from side to side; when *crêpe* is loose, first side is done.

TO FLIP: Shake pan briskly from side to side; then, with a quick movement, push pan forward and draw it back toward you. *Crêpe*

*Measure across cooking surface.

should flip over nicely and land again in pan. Or, turn with a wide metal spatula.

Press *crêpe* with spatula to ensure that it is cooking evenly. A *crêpe* is *bien frisée* (well fried) when it is lightly browned with many bubble holes on its surface. It should be soft and pliable.

If pan is hot enough to start, it is possible to make 2 *crêpes* per minute. Each *crêpe* will cook about 15 seconds on each side. Often, however, the first few *crêpes* are difficult to handle. Be sure to make 6 perfect ones for your *Coulibiac*. Any rejects may be eaten by the cook!

Crêpes made in advance may be covered with a damp towel and left at room temperature or refrigerated. If you refrigerate them, warm them slowly in a low oven, in a covered double boiler, or in an electric frying pan before adding to the *Coulibiac*.

POACHED SALMON

INGREDIENTS

1 1/2 *pounds fresh or canned salmon**
2 *cups dry white wine*
1 *cup water*
2 *shallots or 2 to 3 teaspoons red onion, finely chopped*
3/4 *teaspoon table salt*
4 *turns of black pepper mill, medium grind*

METHOD

Rinse fish in cold water. Combine it with remaining ingredients in a 1-quart saucepan. Bring slowly to boiling point, reduce heat, and poach for 23 minutes, basting and stirring several times. (When poaching, the water should always be kept just under the bubbling point.) Allow salmon to cool in its stock.

Salmon may be prepared ahead of time and refrigerated until ready to use. When ready to use, drain it thoroughly.** Remove skin and bones.

*FOR CANNED SALMON: Use same method of poaching, even though canned salmon is ready to eat. Drain off canned juice, place salmon in colander, run cold water over it, poach as above. Remove skin and bones, if any, after poaching.

**Cooking liquor may be frozen for future use in stocks, for poaching other fish, or as a base for fish sauces.

THE DUXELLES

INGREDIENTS

1 *pound fresh mushrooms*
1/2 *cup chopped white onion*
6 *tablespoons clarified butter*
1/2 *teaspoon table salt*

METHOD

Cut tips from mushroom stems. Wipe with clean damp sponge. Quarter and chop.

Place chopped mushrooms in a clean dishtowel. Gather up towel corners, twist into a sack, and squeeze mushrooms to remove all moisture. (You'll be surprised at the amount that comes out.)

In an 8-inch frying pan, one large enough so that vegetables will not be crowded, heat butter until it sings. Sauté onions until glossy; add mushrooms and sauté for 1 minute. Sprinkle with salt. Remove from pan into a bowl with a slotted spoon so that juices stay behind.*

Duxelles can be made in advance; cover and refrigerate.

HARD-BOILED EGGS

INGREDIENTS

4 *jumbo or extra large eggs*

METHOD

In a 1-quart glass or enamel saucepan, cover eggs with cold water. Bring to boiling point, uncovered, over medium heat. When a rolling boil is reached, reduce heat and simmer gently for 12 minutes.

Remove from heat, pour off hot water, and run cold water over eggs to cool them immediately. Shell; chill in refrigerator before slicing.

Eggs can be boiled several days in advance. If you are keeping them for several days do not shell before refrigerating.

*Save mushroom juice; store it in refrigerator for future use in making pan gravy or soup.

When ready to assemble your *Coulibiac,* slice the eggs 1/8 to 1/4 inch thick. To facilitate slicing, dip knife in hot water between cuts. If eggs are sliced much in advance, place slices on an enamel, pottery, or glass dish and cover with storage wrap.

TO ASSEMBLE THIS MASTERPIECE

INGREDIENTS

1 *egg, uncooked*

METHOD

Take *brioche* dough from refrigerator an hour before rolling out; roll out 3 to 4 hours before baking.

Have *crêpes,* salmon, *duxelles,* and sliced eggs at hand. It is easier to assemble the *Coulibiac* if all fillings are cold except the *crêpes,* which should be warm enough to be supple.

Sprinkle work surface and rolling pin lightly with flour. Knead dough just enough to flatten it (a second or two). Roll out to about a 17-inch circle, flipping it over several times to make sure dough is not sticking; sprinkle with more flour as necessary.

Roll edges thinner than center.

Now, cut out a 14 by 16-inch rectangle (step 1 in the figure on page 276); flatten edges. Reserve extra pieces for decorating your *Coulibiac.*

In a small bowl, mix the raw egg with a fork for a half second, just enough to blend white and yolk. Using a pastry brush, coat center of rectangle lightly with egg (step 2). This will give dough more strength to support the filling.

Now, add filling as follows, packing firmly and neatly with a spoon:

1) Place 3 *crêpes* on center of dough; they should overlap each other by about an inch (step 3).

2) Spoon on a layer of the *duxelles* about an inch thick.

3) Add a layer of salmon 1 to 2 inches thick.

4) Arrange egg slices for a fourth layer.

5) Repeat mushroom, salmon, and egg layers until filling has been used up.

6) Finally, place last 3 *crêpes* on top, overlapping each other as before. Brush *crêpes* with beaten egg.

Now, cut a 2-inch wedge out of each corner of the dough so that it can be more neatly folded over filling (step 4). Bring up short sides and fold over one at a time, pulling them gently to fold

tightly over the top. Brush edges with egg to seal. Repeat with two longer sides (step 5).

Use a Teflon cookie sheet if you have one, or lightly butter a regular sheet. Place *Coulibiac* upside down on sheet. (It is not as fragile as it might appear.)

Roll out remaining dough until paper thin; cut into strips and roll between the palms of your hands to form ropes 9 or 10 inches in length. Place 10 to 12 of these ropes parallel to each other on top of *Coulibiac* across its width. Patch several ropes together to surround base.

Allow to rest in refrigerator from 1 to 3 hours.

DORURE AND BAKING

INGREDIENTS

1 *egg yolk*
1 *teaspoon water*
dash of salt

METHOD

The *Coulibiac* takes just under an hour to bake. When ready to bake, preheat oven to 400° F.

Combine egg yolk, water, and salt with a fork to make *dorure* (glaze). Just before putting *Coulibiac* in the oven, coat it thoroughly with the *dorure*. Wipe up any which may spill onto cookie sheet.

Cut two little holes through top of dough into the filling; make two tiny funnels of aluminum foil and place them in the holes so that steam can escape during baking (step 6).

Place on middle rack of oven and bake 10 minutes at 400° F. Reduce heat to 350° F. and bake 35 minutes longer. Check during baking period; if crust is getting too dark, cover with aluminum foil.

Allow *Coulibiac* to stand at room temperature 20 to 30 minutes before slicing.

Coulibiac can be baked a day ahead. Cool completely, cover, and refrigerate. Reheat in a 200° F. oven for 1 1/2 hours.

TO SERVE: Place a bread board on a silver tray and transfer *Coulibiac* onto board. Replace funnels with sprigs of fresh parsley. Decorate platter with more sprigs (step 7).

Slice between ropes with a serrated bread knife.

Coulibiac can be served simply with sour cream. However, the classic way to serve it is with sour cream, *Sauce Bâtarde* (a lemon-flavored egg sauce), and *Sauce Beurre Blanc* (a white butter sauce). Recipes for these sauces follow.

Pour sauce (or sauces) into gravy boat; scoop sour cream into a bowl. Spoon one or two tablespoons of sauce or sour cream on each portion.

Coulibiac may be eaten hot, warm, or cold. It makes a delicious main course for a cold buffet.

SAUCE BÂTARDE

INGREDIENTS

2 *tablespoons clarified butter*
2 *tablespoons all-purpose flour*
2 *cups hot water (not boiling)*
2 *egg yolks*
1 1/2 *teaspoons table salt*
1 1/2 *tablespoons lemon juice*
4 *tablespoons whipped sweet butter*

METHOD

Make a *roux:* In a heavy 1-quart saucepan, place butter over medium heat; gradually blend in flour with a whisk; cook half a minute to allow *roux* to swell.

Whisk in hot water, then egg yolks. Continue to whisk. Heat to point just before boiling over medium heat. (This will take 7 to 10 minutes.) By then, sauce will begin to thicken.

Blend in remaining ingredients. Be sure sauce does not boil after adding the butter.*

Keep sauce hot in a double boiler.

SAUCE BEURRE BLANC

Beurre Blanc is a fine sauce to accompany any fish which has been poached or broiled. It may be served with the *Coulibiac* instead of the *Sauce Bâtarde* or as a second sauce, the diners savoring a bit of both.

The sauce should have the consistency of a creamed soup, neither too thick nor too thin. It may be made ahead of time and kept warm in a double boiler or, if stored, reheated in a double boiler.

*If your sauce should curdle, don't panic. First, whisk in 1 to 4 tablespoons hot water. Then break 1 egg yolk into a bowl and whip the curdled sauce into it. *Voilà!*

INGREDIENTS

10 *shallots, peeled*
3 *tablespoons dry white wine*
6 *tablespoons white vinegar*
1/2 *pound unsalted butter*
1 *tablespoon hot water*
1/2 *teaspoon table salt*
4 *turns white pepper mill, fine grind, or scant* 1/8 *teaspoon ground white pepper*

METHOD

There is one extremely important key to success here: The correct temperature of the saucepan. If it is not hot enough, the ingredients will not bind together; if it is too hot, the sauce will curdle. Keep over a medium heat, adjusting your heat source as necessary.*

This recipe utilizes clarified butter, but the *petit lait* (whey) and the froth are important components to its consistency. Thus, the clarifying should be done during the preparation of the sauce.

Mince shallots directly into a 1-cup saucepan, so that no juice will be lost. Add wine and vinegar; stir together. Cook very slowly, uncovered, over a low to medium heat until all liquid has evaporated. Complete reduction will take about an hour.

Meanwhile, in a quart saucepan, slowly melt butter over low heat, being careful that it does not cook. When completely melted, remove pan from heat. Skim froth from surface and set it aside to use later.

Set melted butter aside for 5 minutes to permit suspended white substance (*petit lait*) to settle to bottom of pan.

Stretch a damp cheesecloth, triple thickness, over a small bowl and carefully pour melted butter through the cloth, being careful not to pour out the precipitated particles.

To the *petit lait* remaining in the pan, add the froth which was previously skimmed from the surface. Add the hot water and whisk. Continue whisking and add half the clarified butter, a little at a time, then add half of the cooked shallots.

Now return pan to low to medium heat. Whisk in remaining clarified butter, then remaining shallots, watching temperature carefully. Add salt and pepper. Sauce is done. Keep warm in double boiler.

*If the pan seems to have gotten too hot, plunge it immediately into a bowl of cold water to cool it down a bit. If the sauce curdles, place 1 tablespoon of hot water in another saucepan and slowly whisk the curdled sauce into it, a little at a time. This should eliminate the curdle.

Rôti de Dinde Farcie

ROAST TURKEY WITH A CHOICE OF STUFFINGS

The French word for turkey, *dinde*, derives from *d'Indies*, meaning "from the Indies." The West Indies was the name for the continent of North America at the time the Jesuits first introduced turkey to France. Since then it has become one of the traditional fares for the *réveillons* of Christmas and the New Year, along with goose and duck.

Look for a good fresh turkey with soft, clean, unbruised skin. A 10- to 12-pound dressed turkey will yield 10 to 12 servings. For larger gatherings, the French prepare two smaller turkeys instead of one large one, which might not be as tender.

Some people think that roasting is the easiest way to prepare meat. For me it is the most tiresome, as it requires so much basting and turning. With a turkey, this is done every 15 to 20 minutes for 3 to 4 hours. Basting makes the meat succulent, and prevents the skin from bursting.

Following the instructions for roasting the turkey and making the gravy, you will find several suggestions for stuffing the bird.

TO PREPARE AND ROAST THE TURKEY

INGREDIENTS

12 *large black olives*
4 *tablespoons Cognac*
1 *10- to 12-pound turkey*
1 *heaping tablespoon salt*
12 *to 16 tablespoons clarified butter*

USEFUL UTENSILS: *Trussing needle and string, goose-feather brush*

METHOD

Twenty-four hours or more ahead of time, split olives in half lengthwise; remove pits. Place in a small bowl and cover with Cognac. Cover with storage wrap and allow to steep.

Remove turkey innards usually stored in cavity: heart, neck, and gizzard will be used in the bouillon; liver and whatever fat is removed from body cavities may be used to make a spread (see recipe on page 288). Wipe cavities dry with paper toweling. (If frozen turkey is being used, follow directions for defrosting; usually 2 days in refrigerator are required for a 10- to 12-pound turkey. Rinse cavities with cold running water; drain; dry thoroughly.)

Rub cavities and outside of turkey with salt and some of the Cognac in which olives have been steeping. Reaching up through the neck cavity, slip steeped olive halves between skin and flesh along breastbone, loosening skin with fingers.

Choose a stuffing to suit your taste from those on pages 284–287. Stuffing may be made in advance and refrigerated. It should be cold when placed in the turkey. Stuff the bird when ready to roast, filling cavities loosely so that stuffing can expand. Turkey may be stuffed a day in advance *only if the stuffing is absolutely cold.*

TO CLOSE CAVITIES: Pull neck skin back tightly over back and hold with poultry lacers; pull skin of body cavity together and secure with poultry lacer and string. Or truss.

TO TRUSS: The purpose of trussing is to have the bird hold its shape during and after cooking. Legs and wings are bound tightly together against the body with string. The string is passed through parts of the body with the aid of a trussing needle which is from 10 to 12 inches long.

Cut a double width of string about 2 feet long; thread needle; tie a knot about 3 inches from the ends, enough to tie when finishing off.

Place bird on its back with tail section toward your left hand, if you are right-handed. (Reverse these instructions if you are left-handed.) Pick up legs with left hand and push them into an upright position.

Insert needle through body from just above thigh joint nearest you. Needle should come out at the same point on the opposite side and not hit any bones if placed properly. Pull string through as far as knot.

Push legs back down; pass string over far leg; insert needle down through tail section, catching skin to pull it over body cavity. Then bring it back up through tail section again; pass string over second leg and tie securely with knotted end.

Turn bird onto breast with hind part toward left hand. Re-thread needle, again with about 2 feet of string, doubled. Knot about 3 inches from ends. Insert needle through back just above hip joint and pull string through as far as knot.

Turn turkey so that head section is now toward left hand. Pass needle through wing at its tip; bring it out again through skin at the wing joint. Reinsert needle again about 1 inch away through wing skin, passing it through left-hand side of body and coming out at the base of the neck. Pick up neck skin in two places and pull it back tightly over body. Thrust needle down through body, coming out through webbed skin at wing joint. Pull string through. Keep wing close to body, pass string over wing bone, then, from the top downwards, plunge needle in and out of body to catch wing tip. Pull tightly and tie with knotted end.

When ready to roast the turkey, preheat oven to 500° F. Have clarified butter warm in a small pan. Place turkey on rack in roasting pan. Baste bird on both sides with butter. Roast at 500° F. for 5 minutes on each side, basting each time bird is turned. Then reduce heat to 300° F. and roast 20 minutes per pound: 4 hours for a 12-pound turkey; 3 hours for a 10-pound turkey. This frequent basting prevents the skin from cracking during roasting. If bird becomes too brown, cover with aluminum foil.

When bird is done, turn off oven and open door; allow turkey to stand 15 to 20 minutes so that juice can set before it is carved. Transfer bird onto board or cookie sheet to remove poultry lacers and string.

PREPARING THE GARNISH

In addition to a bed of watercress to decorate the platter and paper frills* to adorn the legs of the turkey, the French often prepare a *hâtelet* to decorate the bird. This is a skewer with a decorative head, on which are displayed perfect examples of whatever ingredients are used in the stuffing: mushrooms, olives, cooked onions, chestnuts, and a small heart of Bibb lettuce for color. The *hâtelet* is inserted in the breast of the bird at a 45 degree angle.

INGREDIENTS

1/4 *to* 1/2 *pound large, firm, white mushrooms*
8 *tablespoons lemon juice (1 lemon)*
1/2 *cup cold water*
2 *tablespoons unsalted butter*

1 *heart Bibb lettuce*
4 *to* 6 *black olives*
2 *ounces (1 bunch) watercress*

*For instructions on making paper frills, see page 59.

METHOD

To prepare *champignons au blanc* for your *hâtelet,* choose large white mushrooms. Combine lemon juice and water in a quart saucepan. Wipe mushrooms clean with a damp sponge, cut tips from stems, and peel them to make them even whiter. Drop them into the lemon water as they are peeled. When all are done, add butter, cover, and bring to boiling point over high heat. Boil 1 minute, covered. Remove from heat, remove cover, and keep in lemon water until ready to use.

Just before serving, pierce mushrooms, olives, and lettuce hearts with the *hâtelet,* forming a decorative pattern. Set aside until ready to use. Wash watercress in several changes of water and reserve for decorating platter.

THE GRAVY

INGREDIENTS

turkey gizzard, neck, and heart
1 *medium carrot, scraped*
1/2 *medium yellow onion, unpeeled*
bouquet garni (6 celery stalks with leaves plus 12 sprigs parsley)
3 1/2 *cups cold water*
1 *tablespoon coarse salt or 1/2 tablespoon table salt*

METHOD

PREPARE BOUILLON: While turkey is roasting, combine the ingredients listed above in a 2-quart saucepan. Cover and bring to boiling point. Simmer 1/2 hour with cover ajar. Remove all solids and reserve for making gravy. You should have about 1 cup of liquid.

Bouillon may be made a day ahead, if desired.

When turkey is ready, reheat bouillon. Remove rack from roasting pan and place pan over high heat on top of stove. Add bouillon, scraping loose any solid particles with a wooden spoon. Deglaze for about 3 minutes. Taste; add a little salt and pepper if necessary. If there is any Cognac left over from the steeped olives, add it to the gravy. Keep warm over low heat until ready to serve; then pour into gravy boat.

TO SERVE: Lay a bed of watercress on a large silver tray or serving platter. Place turkey, breast up, on bed; put paper frills over leg ends. If using a *hâtelet,* insert tip into turkey breast just above the breastbone, at a 45 degree angle. Bird is now ready to be presented at the dinner table.

Provide carving knife and fork and poultry shears for cutting and dismembering bird, as well as a large spoon and serving dish for the stuffing.

If there is no convenient sideboard or tea table on which to carve the turkey, return it to the kitchen for carving after all have feasted their eyes upon it. It is difficult to carve properly on a decorated platter.

Farce aux Marrons

CHESTNUT STUFFING

The stuffing recipes that follow will make enough for a 10- to 12-pound bird.

INGREDIENTS

5 *pounds fresh chestnuts*
16 *tablespoons unsalted butter*
1 *celery heart, washed and cut into* 1-*inch strips*
1 *teaspoon table salt*
3 *cups hot chicken bouillon**
6 *bay leaves*

METHOD

Preheat oven to 500° F.

With a sharp paring knife, slit chestnuts to prevent bursting during roasting. If slit on their convex side, they will be easier to peel. Spread out on a cookie sheet and roast for 15 minutes.

Remove shells while they are still hot; use potholders to hold them.

Select about 20 of the best ones and set aside to prepare separately for decoration.

Heat butter in a large pan (I use a 6-quart Dutch oven). Sauté celery strips until glossy. Remove them with a slotted spoon and sprinkle with salt.

*Use homemade stock, p. 19, or 3 packaged chicken cubes combined with 3 cups of water and simmered 5 minutes.

Add chestnuts to butter; toss gently until coated; sprinkle with salt.

Pour on hot bouillon, add bay leaves, cover, bring slowly to boiling point, then simmer gently for 30 minutes. Add sautéed celery just before chestnuts are done.

Cool completely before stuffing turkey.

Chestnuts prepared in this way also make a delicious vegetable.

TO PREPARE CHESTNUTS FOR DECORATION

INGREDIENTS

20 *chestnuts*
2 *tablespoons unsalted butter*
1 *celery stalk*
1 *cup chicken bouillon**

METHOD

Toss chestnuts in butter and simmer as described above, being especially careful that chestnuts do not break. The simmering should be as steady as possible.

These perfect whole chestnuts may be used on *hâtelets* or as garnish around the platter.

*Use homemade stock, p. 19; or 1 chicken cube combined with 1 cup of water and simmered 5 minutes.

Farce de Chair à Saucisses

HOMEMADE SAUSAGE MEAT STUFFING

INGREDIENTS

4 *pounds pork shoulder blade**
1/2 *teaspoon thyme*
1/2 *teaspoon coriander, crushed*
1/2 *teaspoon sage*
1/2 *teaspoon freshly ground white pepper (medium grind)*
3/4 *teaspoon table salt*

4 *slices white bread*
2 *cups cold water*
3 *whole eggs (jumbo)*

4 *tablespoons clarified butter*
6 *teaspoons chopped shallots*
7 *teaspoons chopped garlic*
6 *tablespoons chopped parsley (about 12 sprigs)*
1/4 *cup Cognac*

METHOD

Cut meat in cubes and chop or grind a small quantity at a time using a meat grinder, food processor with a steel blade, or blender. (If you are using a blender, chop a very small quantity at a time.) Put the chopped meat in a 3- to 4-quart bowl and add herbs and seasoning.

Soak bread for 5 minutes in cold water; squeeze out moisture and crumble into chopped meat. Add eggs and blend well using fingers or pastry blender.

Heat butter in a 12-inch frying pan over medium to high heat. Add chopped pork mixture and toss until meat loses its raw appearance (about 5 minutes). Cover pan and cook over medium heat for 30 minutes. Check every 10 minutes to make sure meat is not sticking to pan.

*This recipe can also be made using 4 pounds sweet Italian sausage instead of the pork. If you make it with sausage, however, you should eliminate the coriander, sage, pepper, and salt, and reduce the garlic to 4 teaspoons.

Using a slotted spoon to drain off any fat, transfer meat to mixing bowl. Blend in shallots, garlic, and parsley. Add Cognac a little at a time.

Cool stuffing completely before inserting into bird. It may be made several days in advance and refrigerated.

Farce au Riz, Champignons, et Poivrons Verts

RICE, MUSHROOM, AND GREEN PEPPER STUFFING

INGREDIENTS

8 *tablespoons clarified butter*
2/3 *cup chopped white onion*
4 *cups long-grained rice*
4 *tablespoons unsalted butter (at room temperature)*
8 *cups hot chicken bouillon**
bouquet garni (10 *sprigs parsley tied with 4 bay leaves)*-
2 *to* 2 1/2 *teaspoons table salt*
4 *additional tablespoons unsalted butter (at room temperature)*

2 *pounds fresh mushrooms***
3 *pounds sweet green peppers*
1 *cup clarified butter*
table salt
1/4 *cup chopped fresh parsley*

METHOD

Heat clarified butter in a 4-quart pot; toss in chopped onion and sauté until glossy. Pour in rice and toss until glossy.

Add the additional butter, hot bouillon, and *bouquet garni.* Cover and bring to boiling point over medium heat. Cook 20 minutes, boiling gently. Liquid should be absorbed in this time.

Remove *bouquet garni.* Stir in salt. Add remaining butter and set rice aside until other ingredients are ready.

Remove tips from mushrooms; wipe with damp sponge; chop coarsely.

Wash green peppers under cold running water; cut in half lengthwise; remove seeds; slice into thin strips.

*Use homemade stock (page 19) or 8 chicken cubes simmered 5 minutes in 8 cups cold water. If you use chicken cubes, taste before salting.
**Set aside 13 of the largest and firmest for garnishing.

Heat butter in 12-inch frying pan over high heat for about a minute; toss in mushrooms and sauté 1 minute. Remove with slotted spoon into a mixing bowl; stir in chopped parsley.

Toss pepper strips into the hot pan and sauté until coated with juices (about 1 minute). Remove from heat and sprinkle with salt.

Combine mushrooms and peppers with the cooked rice. It may be made several days in advance and refrigerated. Be certain stuffing is completely cooled before inserting into bird.

FOIE DE DINDE HACHÉ (Turkey Liver Spread): This recipe is a good way to make use of the turkey liver and excess fat from the turkey cavities. It makes a nice appetizer or hors-d'oeuvre; save it for New Year's Day or for a special treat later. With 1 egg it yields 1/2 cup, enough for 2 persons as an appetizer. With 2 eggs it will provide enough to spread on 16 crackers.

INGREDIENTS

liver from 10- *to* 12-*pound turkey*
1 *or* 2 *hard-boiled eggs*
fat removed from turkey cavities
1/2 *cup coarsely chopped yellow onion*
1/8 *teaspoon salt*
1 *turn black pepper mill, medium grind*

METHOD

Remove any green parts and connective tissue from liver.

Place eggs in an enamel or glass 1-quart saucepan; cover with cold water. Bring to rolling boil, uncovered, over medium to high heat. Reduce heat so that water boils gently and time for 12 minutes. Pour off boiling water and run cold water over eggs at once. Shell, then chop finely.

Melt turkey fat in a 6-inch frying pan over medium heat. (This will take about 15 minutes.) When fat has melted, raise heat to high, add onion, and toss until glossy. Put in liver and sauté until well seared on each side (about 5 minutes).

With a slotted spoon, remove onion and liver onto chopping board. Reserve melted fat. Using a paring knife, chop liver as finely or as coarsely as you like. Sprinkle with salt and pepper.

Place in serving dish or mixing bowl and stir in the melted fat remaining in pan. Spread can be eaten at once. It can also be refrigerated. It will keep several days.

TO SERVE: As an appetizer, present the *Foie de Dinde Haché* in individual portions on lettuce leaves. It can also be served as an hors-d'oeuvre spread on plain crackers, garnished with a bit of parsley.

Chou Rouge à la Flamande

BRAISED RED CABBAGE WITH APPLES
AND CURRANT JELLY

Red cabbage prepared in this way makes a wonderful accompaniment for roasted poultry of any kind. The following recipe will serve 10 to 12.

INGREDIENTS

5 *pound head of red cabbage*
3 *quarts cold water*
3 *tablespoons coarse salt or* 1 1/2 *tablespoons table salt*

5 *heaping tablespoons vegetable shortening*
3 *to* 4 *teaspoons table salt*
7 *tablespoons white vinegar*
2 1/2 *to* 3 *pounds apples (Cortland or Baldwin)*
1 *12-ounce jar currant or cherry jelly*

METHOD

Remove base and outer leaves from cabbage; quarter; remove core. Wash under cold running water.

In the meantime, bring salted water to a rolling boil in a covered pot. If you do not have a kettle large enough to cook cabbage all at once, drop in half at a time. Wait until water again reaches a rolling boil and boil, uncovered, for 15 minutes. Transfer cooked cabbage to a colander (use slotted spoon or tongs if water is to be reused for other half of cabbage) and pass under cold running water. This stops the cooking action.

Squeeze moisture from a handful of cabbage, place on cutting board, and shred with a large knife. Repeat until all cabbage is shredded.

Dry the pot used for boiling with a paper towel; melt shortening in it over high heat. When it begins to smoke, sauté cabbage, tossing constantly with wooden spoon, for about 5 minutes.

Sprinkle cabbage with salt. Stir in the vinegar, 1 tablespoon at a time. The vinegar will restore the beautiful purple color to the cabbage as well as giving it a tart taste. Reduce heat, cover, and simmer for 60 minutes, tossing from time to time.

While the cabbage is cooking, peel, core, and quarter the apples. When the cabbage has cooked for 30 minutes add the apples and continue cooking.

Fifteen minutes after apples have been added, mix in the jelly. Cook the mixture 15 minutes longer. Taste, and if necessary, add another 1/4 teaspoon of salt.

TO SERVE: I like to present this colorful vegetable in a pure white dish. For an informal meal, the cabbage may be eaten with the meat course. If you are dining formally, as for *le réveillon,* you should enjoy it after the roast.

Salade d'Épinards

SPINACH SALAD WITH A MUSTARD-GARLIC DRESSING

This particular dressing seems to bring out the special qualities of spinach. Because it may be tossed in advance and retain its crispness, *Salade d'Épinards* is an excellent choice for large gatherings.

The spinach may be prepared 2 or 3 days in advance and refrigerated; dressing should be assembled as near to serving time as is convenient. The recipe will serve 12.

INGREDIENTS

3 *pounds fresh spinach*
3 *teaspoons chopped garlic*
18 *turns of black pepper mill, medium grind (a scant 1/2
   teaspoon)*
2 1/4 *teaspoons table salt*
6 *teaspoons Dijon mustard*
3/4 *cup red wine vinegar*
1 1/2 *cups salad oil*

METHOD

Snip off most of stems of spinach; wash in a large pan, changing water several times. Drain in a colander or salad basket. Dry between paper or linen towels. When thoroughly dry, break into bite-sized pieces with your fingers. Spinach may be wrapped and stored in refrigerator until ready to serve.

In a salad bowl of at least 5-quart capacity, mix the garlic, pepper, salt, mustard, and vinegar in the order listed. Mix well, then whisk in oil. If your bowl is too small to contain all the greens, divide the ingredients between two bowls.

When ready to serve, add spinach to bowl; toss well.

TO SERVE: Pass the bowl of salad around after the vegetable course. Provide each person with a small salad plate.

Bûche aux Marrons

PURÉED CHESTNUT LOG FLAVORED
WITH SEMI-SWEET CHOCOLATE AND RUM

Bûche aux Marrons or *Bûche de Noël* (Christmas Log) is a fascinating confection traditionally served in France during the winter holidays. It is a perfectly appropriate dessert for any of the winter months when chestnuts are in season. When I prepare it, I always remember the chestnut vendors, *les marchands de marrons*, of Paris. Wherever they set up shop, in front of a *bureau de tabac* (a tobacco shop) or a café, they were the attraction of the neighborhood. What a pleasure it was to be warmed by their hot braziers and to inhale that special charred fragrance while waiting for a little bag of hot roasted chestnuts.

Prepare *Bûche aux Marrons* at least a day ahead and refrigerate it to set the shape. If properly chilled and covered, it will keep several days; it freezes well, too.

PREPARING THE CHESTNUTS

INGREDIENTS

3 *pounds raw chestnuts or* 1 *pound shelled, dried chestnuts**

USEFUL UTENSIL: *Food mill*

*Only 2 pounds are used in the recipe, but always buy extra, as it is impossible to tell before peeling whether chestnuts are good or not. Buy 2 pounds, then buy 1 more pound, separately. Keep them apart during roasting and replace any discarded from the 2 pounds, one for one. This will yield 4 cups puréed. One pound of dried chestnuts will yield a little more than the 4 cups needed.

METHOD

Preheat oven to 500° F.

With the point of a small knife, slit outer covering of each chestnut. This is important, for if there is no way for the steam to escape, the chestnuts will burst all over the oven!

Scatter the 2 pounds of chestnuts on a cookie sheet and roast for 15 minutes. Then roast the 1 pound. Peel the first batch while the second is roasting. It is easier to peel them when hot, but harder on the fingers. Use a potholder. The inner membrane should come off with the shell. Some will be stubborn, but don't worry; these will come off easily after boiling.

Discard any imperfect nuts (those that are wizened or have mold or black spots on them). A healthy chestnut is plump and shiny; its outer shell comes off easily after roasting.

Cover peeled chestnuts with warm water in a 4-quart pot. Bring to boiling point, with cover on, and simmer gently for 30 to 45 minutes. Test after 30 minutes; when chestnuts are very soft, they are done. (Dried chestnuts will take from 1 1/2 to 2 hours to cook and will absorb quite a bit of water. Check from time to time and add more hot water as needed. Cook until soft.)

Drain water from chestnuts and purée, using food mill with largest holes or a strainer. (A food processor will not give the right texture.)

MIXING AND SHAPING THE BÛCHE

INGREDIENTS

1/2 *cup sugar*
2/3 *to* 1 *cup semi-sweet chocolate bits**
2 *cups boiling water*
1/4 *pound whipped sweet butter (at room temperature)*
1 *to* 2 *tablespoons rum (optional)*
salad oil (any except olive oil)

METHOD

Measure 4 cups puréed chestnuts, tightly packed, into a 4-quart mixing bowl. Stir in sugar.

In a separate bowl, melt chocolate bits by pouring water over them. When color turns lighter, pour off water and stir chocolate vigorously with a rubber spatula. Add butter in small chunks and stir. If using rum, add it next, 1 tablespoon at a time, and mix very quickly.

Combine chestnut and chocolate mixtures and blend well. If rum has been used, refrigerate for an hour, until batter stiffens a little.

Place a piece of freezer wrap (about 18 × 24 inches) shiny

*A full cup gives a stronger chocolate flavor.

side up on your working surface.* Grease surface with salad oil, using your fingers to spread it evenly.

Pour batter onto greased surface; bring paper up around sides and roll purée back and forth until it has a cylindrical shape. Push ends inward from time to time, as they tend to become too thin. Continue rolling and shaping *Bûche* with your hands until it looks like a log about 12 inches long and 2 1/2 inches thick.

Cover well with the freezer paper, place on cookie sheet, and refrigerate overnight.

FINISHING AND DECORATING

INGREDIENTS

6 *walnut halves*
crystallized mint leaves (optional)
1/2 *pint heavy cream (optional)*
confectioners' sugar

METHOD

If log has cracked, don't panic; mold it together again with your hand. Slice a thin piece off each end at a slant so that it looks like a sawed log. With a fork, ruffle surface so that it looks like bark. Transfer to serving platter and garnish with walnut meats. Let your imagination play, but don't overdo it. Finish with a few crystallized mint leaves.

Or, if you prefer, use slightly sweetened, stiffly whipped cream to decorate log before garnishing it with walnuts and mint.

TO SERVE: Just before serving, if you have not covered the *Bûche* with whipped cream, sprinkle with confectioners' sugar to simulate snow. (If this is done ahead of time, sugar dissolves.) Cut 1/2-inch slices on a slant; serve with a fork. A dash of slightly sweetened whipped cream may be served with each slice.

Savor with a glass of Champagne or Muscat d'Alsace. You will be asked for just one more sliver of *Bûche,* then another, and another. . . .

*Since freezer wrap has more body, it works better for this recipe than waxed paper or tin foil.

Un Cinq à Sept
A COCKTAIL PARTY

A Choice of Apéritifs

and a

Selection of Fine Hors-d'Oeuvre

To Be Served

from 5 to 7 P.M.

A GATHERING of friends for *apéritifs* may be as formal or as informal as one wants to make it. A Frenchman will often invite a few friends home after work, but seldom is the accompaniment more elaborate than some dried, unsalted nuts, olives, and, perhaps, a selection of cheeses. However, occasionally *une petite réception de 5 à 7* (from 5 to 7 P.M.) may be organized. Any of the dishes presented in this section are suitable for such a celebration. Pick and choose—do as many or as few as you like. The recipes also make appropriate appetizers to serve with the menus included in this book.

The Apéritifs

Here are some suggestions for apéritifs we enjoy serving to our guests.

If the occasion is to precede a very special dinner, I like to serve Champagne. This elegant *apéritif* may also accompany the meal from beginning to end. Choose a Brut (extra dry) for most occasions.

Another wine which may be served with any meal from beginning to end and which also makes a refreshing *apéritif* is Asti Spumante, a sparkling Italian wine made of grapes grown around the town of Asti. It is usually as sweet as a Demi-Sec Champagne, and is a great favorite with those who prefer a sweeter wine. One company makes a dry Asti, which may suit your palate better. Consult your wine merchant.

The *apéritif* specialties of our house, the drinks we most often serve when guests leave the choice to us, are: Pernod, le Kir, sweet or dry Vermouth on the rocks with a twist of lemon, or a Vermouth Cassis.

PERNOD: Anise liquors are sold in the United States under the names Pernod and Anisette.* Those who like the licorice flavor of anise can serve a Pernod in the traditional way: Have ice, small pitchers of ice water, sugar cubes, and spoons available. Measure an ounce of Pernod into a tumbler-style glass. Then let each guest complete the preparation as follows: Hold the sugar cube in a spoon over the mouth of the glass; slowly pour 1 cup of ice water over

*Anisette is sweeter than Pernod, and is served as an after-dinner drink.

it, drop by drop, until cube has dissolved. This takes from 5 to 7 minutes, but it is a pleasant, relaxing pastime which raises anticipation. When the sugar has dissolved, stir drink gently; add ice.

Pernod turns cloudy when water is added. This is because the essences of which it is made are soluble only in strong alcohol; when the water dilutes the alcohol, the essences are precipitated out.

Pernod makes a particularly refreshing drink in the summertime.

LE KIR: Le Kir—a mixture of Cassis, a black currant liqueur, and cold white wine—is another popular French *apéritif*. It is named for a rotund, witty little canon from Dijon, Félix Kir, who won fame during World War II for his brash resistance. After the war, at the age of 70, he was elected mayor of Dijon by his grateful townspeople, who also sent him repeatedly to the National Assembly as their representative. He remained in public life for 22 more years. When the post-war diplomats proved unsuccessful in securing international peace, M. Kir became convinced that peace must come from the bottom up. He became, in his own words, "a traveling salesman of peace." To further this goal he visited Dallas, Texas, in 1957; one souvenir of his trip was a ten-gallon hat which he often wore on the streets of Dijon.

A popular, though controversial figure, Canon Kir loved the province of Burgundy with a passion. In christening le Kir, he was promoting two great Burgundian products. The black currant plants from which Cassis is made are planted among the grape vines and are nourished by the same soil that produces the famous Burgundy wines. The wine originally used in le Kir is Bourgogne-Aligoté, a fruity white regional wine. It is the only wine in Burgundy named after the grape rather than the vineyard in which it is grown.

To prepare le Kir, in a stemmed, crystal water glass or a 6- to 8-ounce tulip-shaped wineglass, measure 2 tablespoons Crème de Cassis and 1/2 cup of chilled dry white Burgundy wine. Stir.

VERMOUTH ON THE ROCKS: Measure about 2 ounces of sweet or dry Vermouth over ice cubes in a short squat glass. Squeeze in a drop of fresh lemon juice; garnish with lemon peel. Stir. For a thirst-quenching variation for hot summer days, serve in a tall glass and add club soda.

VERMOUTH CASSIS: Into a stemmed, crystal water glass or a 6- to 8-ounce tulip-shaped wineglass, measure 1 tablespoon Crème de Cassis, 5 tablespoons sweet Vermouth, 1/4 cup club soda. Add one ice cube; stir.

Sherry from Spain and white or tawny port from Portugal also make excellent apéritifs. If your guests enjoy a sweet wine, you might offer Malaga, a rather sweet red wine from southern Spain, or Banyuls, a naturally sweet French wine made from grapes grown on steep terraces on the jut of land that meets the sea at the southern tip of the Pyrénées.

Les Hors-d'Oeuvre

Hors-d'oeuvre should be light and small to leave room for what is to follow. They are designed to whet the appetite, not satiate it. They are appropriate to serve either at cocktail parties or as appetizers. With these recipes, the host or hostess is free to enjoy the party once guests arrive. All can be prepared well in advance, and last-minute touches can be made just before the first guest rings the doorbell.

Here is a selection of some of the hors-d'oeuvre I like to serve with *apéritifs*. Choose and mix as you desire: make one, several, or all, depending upon the occasion. Generally, 5 to 6 hors-d'oeuvre per person is adequate, but this amount may be adjusted according to the appetites of your guests.

Champignons Farcis

STUFFED MUSHROOMS WITH GARLIC AND PARSLEY

These fresh mushrooms, filled, then covered with snail butter, are guaranteed to open the appetite.

The recipe will provide 20 to 24 hors-d'oeuvre.

INGREDIENTS

1 *pound fresh white mushrooms**
1 *slice white bread with crust removed*
1/4 *cup milk or water*
2 *tablespoons oil*
5 *parsley sprigs, chopped finely*
1/4 *teaspoon salt*

2 *tablespoons unsalted butter, at room temperature*
16 *parsley sprigs, chopped finely*
2 *medium-sized garlic cloves, finely chopped*
1/4 *(scant) teaspoon salt*

fresh parsley sprigs

METHOD

Wipe mushrooms with damp sponge. Cut just enough off end of stem to produce a fresh surface. Separate stems and caps: Holding cap in left hand, with thumb and forefinger of right hand carefully break stem just under cap.

Slice stems, then finely chop, either in chopping bowl or with a sharp knife on a wooden board.

Soak bread in liquid, then squeeze out all moisture. Crumble bread over chopped mushroom stems; mix well together.

Using an 8-inch skillet, place oil over high heat until it sings when a small amount of mixture is dropped into it. Sauté the bread and stem mixture for 1 minute, shaking pan continuously. Add parsley and salt; mix well.

This mixture should be as dry as possible. If any juice has been rendered, press it out with a slotted spoon through a strainer or cheesecloth. Allow to cool.

Now prepare *Beurre Escargot,* a butter mixture similar to that used in preparing snails: Place softened butter in a small bowl. Add chopped parsley, garlic, and salt; work into a paste with a fork.

TO ASSEMBLE: Fill mushrooms with cooled stuffing. Top with a dot of snail butter and spread it over entire surface like an icing.

At this point, mushrooms may be stored in the refrigerator. Place caps, filling up, on a bed of paper towels to absorb any moisture, insert toothpicks in center of each to prevent sticking, and cover with storage wrap. They will keep 2 to 3 days.

---

*Choose them white and firm and of medium size if possible. There will usually be 20 to 24 mushrooms per pound.

Preheat oven to 450° F. Just before you are ready to serve, bake stuffed caps on an ungreased cookie sheet for 5 minutes.

TO SERVE: Cover serving plate with a doily and decorate with fresh parsley sprigs. As an hors-d'oeuvre, *Champignons Farcis* are handled with the fingers.

When served as an appetizer, this amount will serve 5 to 6 persons. Then they are eaten from a small plate with a salad fork.

Canapés la Bécasse Écossaise

SCRAMBLED EGG CANAPÉS WITH ANCHOVIES AND CAPERS

When I catered for cocktail parties, this was one of my most popular canapés. It consists of fluffy light scrambled eggs on crisp toast, topped with anchovies, capers, and grated Swiss cheese, and served sizzling hot from the oven. It also makes a lovely light meal served on whole bread slices.*

Toast and egg may be assembled 2 to 3 days in advance, tightly wrapped, and refrigerated. Some of my students have even frozen them with satisfactory results. Add anchovies, capers, and cheese just before heating. (If anchovies are removed from can much ahead of time, they become too salty.)

The recipe will provide 2 dozen canapés.

INGREDIENTS

1 *loaf sliced, white, firm-textured sandwich bread*
1/4 *pound whipped sweet butter, at room temperature*
7 *jumbo eggs*
4 *tablespoons clarified butter*
4 *tablespoons whipped sweet butter, at room temperature*
6 *tablespoons grated Swiss cheese*
1 *or 2 cans flat fillets of anchovies***
1 *bottle capers in vinegar*
1 *to 1 1/2 cups grated Swiss cheese*

*The amount of eggs given here is sufficient for 10 to 12 whole slices of bread.

**Depending upon the brand of anchovies, one can may not be enough.

METHOD

FOR TOAST: Toast may be prepared in advance and stored in a tight tin.

Preheat oven to 450° F. Remove crust from bread; cut slices in half. Spread softened butter evenly on one side of each slice. Roast in preheated oven, buttered side up, for 3 minutes; turn and roast about a minute longer, watching carefully to be sure toast does not burn. It should be a nice golden brown.

TO SCRAMBLE EGGS: Break eggs into a 4-cup bowl. (Since there are so many, play it safe; break them into a separate dish first in case one should be spoiled.) Stir with a fork so that yolks and whites are lightly mixed. Heat clarified butter in a 10-inch frying pan over medium heat. When butter starts to sing and takes on a nutty aroma, add beaten eggs all at once, stirring continuously with a rubber spatula. Good scrambled eggs should be what the French call "raw" (very soft and smooth), so remove pan from heat while eggs are still runny. Continue to stir; eggs will set from the heat remaining in pan. Immediately stir in whipped butter, a little at a time; then fold in cheese.

If canapés are being made in advance, allow eggs to cool completely before spreading on toast.

TO ASSEMBLE: Spread egg mixture evenly on unbuttered side of toast slices.

At this point, canapés may be stored in refrigerator or freezer, wrapped tightly in storage wrap.

Drain anchovy fillets. Cut each fillet in half lengthwise and cross two halves over top of egg. Place a caper in the angles formed by the anchovies. Sprinkle each canapé generously with grated cheese.

TO BAKE: Just before serving, preheat oven to 450° F. Place canapés on a cookie sheet and bake 3 to 5 minutes, until cheese has melted. (If baked directly from freezer, baking time is about 6 minutes.)

TO SERVE: This canapé is best when still hot from the oven, so place on a garnished platter and pass immediately, or place on an electrically heated serving tray.

Délicieuses au Fromage

DEEP-FRIED SWISS CHEESE PUFFS

These little balls made of beaten egg white and grated Swiss cheese, rolled in bread crumbs and deep fried, are easy to make. They can be prepared several hours ahead and refrigerated. The final frying takes just 5 minutes.

This recipe makes 12 *Délicieuses* the size of Ping-Pong balls. For more, you may double the ingredients, using the same amount of oil for frying.

INGREDIENTS

3 *cups salad oil*
2 *egg whites*
1/8 *teaspoon freshly ground white pepper*
1 *cup grated Swiss cheese (about 4 ounces)*
1/4 *cup bread crumbs*

parsley sprigs, fresh or deep-fried*

USEFUL UTENSIL: *Frying vessel*

METHOD

Heat oil for 10 minutes over medium heat in a frying vessel of 3- to 6-quart capacity. A frying thermometer should register 360° F. to 380° F.

In a 1-quart mixing bowl, beat egg whites at high speed of electric mixer for 2 minutes, scraping sides of bowl with rubber spatula.

Gently fold in pepper and grated cheese a third at a time with rubber spatula.

Shape mixture in small balls; roll in bread crumbs.

If *Délicieuses* are being made much in advance, cover with storage wrap and refrigerate.

*FOR DEEP-FRIED PARSLEY: Drop absolutely dry fresh parsley sprigs into the hot oil. Take them out almost immediately with a slotted spoon and shake to remove excess oil. (They will become a brighter green.)

Oil may be cooled, strained, and stored in a cool place for future use. (Do not refrigerate.)

When oil is hot, drop balls in carefully so as not to spatter fat. All 12 balls may be fried at once, as long as they have room to swim and twirl. They will be done after 5 minutes of frying over medium heat. Most balls will turn by themselves; turn others if necessary. They should be nicely browned all around.

Lift from vessel with slotted spoon, shaking over pan to remove excess oil. Once fried, these balls cannot remain long in a warming oven as they will dry out.

TO SERVE: Place in heated serving dish on a clean linen napkin to absorb any oil.*

Arrange parsley sprigs (fresh or deep-fried) around serving dish. Fried parsley is usually eaten with the hors-d'oeuvre. Serve at once.

Petites Brioches Fourrées au Crabe

BRIOCHES STUFFED WITH CRAB

Miniature *Brioches* are made with traditional *brioche* dough which is shaped into 2 1/2 × 3/4-inch *petits-fours* molds instead of the traditional 3 × 1 1/8-inch molds. They are stuffed with crabmeat and homemade mayonnaise. The following recipe will make 32 of these miniature *Brioches,* or a dozen traditional breakfast buns. Any leftover dough can be made into breakfast rolls; bake and freeze, if desired.

Brioches Fourrées are equally good for afternoon tea.

THE LEVAIN (SPONGE)

INGREDIENTS

1/3 *cup all-purpose flour*
1 *yeast cake*
3 *tablespoons tepid water*
3 *cups tepid water*

METHOD

This traditional *brioche* dough should rise three times, so organize its preparation to fit your schedule. A convenient system is

Directions for folding the napkin are given on page 122.

to start dough about 6 P.M. The first rising is completed by 9 P.M., and the second rising can take place in the refrigerator overnight. Next day the dough is ready to put into molds to rise for the third time before baking.

Measure flour into a small mixing bowl. Crumble in yeast; sprinkle in the tepid water. Rapidly blend all ingredients with fingertips to form a soft ball. (Three tablespoons of water should make it just right, but if sponge is too sticky, add a little more flour; if too dry, sprinkle with a few more drops of water.)

With a small knife cut a cross into top of sponge ball; this helps it to expand when rising.

Measure 3 cups of tepid water into a 4-cup pan and drop sponge in, cross side up. Place in a warm oven to rise 15 to 20 minutes. When ready, sponge will float. It will look very light and be full of bubbles. Lift from water with slotted spoon onto paper toweling; pat to remove excess moisture.

THE DOUGH

INGREDIENTS

2 *cups all-purpose flour*
1 1/2 *teaspoons table salt*
4 *jumbo or extra large eggs**
10 *tablespoons whipped sweet butter***
4 *tablespoons melted butter*

METHOD

Heat a 2-quart mixing bowl by rinsing it in hot water. Wipe dry.

Measure flour into heated bowl. Make well in center of flour. Add salt, *levain,* and eggs. Mix together well with hands. (This is a little messy, but it is the only way to get a good *brioche* dough unless you have a dough hook on your electric mixer.)

Work dough vigorously, slapping and pulling it 200 times, until it is very elastic.

Measure butter into a small bowl and work with fingers to make it pliable. Take a handful of the dough and work it into the

*Take from refrigerator 2 hours before using.
**Take from refrigerator 1/2 hour before using.

butter for about 1/2 second. Transfer this mixture back to the large bowl of dough and work together, slapping and pulling, for 2 more minutes.

Scrape dough from sides of bowl; wipe inside rim of bowl with damp paper towel to clean; cover bowl with clean linen towel and let rise in warm oven for 3 hours. (If you have a gas stove with a pilot light, place bowl near pilot and dough will rise perfectly. Or you can place dough in a cold oven on shelf above a large pan of hot water. Close door; turn on heat at 400° F. for exactly 60 seconds. Turn off heat and dough will rise perfectly.)

After 3 hours, remove dough from oven and deflate by folding it over several times. Cover again with towel and place in refrigerator to rise for a second time, overnight.

Molds may be buttered well in advance. Coat them with melted butter while dough is rising.

Next day, take dough from refrigerator and deflate again by folding it over; dust hands and dough slightly with flour if necessary.

Transfer dough to lightly floured working surface; shape it into a ball; cut ball in half. Work with one half of the dough at a time. Roll out one half into a cylinder about 23 inches long and 1 1/4 inches in diameter. This will be enough to fill 16 *petits-fours* molds. Slice off 16 1-inch pieces of dough. Roll each of these into a ball and place in molds. They should fill the molds about 2/3 full. Cut the rest of the cylinder in half lengthwise and slice each half into 8 pieces. Roll these small pieces into cone shapes.

Make an indentation in the top of each dough ball and insert the narrower end of a cone into the hole, being sure cone sticks well up so that it will not be swallowed by rising dough. Set filled molds aside to rise while repeating procedure with other half of dough.

When all molds are filled, place on cookie sheet and set in a warm oven again to rise 15 to 20 minutes, uncovered.

THE DORURE (GLAZE)

INGREDIENTS

1 *egg yolk*
1 *teaspoon cold water*
1/8 *teaspoon table salt*

METHOD

Combine egg yolk, water, and salt and blend with a fork. Using a goose-feather pastry brush, coat top of *Brioches* with *dorure.*

With a pair of kitchen shears, cut three or four slashes across each *brioche* head near the cone so that the cone can expand while baking.

Preheat oven to 425° F. and bake on middle rack for 12 minutes.

Brioches may be frozen after they are baked and completely cooled. They will take 2 hours to defrost at room temperature.

THE FILLING

INGREDIENTS

1 1/2 *cups crabmeat (about* 12 *ounces)*
1/2 *cup homemade mayonnaise**
paprika

fresh parsley sprigs

METHOD

Drain off all liquid from canned or thawed crabmeat. Shred meat and remove any cartilage.

Mix crabmeat with mayonnaise. Slice off top third of *Brioches.* Cut a small hole in center of each bottom section; spoon in crab, sprinkle with paprika, and replace top.

TO SERVE: Place in paper *petits-fours* cups.

Arrange attractively on doily-covered tray; decorate with parsley sprigs.

Rillettes

PORK SPREAD WITH GARLIC AND ONION

What Frenchman is not familiar with this most universal of delicatessen products? Every province, township, and village in France has its own variety of *Rillettes,* a meat pâté used either as

*Directions for making homemade mayonnaise are on page 235.

an appetizer or as an hors-d'oeuvre. *Rillettes* from *les charcuteries* of Normandy are of rabbit meat; from Angers, of goose. But the most acclaimed *Rillettes* come from Le Mans and Tours, cities in the valley of the Loire. They are made from a combination of pork and goose meat and just plain pork, respectively.

My *Rillettes* is an adaptation of a recipe given me by an old friend, whose family for generations had lived in the Province of des Deux-Sèvres, just south of the Loire. It is made from pork, which is always available. We like it because it is not as greasy as most *Rillettes*. It has a rather coarse, stringy texture, not smooth like a liver pâté. Although some fat will be apparent as it cools, do not remove it, for this would change the personality of this provincial delicacy.

Rillettes will keep well for several weeks refrigerated; it may also be frozen if you wish. It makes a distinguished hors-d'oeuvre to have on hand for large or small gatherings.

The recipe that follows will make 3 to 3 1/2 cups of *Rillettes*, enough to serve 30 as an hors-d'oeuvre.

INGREDIENTS

2 1/2 *to 3-pound pork butt with bone*
3 1/2 *cups cold water*
1 *teaspoon table salt*
10 *turns of black pepper mill, medium grind (a scant 1/4
    teaspoon)*
1/2 *teaspoon dried thyme*
1 *large garlic clove, peeled*
1 *large bay leaf*
1 *whole small yellow onion (about 1/4 pound), peeled*

METHOD

The butt is that part of the pork shoulder nearest the neck. It may be sold already deboned. In that case, ask the butcher for the bone, as it adds extra flavor to the *Rillettes*. Since meat is always a little more expensive when purchased with the bone removed, you may want to remove it yourself. This process can be done at home easily; all that is required is a little patience and a good sharp knife.

TO DEBONE: Cut through meat to the bone all along length. Slowly, inch by inch, sever meat from bone with a scraping motion of the knife, pulling the meat away with the other hand. That's all there is to it.

Next, cut meat into thin 2 × 1/2-inch strips, or into 2-inch cubes. Combine all ingredients, including bone, in a 4- to 6-quart pot (a Dutch oven is good). Set lid ajar, and simmer 5 hours. (In 3 hours the meat is edible, but the additional hours of simmering will heighten the flavor of the seasonings.) Liquid should be nearly evaporated when done. Check from time to time to be sure that the mixture is boiling gently and stir with a wooden spoon. Meat should not stick to pan bottom.

Remove bay leaf and bone; then mash meat with wooden spoon. (*Do not* use a blender, grinder, or food processor, as these implements destroy the desired texture.) When cool, store in glazed earthenware, stoneware, or glass containers. If there is any liquid left, pour over packed *Rillettes.*

TO SERVE: Remove *Rillettes* from refrigerator at least 1 hour before serving so that it will be easy to spread.

For an hors-d'oeuvre, spread *Rillettes* on crackers or small rounds of rye bread. It makes a delicious appetizer accompanied by crusty French bread.

Jeu D'Échecs

TINY SANDWICHES WITH EDIBLE CHESS FIGURES

Here is a whimsical presentation of hors-d'oeuvre, a chess board made of 64 small sandwich squares topped with edible chess men. It will delight guests, but beware: If there are youngsters in the group, the chessmen will disappear quickly.

You may be surprised to find that the *Jeu D'Échecs* can be made up in less than an hour, something which cannot be said about many a simple-looking hors-d'oeuvre.

Use it as an amusing centerpiece, and have extra sandwiches ready as replacements.

For your sandwiches, use your favorite fillings or pick from the following suggestions: pickled tongue, cream cheese topped with thin slices of smoked salmon, *pâté de foie gras,* a spread of sardines and sweet butter, black caviar (if you feel like splurging), crabmeat with homemade mayonnaise, imported Swiss cheese, thin slices of cucumber, egg salad, *Rillettes.* The larger the variety of fillings, the more delights the chess board holds.

INGREDIENTS

1 *loaf dark bread, preferably a square loaf of Westphalian pumpernickel bread*
1 *loaf white, firm-textured sandwich bread (thin sliced)*
2 *lemons*
3 *hard-boiled pullet eggs*
1 *medium carrot, cut into 10 round slices about 1/4 inch thick*
2 *regular frankforts or 1 small jar of cocktail frankforts*
1 *small can of black olives*
1 *small jar of green olives*
1/4 *pound smoked Nova Scotia salmon**
4 *whole cooked jumbo shrimp in their shells, or 1 can artichoke hearts*
1 *small jar capers*
1 *small jar cocktail onions*
1 *small jar marinated whole button mushrooms*
1 *small jar French or American gherkin pickles*
toothpicks

METHOD

You will need a flat surface about 14 × 20 inches on which to lay out the sandwiches. If you do not have a bread board large enough, cut a piece of cardboard to size, wrap it in aluminum foil, and cover with a doily.

Cut crusts from bread, then quarter each slice to make at least 64 squares from each loaf. This will make 32 dark and 32 light sandwiches.

Spread with a variety of fillings of your choice.

Arrange filled sandwiches on prepared board, alternating dark and light squares as on a chess board. Cover with a clean damp linen towel to keep moist.

TO MAKE CHESSMEN: Secure all portions of each figure with toothpicks or pieces of toothpicks; then secure each figure upright with as many toothpicks as needed on top of the appropriate square. Chessmen should be placed along one end of row of squares in the following order: castles or rooks on the 2 end squares, the knights on the second squares in from either end, bishops on the third squares in, the king and queen on the middle squares. Place pawns across second row. Secure second set of figures on opposite side of the board.

*Ask your grocer for large whole slices.

1) Queen: Parts needed are large carrot round, 1 small carrot round, 1/4 lemon wedge, 1 round lemon slice, 1 piece of salmon, a piece of gherkin, and an onion. Cut 1 lemon in half lengthwise, then quarter one half, lengthwise. Secure lemon wedge to large carrot round for a base; drape salmon over cut side of lemon for a cape; secure round lemon slice for a collar, gherkin for a head, small carrot round for hat rim, and top with onion. (Make 2.)

2) King: Use large carrot round for base, hard-boiled egg for body, a slice of salmon for his cape, a black olive for his head, and the round end of the third hard-boiled egg white for a hat. Place 2 or 3 capers for buttons on front of body. (Make 2.)

3) The Bishops: Use a large carrot round for a base, a whole gherkin for the body, an onion for the head. (Make 4.)

4) The Knights: Simply secure the whole shrimp in its shell in an upright position on its appropriate square. Or, if you are using the artichoke hearts, secure 2 on a toothpick and top with a tiny shrimp. If you are using just the small shrimp, secure 3 or 4 on a toothpick. (Make 4.)

5) Castles or Rooks: Cut cooked frankforts in half or use whole cocktail frankforts. Top them with a mushroom. (Make 4.)

6) Pawns: Use 8 black olives on one side of the board and 8 green olives on the other side. If they tip, slice off a bit of the base.

Les Vins de France

ABOUT FRENCH WINES

"**A** MEAL without wine is like a day without sunshine." Most Frenchmen would agree with Brillat-Savarin on this point. For a French housewife to plan a meal without considering the wine to accompany it would be like forgetting sauce for the lamb or butter for the bread. Because wine is an integral part of French meals, I have included with each menu suggestions for the type of wine which will bring out the best in the various dishes.

These suggestions are my personal preferences and are given as a guide for those who are, as yet, unfamiliar with many wines. I hope the information provided will help pave the road which leads to one of life's major pleasures.

I don't claim encyclopedic knowledge of wines. There are many excellent treatises on the subject. Some are definitive studies by people who have spent a lifetime in the field, either as professionals or as devoted amateurs. Others are excellent introductions which will entertain as well as instruct. You may be interested in turning to them as your interest grows. But I can share with you the tradition and experience that stem from my French family background.

Many French youngsters are allowed watered wine every night at dinner. Before I was old enough to acquire any preference, I felt it a supreme privilege to be sent with the cellar key to fetch a bottle for my father. It was an adventure that took courage, descending the dimly lit stairs, and returning, cradling the precious bottle in my arms.

Like most Paris apartments, our flat came with its own small cellar and, like most Parisians who enjoyed wine, my father kept his *cave* as a wine cellar. Since there was no central heating, the temperature winter and summer remained about the same and, at least where we lived, there was little underground vibration from the traffic. My father always kept his *cave* well stocked.

Monsieur Henri, as my father was called affectionately by his friends, acquired a reputation as a *bon vivant* for his good table and his good cellar. The credit for his "*bonne table,*" of course, goes to my mother, who seldom knew what it was to cook for only her family of four. Ten was the usual minimum for lunch and dinner, for Monsieur Henri took his meals surrounded by a little court of friends, employees, and business associates. I have wondered often if being such a marvelous cook was an asset for my mother.

Twice a year our cellar was restocked, and Monsieur Henri presided over the affair with great solemnity. First, there would be a family conference, then a meeting with the *négociants en vins,* the wholesale merchants representing the various wine houses. The selections were intensely discussed. My father was particular about the *négociants* with whom he traded, for so much depended upon their expert advice. He never could be fooled twice.

Monsieur Henri took care with his purchases: an adequate supply of bottled wines, some of the better vintages for Sunday dinners and special occasions; some *apéritifs* to be enjoyed by our little group; a few *digestifs* (after-dinner brandies); and perhaps a few bottles of Champagne or another sparkling wine. But he took special pains with his largest purchase, a generous supply of the *petits vins du pays,* table wines which would be served with our meals day after day.

It was for these *vins du pays* that the *négociant's* honest advice was particularly important. Unavailable as such in the United States, *vin ordinaire* is usually a blend from the lesser vineyards of a wine district which is sold in bulk and costs less than bottled wine. In off years it can be a better buy than a "*château*" product. My father was a purist: He had to make sure he was buying an honest regional wine, unadulterated with a more prolific southern wine or one of the imports from Algeria or Spain with which so much of the *carafe* wine of France is stretched. Usually he chose well, and his *vins du pays* made excellent drinking.

The day the wine was delivered was a special one. It was exciting to watch the large cask of *vin ordinaire* being brought in on the stooped shoulders of the carrier, and to wait for the wine to rest until an appropriately clear dry day when a man would come to bottle it for us. From my perch on the cellar stairs I could see what was happening below and enjoy the lovely aroma the bottler released. Even for a child, a well-stocked cellar provided a sense of security and well-being.

During the winter months, Father made a special ritual of Sunday. It was our only family day, and he cultivated an atmosphere of deliberate leisure. Mother always prepared a dish of which he was particularly fond, and then, as a family or with one or two friends, we would spend the long afternoon savoring the food and one of the special bottles he would select from his cellar, a wine he thought would go especially well with what Mother was cooking.

If it was a white wine, he chilled it in ice for a half hour before it would be served. If it was a red wine, he carefully uncorked it about an hour before it would be poured, to allow it to breathe. It is this process of oxidation which releases the bouquet of a good red wine and brings out its full flavor.

These meals were an education, for like all true oenophiles, Monsieur Henri knew his wine lore. As we slowly sipped, he would point out the qualities of the wine he had chosen, analyzing its characteristics. Wine has its own vocabulary: tender, mellow, soft, light, delicate, vigorous, robust, full-bodied, masculine, young, fresh, balanced, elegant, breeding, bouquet. All are words which become meaningful when one compares one wine to another.

The first time my husband came home to meet my parents, Monsieur Henri must have known it was an important occasion in our lives, for he produced one of his special bottles. My husband recalls how fascinated he was by the way my father handled the bottle and by the reverent look on his face when he examined the label. He tells how, after pouring his own glass, my father sniffed it, held it to the light to admire its color, wet his lips, then took a small sip and rolled it around on his tongue before swallowing. His expression turned to one of delight. He filled our glasses and waited eagerly for our reactions. Then he tried to share with us all the things he tasted in the wine. He described the area from which it came, the soil upon which the grapes had been grown, the way in which the vines were pruned, and the variations in the way the vintners fermented and stored their product. He enjoyed recounting the legends and history connected with the region and the vineyard.

The wisdom of an oenophile is acquired throughout a lifetime of pleasurable experiences in educating the taste buds to detect, in a thimbleful of liquid gold or a drop of sparkling ruby, the intensity of sunlight or the character of soil. Monsieur Henri did not pretend to have attained such heights. He was, after all, a man of modest means, who worked hard six days a week, with little time for extended pleasures. But for us, he opened up a world which has enriched our lives ever since.

Just as one's pleasure measurably increases if one knows whether he is biting into a Winesap or a McIntosh, viewing a da Vinci or a Monet, listening to Debussy or Stravinsky, so one's appreciation of wines increases the more one knows about them.

About Wine Making

Three things, apart from the skill of the vintner, are important to the production of good wine: the grapes, the soil, and the climate.

Of the over two dozen species of grapes known throughout the world, only one, *Vitis vinifera*, a European native, is used to produce wine of quality. This is a different species than the table grape, which grows a larger, pulpier fruit. Wine grapes are juicier, more acid, and contain all the elements necessary to turn them naturally into a fermented drink. No additives are needed in any of the better wines.

Of this species, there are some 18 varieties which predominate in the major wine-producing areas of France. Their names have a ring familiar to every wine lover: *chardonnay, gamay, cabernet-sauvignon, pinot, merlot, muscadelle, gewürztraminer.* Through centuries of trial and error, growers have discovered which grape will produce best on which parcel of land. This has been determined with such precision that in France it is now decreed which grape may be grown in which vineyard. There are restrictions, too, on the way in which vines can be trimmed, and how many grapes can be produced in a particular vineyard to keep up its standard of quality. Vineyards are usually capable of producing far more than is allowed, but it is quality, not quantity, which dictates the standards.

Soil is the next major consideration. The same grape grown in different soil produces an entirely different product. The soils upon which the wine grape flourishes are usually considered poor for other crops. Although vines will yield prolifically on fertile lowland soils, the wine made from such grapes is flat and dull, and lacks character. A soil of chalk, gravel, sand, or clay, rich in minerals and with good drainage, has proven best.

More than any other product of this globe, wine has a truly indigenous character. By its very nature it is a double concentrate of its environment. First, the grape itself is the direct product of that one particular spot of earth into which the vine sinks its roots, sometimes to a depth of 30 feet, and from which it absorbs the elements so vital to its character. Secondly, these elements "work" when pressed out, and translate themselves into texture, bouquet, flavor, body, balance—all the qualities essential to good wine.

There are definite climatic limits to the growth of wine grapes: in Europe, this is roughly between the thirtieth and fiftieth parallels north. Although the vines may grow prolifically in sunny southern lands, they produce a wine of little character. In many cases, the more hostile the climate, the more barren the soil, the greater the wine. It is the struggle which seems to produce quality in wines, as well as in human beings.

Wine probably had its origin somewhere in the Middle East. Archaeologists have not yet determined whether Stone Age man drank the fermented juice of grapes, but references to wine are as old as written records. It has been described as a gift from the Gods—from Osiris, Dionysus, and Bacchus. The Hebrews credited Noah with its creation, and the Old Testament is rich in references to it. Egyptian Pharaohs attached such importance to it that they had their wine jugs buried with them.

But as grape cultivation spread from Greece to Rome, Spain, and Gaul, wine from the more northerly country took precedence each time over that of its southern predecessor. During the height of the Roman Empire, wines from Gaul were recognized as superior, a position French wines have held to this day.

The Phoenicians are usually given credit for introducing the cultivation of the vine to French soil when they colonized the harbor around Marseille. From there, viticulture spread up the Rhône and the Saône, through the area that is today the wine region of Burgundy. Pliny was praising the wines of the Rhône and the Gironde in the first century A.D.

It is because the area in which the grapes are grown makes such a difference in the characteristics of a vine that, by law, a bottle of French wine must be labeled with the name of the region from which it comes—its *Appellation d'Origine*. More important to the label, however, are the words "*Appellation Contrôlée*," which guarantee that the wine not only comes from the geographical location named, but that it has been produced under the conditions specified for viticulture in that area: that is, with the right grapes, pruned, cultivated, harvested, and fermented in the tried and true fashion.

There are some fine points to be understood when reading a label on a bottle of French wine. The illustrations on pages 316–317 may help. The smaller the geographical region specified under the *Appellation Contrôlée*, the better the wine. For example, a label which reads *Appellation Contrôlée* Bordeaux, merely means that although the wine was produced under specified conditions, it could come from anywhere in Bordeaux and is probably a blend of wines from many of the lesser vineyards. Such a mixture is not necessarily bad, but one should not expect the quality of a more renowned Bordeaux. These will be labeled with a more specific name, such as the district from which they came, the *commune* within that district, or better still, the specific vineyard, estate, or *château* within that *commune*. Usually only classified growths are bottled on the estate. "*Mis en bouteilles au château*" for Bordeaux, or "*Mis en*

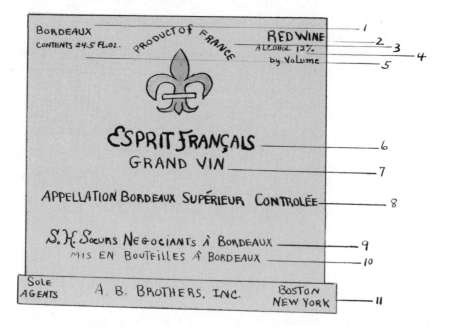

READING A FRENCH WINE LABEL: Wine labels—above, a regional wine, and on page 317 one bottled on an estate. By examining the labels carefully, you can see the differences in the two wines. Important elements are: (1 and 19) The region of origin. (2 and 18) The type of wine. (3 and 16) The country of origin. (4 and 20) Alcoholic content by volume. (5 and 21) The quantity per bottle. (6 and 14) The name of the wine. Number 6 is a trade name made up by the producer for this wine and no other; 14 indicates a *château* product—a wine made from specified grapes grown within a limited area and pruned, cultivated, and handled in a way prescribed by law. (7) No official significance—just the enthusiasm of the grower. (8) A legal guarantee that the wine was made in Bordeaux of grapes grown in Bordeaux under all the rules prescribed by law. The word "superior" has no legal meaning. (9) The producer/shipper who bought freshly pressed wines from various vineyards in Bordeaux, and aged, bottled, and shipped them. (10) Simply means that the wine was bottled somewhere in Bordeaux. (11) The name of the importers—usually a separate label. (12) The year or vintage. Most fine wines carry this on the label. You can check on the quality of a particular year by looking it up in a list of vintages. (13) This statement, often diagonally printed, indicates that the wine was bottled on the estate where it was grown and produced. (15) A guarantee that this wine was produced under all the rules prescribed for the particular estate where it was bottled. (17) An official sign that the vineyard was rated as a first class growth when the finest vineyards were classified in 1855.

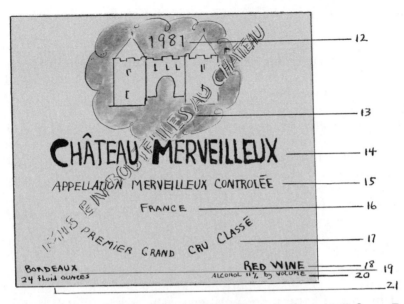

bouteilles au Domaine" or *"Mis en bouteilles à la Propriété"* for a Burgundy, mean that the grower stands behind his product and is proud to have it known that it comes from his cellars.

Because the micro-environment of the vine is so important, a wine made in the United States and labeled "Claret" or "Burgundy" or "Champagne" will have little resemblance to the French product. Even though the same grape is used, soil, climate, and viticulture practices differ. Innoculating the juice with yeast from France may improve the end product, but it does not turn it into a wine from French soil. This is not to say that a good American wine is not better than an inferior French one. But it might be less confusing if it had a name of its own.

Principles of Wine Making

Although details of the wine-making process vary with the region and the wine, the principles are essentially the same everywhere. First, the grapes must reach a certain maturity so that they will contain enough sugar to ferment properly. This is why the date of the harvest has always been so important. From earliest times, the responsibility for the harvest has been vested in a trusted authority. Today there is an instrument for measuring the percentage of sugar in the grapes, which takes the guesswork out of the decision.

The grapes are picked by hand, transferred from the pickers' baskets into large carts or trucks, and taken directly to the press houses. There the stems are usually removed, either by hand or by machine, since they produce too much tannin if left on. Then the grapes are pressed. For white wines, the *must,* as the juice is called, is separated immediately from the skins, drawn off into tanks and allowed to ferment. (Not all white wines are made from white grapes.) For red wines, the skins and must are fermented together for a certain period, usually 1 to 2 weeks. For rosé wines, the skins are in contact with the must for a shorter time.

Fermentation is the spontaneous action of the yeast present in the grapes and in the atmosphere which creates enzymes which in turn convert the sugar into alcohol. The maximum percentage of alcohol which will occur naturally is a little over 14 percent by volume. In poor years, when there has not been enough sunshine to mature the grapes properly, sugar may be added legally to the must in some of the more northern regions in order to bring the wine up to its standard alcoholic content, a process known as *chaptalization* (after Jean-Antoine Chaptal, the man who invented it).

After the initial fermentation has stopped, the wine is drawn off into casks or vats. Oak is traditionally the best material, but today the containers are sometimes glass lined or made of stainless steel. In these vats the secondary fermentation takes place. Carbonic gases are released during fermentation through a loose bung hole in the top of the vat and solid matter, called *lees,* is deposited at the bottom.

After 4 or 5 months, the wine is racked, a process which is repeated three or four times during the first year. Racking simply means separating the wine from the lees by pouring it into clean casks.

To remove the last of the impurities to make a clear liquid, the wine is refined. Traditionally this has been done by adding egg whites, isinglass, or blood, which attracts the impurities and drags them to the bottom. Today a chemical pill performs the same function.

Finally, the clear, bright wine is racked into a clean cask to mature before bottling. For the better wines, this process could take several years. The wine will reach its final growth in the bottle.

Wine, like cheese, is a living thing. It has an infancy, a childhood, maturity—the point at which it is best consumed—and an old age, in which it declines.

Some of the better wines mature slowly. The greats of Bordeaux, for instance, are sometimes still at their peak after half a century. But the pace of the modern world does not encourage such slow development, and soon the peaks of greatness may be a thing of the past.

However, some feel that we live in the Golden Age of wine. It is certainly true that wine has improved over the years. The rough wines drunk by the Romans, spiced, salted, honeyed, and watered, would be unpalatable today. With their scientific knowl-

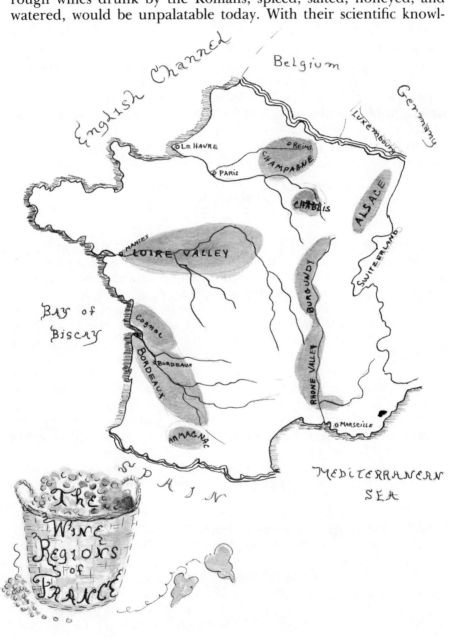

edge of wine making and the new technology of the past century, vintners are capable of producing wines that are consistently better than ever before. These wines age rapidly and are drinkable when very young. The current demand for wines makes it profitable to do this. Yet, ironically, the same techniques which make it possible to meet the growing demand for wine and to raise its general standard, prohibit the development of traditional greatness.

In the discussion of the various wine regions that follows, I will not attempt to list the growths or ratings of wine or to indicate noble vintages. (The vintage is simply the year in which a wine was produced; there can be exceptionally good years.) There are many books and tables published which will give both. Rather, I will offer only a brief introduction to familiarize the reader with the geography and the place names of French vineyards. Specific mention will be made only of those wines suggested for the menus.

Bordeaux

Any discussion of French wines usually begins with the region of Bordeaux, for it is the largest quality wine area, and it also produces the greatest variety of wines, some of these, without doubt, are among the finest wines in the world.

Bordeaux is in the southwestern corner of France. The region is drained by two major rivers, the Garonne and the Dordogne, which together form the broad tidal Gironde 60 miles from its delta in the Bay of Biscay. The city of Bordeaux, which lies 13 miles above this confluence on the Garonne, was already a port when Caesar conquered Gaul. A few wines were made in the region even then, and by the fourth century A.D. Ausonius, a native of the area and son of a Roman senator, retired from a career which took him all over the Empire, returned to Bordeaux, and wrote this couplet:

> *O patria insignem Baccho*
> *Terre aimée de Bacchus*

When Eleanor of Aquitaine married Henry Plantagenet in the twelfth century, the region came under British rule, and it remained an important part of the British Empire for three centuries. It was during this time that wine became the major business of the area. Bordeaux produced the famous British claret (from the French *clairet,* a light mixture of red and white wines, more popular in that day than a full-strength red). British merchants and shippers established their headquarters in the city of Bordeaux. To this day, many of the major wine dealers are of foreign origin—British, Dutch, or German—some from families who have run the same firm for hundreds of years.

Except for special growths, which are cared for and bottled on the estates where they are grown, most Bordeaux wines are delivered in casks to the shippers, who are responsible for the end result. In addition to storing the wine under proper conditions until it matures, bottling it, selling it, and shipping it, they blend wines from the same districts, carefully balancing the assets of each in an effort to create a consistent quality year after year. The best of these are shipped under regional or parish names.

Of the 39 individually recognized districts of Bordeaux, there are 5 principal ones to remember:

Médoc lies northwest of the city of Bordeaux on a low spit of land once reclaimed from the sea much as Holland has been. It is about 50 miles long by 5 miles wide, and is bordered by the Bay of Biscay on one side and the Gironde on the other. Just north of the city, in the area known as Haut-Médoc, the soil is well-drained, loose gravel, but it gradually becomes more sandy towards the end of the spit. It is from the area of Haut-Médoc that the most elegant, light-bodied, full-flavored wine in the world is produced, chiefly from *cabernet-sauvignon, cabernet franc,* and *merlot* grapes. Three parish names to look for are Margaux, Pauillac, and Moulis. A bottle from a vineyard within one of these parishes is sure to be of good quality.

The growth classification made for Médoc in 1855 remained intact until 1932, when the *Syndicat des Crus Bourgeois du Médoc* completed its first classification. A new listing of Crus Bourgeois

was made in 1966, and it was revised again in 1978. This classification can be a guide to excellent values from a large number of *châteaux* that were not in the original Médoc classification.

Graves extends for 40 miles southeast of Bordeaux along the western bank of the Garonne. It is about 12 miles wide. Its name comes from the gravelly soil which predominates. Better known for its dry to mellow whites, which have a delicate bouquet and fruity flavor, it is also the home of one of the oldest red wines. This is Château Haut-Brion, known to seventeenth-century British as "Ho Bryon" or "Obrian."

The vineyards of Saint-Émilion rise up the slopes onto the plateau east of the Dordogne. They contain the only vines grown at any height in the Bordeaux region. This hillside growth is said to be what gives them their resemblance to the Burgundies. They are the most masculine wines of Bordeaux; full-bodied, robust, powerfully fragrant reds. One of the best growths of Saint-Émilion is that of Château Ausone, said to be on the site of a villa which belonged to Ausonius, the Latin poet.

Sauternes, the fifth major district in Bordeaux, lies farther along the Garonne beyond Graves. It is from here that the most luscious, naturally sweet wine in the world comes. The grapes which produce these white wines are the *sauvignon, sémillon,* and *muscadelle,* but the method that produces the sweet wine is entirely different from that used for other wines. The grapes are allowed to stay on the vines until they are overripe and are attacked by a particular mold, called by the French the *"pourriture noble,"* the noble rot. This mold feeds upon the juice of the grapes, reducing their liquid content and increasing the percentage of sugar they contain. The harvest is accomplished almost grape by grape, pickers gathering only those covered with the grayish film, sometimes culling the fields as many as five times. Even after the natural yeasts have converted as much of the sugar as possible to alcohol, there is still an excess of sugar which creates the natural sweetness of the wine. The mold itself imparts a nutty flavor, for which it is sometimes necessary to develop a taste. Barsac, a village within the district of Sauternes, may label its wines either Barsac or Sauternes.* The wines have the same qualities, except that those labelled Barsac may be less sweet. Natives of the region have a saying: "Barsac is the male and Sauternes, the female." From the 1855 classification, the Grands Crus of Barsac are Château Climens and Château Coutet. The Premier Grand Cru of Sauternes always has been from Château d'Yquem.

*It may be helpful to note that the French Sauternes is always spelled with a final "s."

Bourgogne (Burgundy)

After discussing the region of Bordeaux, one naturally turns to Burgundy, the oldest wine-producing area in Europe, and to some oenophiles, the greatest. Happily, this dispute will go on and on. Certainly the top vineyards of Burgundy rank with those in Bordeaux.

The name comes from that of the old Germanic tribe, the Burgundii, who conquered what is now the eastern edge of France in the sixth century. At that time, grape vines were already there and flourishing, bordering the Phoenician tin route that ran up the Rhône and Saône and finally down the Seine to England. In fact, the peasants had been so busy growing vines, that a Roman Emperor in the first century A.D. ordered them to pull up all the vines and replace them with wheat. During the Middle Ages the region became a duchy, and its powerful dukes struggled with the French kings for supremacy. This period saw the rise of the great vineyards, fostered by the rich dukes and by the Church, which held vast tracts tilled for the glory of God and the support of His Church. After the Revolution, these great vineyards were broken up, sold, and resold, so that today there are over 100,000 parcels of land, each separately owned. (The vineyards of Bordeaux escaped this fate only because a great effort was made to reunite them.)

Because of this division bottles of Burgundy which bear the

same vineyard name can differ greatly in their contents. When buying a Burgundy, it is important to be able to recognize the name of the grower as well as the shipper. Here is where a good wine merchant can be of inestimable value.

Today the name Burgundy is no longer an official regional name; it applies only to a long, narrow string of vineyards which extend from those of Chablis, 100 miles southeast of Paris, to the Rhône, some 225 miles south. All of the great Burgundies are produced at the northern end of this strip, in a short stretch no more than 25 miles long by 1/2 mile wide.

The exception is Chablis, which is in a class by itself. The district of Chablis lies like a disconnected head above the long serpentine body of the rest of the region.

Here the *chardonnay,* the same white grape used in the vineyards father south, produces what by many standards is the finest, lightest, driest white wine in the world. Close to the northern limit for wine cultivation, the chalky hillsides, which are a rare outcrop of bituminous clay, give to Chablis the taste of flint and the color of "springwater in sunlight," a pale yellow with faint flecks of green.

The vineyard slopes rise above the quiet country town which gives its name to the wine, and are drained by the placid Serein, the Serene River, which eventually flows into the Seine. To the industrious Cistercian monks goes the credit for developing the qualities of Chablis, which have changed little since the Middle Ages.

Less than 1,000 acres produce classic Chablis. Not all are under cultivation at once, as some fields are allowed to rest for up to 40 years. The steep chalk slopes are not conducive to mechanization, and after a heavy rain the peasants carry the soil which has washed away back up the slopes in baskets. Because of its northern position, the area is subject to early and late frosts and hail, the worst enemies of the vine. For all of these reasons, a good Chablis is rare and expensive. To experience that *finesse,* lauded through the ages, one must have a bottle labeled Grand Cru or Premier Cru. An *Appellation Contrôlée* Chablis or Petit Chablis are wines which have been made within the district, but they are more likely than not a poor wine made from grapes grown on inferior slopes and bottled outside the district. Unless you can find a bottle of Cru Chablis at an affordable price, it would be better to try another dry white wine, such as one of the Loire wines, with your oysters.

The Golden Slope (Côte d'Or) is actually a low range of hills too poor to grow anything but vines. Their magic lies in their limestone soil and their southeast exposure, which gives them the maximum advantage of the sun's rays. Even on this Golden Slope, however, it is only in a narrow strip, midway between top and bottom, that the best of the vineyards lie.

The Côte d'Or is divided naturally by a break in the hills into two parts, the Côte de Nuits to the north, the Côte de Beaune to the south. From the Côte de Nuits come the most fragrant, full-bodied, generous red wines in the world. These wines are never a blend of grape varieties, the best of them coming from the *pinot noir*. One of the most famous of these is Chambertin, a wine first made famous by Napoléon, who took a load of it with him to Moscow in 1812. Chambertin comes from only 70 acres, and the first name identifying the wines classified as Chambertin is important. For example, in 1847, clever wine growers arranged that the town of Gevrey change its name, by use of a hyphen, to Gevrey-Chambertin; the wine grown there bears its name. In that way they shared the popularity and glory brought to Chambertin by the Emperor. Many small vineyards have classified their wines as Chambertin (for example, Charmes-Chambertin), and it is important to become familiar with a reputable merchant who knows the merits of a particular bottle. Some Burgundy *communes* have officially hyphenated their names with that of their best vineyard to entice the unwary buyer. There are, however, other vineyards entitled to a Grand Cru *Appellation Contrôlée* which have also hyphenated their vineyard names with that of Chambertin. A good wine seller can be a great help.

Clos de Vougeot is the largest vineyard of the Côte d'Or, 130 acres. Like all the others, it is now subdivided among some 50 small owners. The vineyard was set out originally by the Cistercians, who also built the imposing castle which still stands inside the walls. The building today is the headquarters of the *Confrérie des Chevaliers du Tastevin* (the Brotherhood of the Knights of the Tasting Cup). The Brotherhood was founded in 1934 to promote things Burgundian, particularly the wines. The honor of membership in the society has been bestowed upon noted epicureans around the world. Colorful, ceremonious banquets are held throughout the year in a grand old hall of the *château*.

The most famous vineyard of the Côte is also its smallest, being only 4 1/2 acres. It is Romanée-Conti in the *commune* of Vosne-Romanée. (Again, the commune, Vosne, has been hyphenated with its most famous vineyard, Romanée.) The name derives from the fact that the site was once a Roman camp and the vineyard once the proud possession of a prince of Conti. Romanée-Conti is a wine given the best of superlatives by the experts: It is "perfectly balanced" and was once described as "bottled velvet and satin." In another 150 acres of Vosne-Romanée are several other vineyards which stand a close second to this prince of wines, among them La Tâche, Le Richebourg, La Romanée, and La Romanée Saint-Vivant.

If the Côte de Nuits produces the unsurpassed reds, the Côte de Beaune produces the "divine Montrachet," that "quintessence of the chardonnay," a golden, full-bodied wine, to many tastes the greatest white wine in the world. The name itself means Bald Hill, a reference to the scrubby, calcareous slope on which the vines grow. Since its 19 acres of vineyard straddle two *communes*, that of Puligny and Chassagne, both hyphenate their names with that of Montrachet.

The Côte de Beaune also produces its quota of excellent reds. All of them, however, are somewhat lighter in character than those grown to the north. Beginning at the north are the vineyards of the *commune* Aloxe-Corton, which vie in quality with the more northern wines. One of its vineyards was once owned by Emperor Charlemagne and still bears the name Corton-Charlemagne.

The capital of the entire region is the medieval city of Beaune. Not only does the district produce a quality of good wines under the *Appellation Contrôlée* Beaune, but it is here that most of the Burgundian shippers have their headquarters. Here also is the famous *Hospices de Beaune,* a charitable institution which dates from the fifteenth century. It is supported solely by the proceeds from its many vineyards, most of which have been bequests. Each year on the third Saturday in November, wines from the *Hospices* vineyards are auctioned off, the prices they bring setting the scale for all Burgundies that year. The auction, until a few years ago when the crowds became too large, took place in the picturesque court-yard of the *Hospices,* draped with ancient tapestries for the occasion. The bidding ends when a candle, lit at the start of each sale, burns out.

South of Beaune are two communes which produce probably the best-known Burgundies, Volnay and Pommard, which are usually sold under their *commune* names. These wines are lighter and more delicate than most Burgundies. The southern end of the Côte de Beaune produces its best whites, the Montrachet already mentioned and those from Meursault, dry and delicate.

Southern Burgundy is subdivided into three main districts: the Côte Chalonnaise, the Mâconnais, and the Beaujolais. Although none of the wines from this region are classed with the greats, it produces many drinkable wines at reasonable prices. Mercurey, one of the best of the reds from the Côte Chalonnaise, takes its name from the ruins of a Roman temple honoring the messenger god. The vineyards here are said to be older than the Roman occupation.

The best-known white wine of southern Burgundy is probably

Pouilly-Fuissé, a dry, fruity wine, named for two villages in the Mâconnais and not to be confused with Pouilly-Fumé, the dry, flinty white wine of the Loire Valley. As always, it is important to look for a vineyard name on the label.

Beaujolais, the southernmost district of those classified as Burgundies, produces a wine of entirely different characteristics. It is the product of the *gamay* grape, outlawed in the north as a "very bad and disloyal plant" for producing poor wines. This grape was brought back from the Middle East by Crusaders in the twelfth or thirteenth century. The vines flourished on Burgundian soil, but the wine was coarse and harsh. Punishment for growing the *gamay* on prime vineyard lands is severe. In Beaujolais, on granitic soil and in stronger sunlight, the *gamay* comes into its own. Here it produces one of the most popular *carafe* wines in France, a wine that is fresh and drinkable when young. Moulin-à-Vent and Fleurie are two of the better *Appellations Contrôlées* of Beaujolais.

Côtes du Rhône

South of the Burgundy region, bordering the Rhône on its 150-mile meanderings to the sea, are the prolific vineyards of the *Côtes du Rhône*. These southern vineyards are planted with the *syrah* grape, which the Crusaders brought from Persia. Most of the wines end up as *carafe* wines, but there are several notable exceptions known as the classic growths of the Rhône. Among these are the vineyards of Hermitage, named after the Hill of the Hermit upon which they grow. The hermit was a Crusader who spent his life after his return on the hilltop. The reds are strong, deep-colored wines which age well; the whites, honey-colored with a dry mellowness.

Another classic growth is Châteauneuf-du-Pape, one of the strongest red wines of France, deep purple with a rich flavor. Its name comes from the fact that the vineyards in the area were developed under the watchful eyes of the Popes when they resided in Avignon in the fourteenth century. It remained a relatively obscure wine until a venerable nineteenth-century *marquis,* noted for his prowess around the court, revealed that the secret of his vigor was the wine from his vineyard on the Rhône. Its aphrodisiac properties are touted to this day.

Last, two of the best rosés of France, tart and fruity, come from Tavel and Lirac. They are made predominantly from the *grenache* grape.

Champagne

Champagne, the King of Wines, comes from the smallest acreage of vineyards in the country, the area around the old cathedral city of Reims in the northeastern corner of France. It was in Champagne country, along the River Marne in the villages of Épernay, Hautvillers, and Château-Thierry, that Allied troops turned the tide of World War I.

Even before they began to sparkle, the wines of the region were known as the Wine of Kings, for the thirteenth-century cathedral was the site of coronations, and the coronation wine was from Champagne.

It was not until the seventeenth century that the natural effervescence of Champagne was encouraged and captured. Like the Vouvrays of the Loire, Champagne undergoes a second fermentation in the first spring after the harvest. Even if the wine is kept underground at a constant temperature, at the time the sap rises in the vines, the wine begins to bubble. This phenomenon is still unexplained by science. Without proper containers, however, the gases are lost. It took the time and patience of a Benedictine monk, Dom Pérignon, named cellar master of the Abbey at Hautvillers in 1688, to make Champagne as we know it today. After observing this second fermentation, he found that if the glass of the bottles were thickened, they could contain the pressure, which sometimes built up to six times that of the atmosphere. In place of oiled cloths, he used cork for the first time and tied it down so the pressure would not expel it. Until his death at an advanced age, he experimented in blending wines from the various vineyards of the region, an art continued to this day by each firm that makes Champagne. For, with one or two exceptions, Champagne is always a blend.

The chief grapes used are the *pinot noir*, the grape that produces those deep red Burgundies, and the white *chardonnay*. But in Champagne the soil is chalk, and the method of production differs. The whole process of making Champagne is so specialized that no individual makes his own. It is the continuous work of a series of experts. The grapes are sold prior to harvest to one of the large Champagne companies, at a price previously set by authorities in the region.

During the harvest, the grape bunches are carefully sorted, and any imperfect grapes are discarded. Great care is taken that they are not bruised on their way to the press houses, where they are taken as quickly as possible. These press houses are scattered throughout the vineyards so that the delicate grapes will not have to travel far.

The grapes are pressed quickly in large, shallow bins which allow the juice to run off immediately so that it won't be colored by prolonged contact with the skins, as a greater proportion of the grapes are black. After a short settling period, this must be racked off into 200-quart barrels and trucked to the central storage cellars in Reims or Épernay. These cellars consist of miles of underground galleries carved into the chalky subsoil. The oldest cellars around Reims were built as quarries to produce building stone for Roman cities. These galleries make perfect storage cellars. They are dry, with a constant temperature of around 50° F. The first fermentation takes place here, but stops with the onset of cold weather. During the winter the cellar masters taste and blend, trying to produce the standard for which their firms are known. These blends are then bottled by March before the second fermentation, which will take place in the bottle. The bottles are then stored deep inside the galleries. Here, for a year, they will rest while the by-product of this second fermentation collects as a deposit.

The trick is to get this deposit into the neck of the bottle next to the cork so that it can be removed without losing any of the sparkle. This is done by placing the bottles in large racks with their bottoms slightly raised. Every day they are given a twist and the rack is tilted a little more by an expert who can handle as many as 30,000 bottles a day. After about 3 months the bottle is bottom up and the neck black with sediment; the wine is crystal clear.

Three lightning fast steps now occur: First, the cork is released, bringing with it the sediment. Then each bottle is given an injection of cane sugar dissolved in Champagne. The percentage of sugar depends upon the type of Champagne desired: Brut has the least added and is always the best, Sec and Demi-Sec are sweeter. Finally, the bottle is recorked and wired. This series of operations is done quickly so that no detectable amount of sparkle is lost. Then the bottles are stored again until the injected liquid is completely absorbed and the wine matures. In the best firms, this process takes 4 to 5 years.

I would like to add a note on the service of Champagne: Time and trouble have been expended to put the bubbles in the wine, and anything that allows them to dissipate before the wine reaches your lips is a waste of the money you paid for your bottle. Champagne should be properly chilled before opening: 1 hour on ice or 2 hours in the refrigerator. The tulip-shaped, all-purpose 8-ounce wineglass is perfect for the service of Champagne; even a tall water glass is better than the popular sherbet type used in the

United States, which gives a wide surface from which the bubbles readily escape.

Champagne is right for any occasion and for any meal. Like most sparkling wines, it makes an excellent *apéritif* which may be continued throughout the meal and on to the dessert. Madame de Pompadour once said: "Champagne is the only wine that leaves a woman still beautiful after drinking it."

The Loire

The wines of the Loire are as delightful as the countryside in which they are produced. Red, white, or rosé, they are all light, fresh, and delicately fruity, easy to drink and thirst-quenching. Only in recent years have they begun to travel.

Anyone wishing to go on a wine tour might well begin in this garden of France, as famous for its Romanesque churches, Renaissance castles, and pure French tongue as it is for its wine. For this is the *château* country, the pleasure-ground of kings, where every hilltop bordering the river is crowned by a fifteenth-century palace, a remodeled fortress from the feudal era.

This is also the native region of some outspoken men, among them Rabelais, Richelieu, and Balzac, all of whom praised the wines of the Loire above all others. Saint Martin, patron saint of vintners, was from Tours, the wine center of the region. To him is given credit for the discovery of pruning. As the story goes, he kept two vineyards. One he carefully walled off from all encroachment; in the other he allowed his donkey to browse among the vines. To his surprise, he found that year after year, the better wine came from the vineyard clipped by his hungry animal; thus he made the deduction that pruning might add to the quality of wine.

Starting near the mouth of the Loire, the first vineyards of note are those of Muscadet, which produce a light, dry white wine with a definite tang of lemon. They are excellent with all seafoods.

Next come the Angevin wines, by which the Three Musketeers of Dumas lived and fought. The Rosé d'Anjou is sweeter than a rosé from Tavel; its whites are both dry and sweet. The old province of Touraine, with Tours at its center, lies in the heart of the Loire Valley. Just downstream from Tours is the native village of Rabelais, Chinon which, with its sister village Bourgueil, produces the ruby reds, still the best red wines of the valley. Upstream from Tours, in the steep chalk cliffs which rise above the river, are caves which date from prehistoric times. It is here that the sparkling white wines of Vouvray are stored and where some of the vintners make their homes. It is surprising how clean, warm, and comfortable a cave can be. Next to Champagne, Vouvray's Mousseux are considered the best sparkling wines of France. They make a good substitute for Champagne at any time. Like Champagne, their natural tendency to effervesce is encouraged, then captured in the bottle. There are also still Vouvrays, but they do not have the quality that sparkle gives the wine.

Last, but certainly not least, as the river turns south towards its source in the Massif Central, come two very dry white wines, Pouilly-Fumé and Sancerre. Like the Muscadet from the other end of the Loire, these two wines are excellent with seafood, particularly oysters and other shellfish. All of the wines from the Loire, even the reds, are better slightly chilled.

Alsace

The wines of Alsace are the only ones which bear the name of the grape from which they are made rather than the name of the vineyard or district. This is because the original holdings were severely broken up during the 50-year occupation by the Germans following the Franco-Prussian War, from 1870 to 1918. During this time the traditional wine grapes of the region were replaced to produce quantity instead of quality. Since the return of Alsace to France, the vineyards have been replanted. To the vintners of the area, the grape variety is the most important key to the quality of the wine they are producing.

Situated in the northeast corner of France, Alsace is the northernmost district of the country producing wine, and the rigors of its climate add the mark of distinction. All of its wines have a great fruitiness and bouquet, a result of the slow maturation of the grape. The vineyards are situated, like those of the Côte d'Or, on the lower slopes of a mountain ridge that faces southeast, where they can take advantage of the full force of the sunlight which reaches them. Here the mountains are the Vosges, which run parallel to the Rhine for almost 60 miles.

Next to the name of the grape, which always gives its own stamp to the wine, the name of the producer and shipper (always one and the same) is important on the label. Look for the slim, long-necked bottle, called *flûte d'Alsace*. A good wine merchant can be of help.

Four Alsatian wines mentioned in this book are Riesling, Gewürztraminer, Sylvaner, and Muscat d'Alsace. Riesling is a grape variety forced to its noblest character by the northern climate, both in France and in Germany. It is clean, dry, and steely. Gewürztraminer, a word which means "very spicy" in German, is said to have the strongest fragrance and bouquet of any white wine in the world. Although it is a dry wine, containing very little sugar, its heady bouquet makes it taste somewhat sweet. Sylvaner is a dry white wine with a less pronounced bouquet than the others. Its grapes are grown in choice locations and it is fresh and light, an excellent complement to seafood. Muscat d'Alsace is another dry white wine. As its name indicates, it is made with *muscat* grapes, which give it an incomparable fragrance. Although it is a still wine, it can be served, like Champagne, as a before-dinner drink and throughout the meal. It is also a good dessert wine. To my mind and my taste, it is definitely *un vin pour réception* (a wine to serve on special occasions).

Guidelines for Selecting and Serving Wines

Let your personal taste be your guide in selecting wine.

Over the years, as many different shaped wineglasses as there are wines have been developed. However, the clear, long-stemmed, tulip-shaped, 8-ounce wineglass is perfect for all wines, including Champagne. Never fill it to the top; a third to half full is plenty, since you should have room to swirl the wine. A large part of the pleasure of wine is its aroma, the delicate, unique bouquet which also subtly adds to its taste. The tulip shape of the glass is ideal for momentarily trapping this bouquet. Even a tall water glass is better for wine than the small, wide-mouthed cocktail glass or the small wineglass used in so many homes and restaurants, filled to the brim.

If you are serving several wines with a meal, the following rules of precedence may be helpful. Always serve:

1) *Lighter wines before rich, full-bodied wines*
2) *Dry white wines before red wines*
3) *Dry wine before mellow and sweet wine*
4) *Red wine before sweet white wine*
5) *Red Bordeaux before red Burgundy*
6) *White Burgundy before white Bordeaux*
7) *White Burgundy before red Bordeaux and red Burgundy*
8) *Red Bordeaux and red Burgundy before sweet white Bordeaux*

A red wine is best when served *"chambré,"* that is, at room temperature without central heating, about 60° to 65°F. It should be uncorked about an hour before it is to be poured so that it may "breathe." This process of oxidation develops the bouquet, and will bring out the full quality and smoothness of the wine.

White and rosé wines should be served slightly chilled, around 50°F. About 1 hour in the refrigerator or 1/2 hour in an ice bucket should bring them to the right temperature. They should be opened just before serving.

Champagne and other sparkling wines can stand more chilling: 2 hours in the refrigerator or 1 hour in the ice bucket.

Only truly great old red wines need special care and handling. Many oenophiles use a wine basket, the purpose of which is to cradle the bottle in a reclining position when carrying it from storage to table, and to keep it from moving when the cork is pulled. This is necessary with old red wines to avoid disturbing any sediment which may have collected. If there is much sediment, the wine should be decanted before serving. If you pour it slowly, in one continuous smooth motion, the sediment is less likely to mix with the clear wine.

Wine bottles should always be stored on their sides so that the liquid is in contact with the cork to prevent it from drying out and shrinking, thus allowing too much oxidation. Good corks, which come from Spain, permit just enough exchange of gases to allow a wine to mature. Try to purchase red wine a few days before serving it, so that it has time to rest on its side.

Use a good corkscrew, one that exerts the greatest leverage on the cork with the least effort. Be sure to wipe inside the bottle neck before pouring.

Never serve wine with a salad which has a vinegar dressing; vinegar dulls the taste buds.

Find a reliable wine seller whose judgment and knowledge you can trust. Given the enigmas of wine labels, only he can introduce a beginner to the names of reliable shippers and advise about vintages. Also, he can give tips on a wine which may be developing better than was anticipated and which will make a good buy. And he can recommend which wines to save for the future and which to drink immediately.

Un Choix de Vins

The chart that follows lists the wines suggested for the menus in this book. It is not intended to be a comprehensive review of French wines, but to give you an idea of the varieties available. Since white wines are served before reds, I begin with them, moving by regions from the drier to the sweeter wines. The reds follow, arranged with lighter wines preceding those with more body. A few rosés and Champagnes are listed at the end of the chart.

WHITE WINES

WINE NAME	REGION	DESCRIPTION	GOOD WITH
Riesling	Alsace	Very dry	Fish, shellfish, white meat, poultry
Muscat	Alsace	Dry, very fruity	May be served as an *apéritif* and with desserts
Sylvaner	Alsace	Fresh, fruity, light	May be served as an *apéritif;* good with cold cuts, seafood
Gewürz- traminer	Alsace	Smooth, great bouquet	Soufflé, *foie gras,* sauerkraut; could also be served with dessert
Entre-Deux- Mers	Bordeaux	Dry light	Veal, roasted poultry, broiled and fried fish
Graves de Vayres	Bordeaux	Mellow	White meat and poultry with cream sauce
Premières Côtes de Bordeaux	Bordeaux	Mellow	Rabbit and veal with cream sauce

WINE NAME	REGION	DESCRIPTION	GOOD WITH
Sainte-Croix-du-Mont	Bordeaux	Sweet	Fish, shellfish with cream sauce, dessert, fruit
Loupiac	Bordeaux	Sweet	Fish, shellfish with cream sauce, dessert, fruit
Château Rayne-Vigneau	Bordeaux Bommes	Sweet	Dessert and fruit
Château Climens	Bordeaux Barsac	Sweet	Dessert and fruit, *foie gras*
Château Coutet	Bordeaux Barsac	Sweet	*Foie gras,* seafood with cream sauce, dessert and fruit
Château d'Yquem	Bordeaux Sauternes	Sweet	*Foie gras,* seafood with cream sauce, dessert and fruit
Chablis	North of Burgundy	Very dry	Seafood, particularly oysters
Pouilly-Fuissé	Southern Burgundy Mâconnais	Fresh, fruity, dry	Broiled fish, seafood, particularly oysters
Puligny-Montrachet	Burgundy Côte de Beaune	Fine, dry	Fish, poultry, white meat, goat cheese
Chassagne-Montrachet	Burgundy Côte de Beaune	Fine, dry	Fish, poultry, white meat, goat cheese
Meursault	Burgundy Côte de Beaune	Dry, mellow, fruity	Rabbit and white meat with cream sauce
Auxey-Duresses	Burgundy Côte de Beaune	Dry, soft	White meat and poultry with cream sauce

WHITE WINES, CONT.

WINE NAME	REGION	DESCRIPTION	GOOD WITH
Saint-Péray	Côtes du Rhône	Sparkling, fruity	May be drunk as an *apéritif* and throughout the meal with fish, white meat, poultry
Hermitage	Côtes du Rhône	Dry, mellow, fruity	Seafood with cream sauce
Sancerre	Loire Valley	Fresh, very dry	Seafood, snails, white meat, goat cheese
Pouilly-Fumé	Loire Valley	Dry	Seafood, white meat
Muscadet-Sur-Lie	Loire Valley	Dry	Seafood
Muscadet	Loire Valley	Fresh, light	Seafood
Vouvray Brut	Loire Valley Touraine	Still or sparkling, the driest	May be served as an *apéritif*, or with seafood, white meat
Vouvray Demi-Sec	Loire Valley Touraine	Sweet	Fish and seafood with cream sauce
Vouvray-Doux	Loire Valley Touraine	Very sweet	Dessert and fruit

RED WINES

WINE NAME	REGION	DESCRIPTION	GOOD WITH
Bourgueil	Loire Valley Touraine	Fresh	Roast lamb, game (fresh or hung), goat cheese, semi-hard cheese

WINE NAME	REGION	DESCRIPTION	GOOD WITH
Chinon	Loire Valley Touraine	Fruity, light	Roast pork, white meat, game (fresh or hung), semi-hard cheese
Château Margaux	Bordeaux Parish of Haut-Médoc	Light-bodied, delicate, exquisite fragrance	Roast lamb, white meat, semi-hard cheese
Moulis	Bordeaux Parish of Haut-Médoc	Light-bodied, mellow, fine fragrance	Sweetbreads, game and poultry, semi-hard cheese
Pomerol	Bordeaux District	Light to full-bodied, smooth	Roasted poultry, semi-hard cheese
Saint-Julien	Bordeaux Parish of Médoc	Light-bodied, good balance	Sweetbreads, game and poultry, semi-hard cheese
Pauillac	Bordeaux Parish of Médoc	Light-bodied, can have great bouquet and finesse	White meat, roasted poultry
Saint-Émilion	Bordeaux District	Full-bodied, strong bouquet	Red meat, soft cheese, venison
Château Haut-Brion	Bordeaux Graves	Rich, delicate and fruity	Red meat, soft cheese
Fleurie	Southern Burgundy Beaujolais	Fresh	Lamb, semi-hard cheese
Mercurey	Southern Burgundy Côte Chalonnaise	Fruity	Roasted poultry
Givry	Southern Burgundy Côte Chalonnaise	Fresh, light	Roasted poultry
Juliénas	Southern Burgundy Beaujolais	Fruity, light	Roasted and broiled poultry

RED WINES, CONT.

WINE NAME	REGION	DESCRIPTION	GOOD WITH
Moulin-à-Vent	Southern Burgundy Beaujolais	Earthy bouquet	Roasted and broiled poultry
Morgon	Southern Burgundy Beaujolais	Earthy	Red meat and stews in red wine sauce
Mâcon Rouge	Southern Burgundy Mâcon	Excellent body	Red meat, pork, game, soft cheese
Crozes-Hermitage	Côtes du Rhône	Full bouquet	Pork, soft cheese
Châteauneuf-du-Pape	Côtes du Rhône	Full-bodied	Meat in red wine sauce, red meat, game, soft cheese
Pommard	Burgundy Côte de Beaune	Smooth	Red meat in red wine sauce, game
Volnay	Burgundy Côte de Beaune	Delicate, smooth	Poultry in red wine sauce, venison, semi-hard cheese
Aloxe-Corton	Burgundy Côte de Beaune	Warm bouquet, smooth	Poultry in red wine sauce, venison, semi-hard cheese
Romanée-Conti La Romanée, Vosne-Romanée, Romanée Saint-Vivant	Burgundy Côte de Nuits	Very full-bodied, superb bouquet, great balance and finesse	Duck, red meat, soft cheese
Clos de Vougeot	Burgundy Côte de Nuits	Very full-bodied, fine bouquet	Fish in red wine, red meat, soft cheese
Chambertin	Burgundy Côte de Nuits	Very full-bodied, fine bouquet	Fish in red wine, red meat, soft cheese

ROSÉ WINES

WINE NAME	REGION	DESCRIPTION	GOOD WITH
Rosé de Lirac, Rosé de Tavel	Côtes du Rhône	Dry, tart, fruity	May be served throughout a meal; innards, goat cheese
Rosé de Béarn	Southwest of Bordeaux	Dry	May be served throughout the meal; innards, goat cheese
Rosé d'Anjou	Loire Valley	Dry to sweet	Soufflé, cream cheese, dessert, fruit

CHAMPAGNES

Mousseux Brut Blanc de Blancs	Burgundy	Sparkling, extra dry	May be served as an *apéritif* and throughout a meal
Champagne Brut	Champagne	The driest	May be served as an *apéritif* and throughout a meal
Champagne Extra Dry	Champagne	Very dry	May be served as an *apéritif* and throughout a meal
Champagne Dry	Champagne	Dry	May be served as an *apéritif* and throughout a meal
Champagne Demi-Sec	Champagne	Sweet	Desserts and fruits
Champagne Doux	Champagne	Very sweet	Desserts and fruits

Digestifs

AFTER-DINNER DRINKS

Just a word about *digestifs,* drinks which finish off a meal as no other drink can, and are served with or after coffee.

First, there are brandies, the *vins brûlés* ("burnt wines"), as they were called originally. The term "brandy" comes from the Dutch word for burnt wine, *brandewijn,* which was interpreted by the English as brandywine and shortened to brandy. True brandy is wine, usually the newly fermented juice of grapes, which has been distilled twice, then aged. It is said to have been "invented" as an expedient method for shipping wine more economically, the intent being to water it at the end of its journey. But the distilled product itself caught on, and has been one of the luxuries of civilization ever since.

It takes 10 gallons of fermented grape juice to make 1 gallon of brandy. As a distillate, it is a harsh, potent, colorless liquid. It is the aging in charred oak casks that gives to brandy its characteristic flavor and color. The better the brandy, the longer it has aged in the cask. Good brandies are aged up to 25 years. However, many are helped along their way by the addition of sugar, coloring, and water. The more that is added to a brandy, the poorer it is.

The best brandies are French and the best French brandies are from the southwestern part of the country: Cognac, from a small district surrounding the town of Cognac on the winding Charente, just north of the Bordeaux region; and Armagnac, from a small district in the northern Pyrénées, southeast of Bordeaux. The undistilled wines from both districts are indifferent at best, mostly harsh and acid.

In the Gascon country of D'Artagnan, the most famous of Dumas' Three Musketeers, Armagnac is still made by individual producers in small copper stills. In Cognac, the distilling is usually done centrally, with similar equipment.

Every wine region in France produces its own brandies—*Eaux-de-Vie* ("waters of life"), as they are called—from the *marc,* the last pressing of the grapes and pulp. Most *marcs* are consumed locally, either because so little is made or because they are of no great quality.

One *Eau-de-Vie,* Calvados, is worth mentioning because it can be found in the United States. It comes from the region of Normandy, which produces no wine. Calvados is a distilled cider, a fact which easily could be guessed from its aroma. Elsewhere in France, it is known as *le trou Normand* ("the Norman hole"), meaning that it aids digestion by digging a hole in the stomach. For this reason, it is often drunk between courses.

There are other fruit brandies, all exceedingly dry. They include Quetsche, made from purple plums; Mirabelle from yellow plums; Framboise from raspberries; Fraise from strawberries; and Kirsch from cherry pits.

The finest after-dinner liqueurs are also distilled. They are made from crushed herbs and spices: seeds, leaves, bark, roots, and stems. They are usually a mixture of these elements combined with alcohol and sugar. Some of the most commonly used substances are anise, angelica, peppermint, hyssop, sassafras, gentian, fennel, wormwood, coriander, cinnamon, cloves, lemon and orange peel, coffee, and tea. Among the most popular liqueurs are Benedictine, Chartreuse, Cointreau, Grand Marnier, Crème de Menthe, Anisette, and Noyau de Poissy.

Le Plateau de Fromages

THE CHEESE TRAY

A French family luncheon or dinner may or may not include a sweet dessert, but there is always *un fromage,* a cheese, served after the salad, with crusty white or dark bread, crackers, and sweet butter. Butter is a must with some cheese—if not all! An outstanding exception is Swiss cheese, which is delicious with a strong mustard.

For guests, there should be a tray of assorted cheeses, served with fruit knives and forks. As Brillat-Savarin said, "Dessert without cheese is like a beautiful woman with only one eye." Climax the simplest meal with cheese and a fresh fruit in season, and you have had a feast.

Perhaps this fondness for cheese arises from the fact that for centuries it has been a nation-wide product in France. Over 400 rural districts produce their own distinct varieties. Some of them, like French wines, are known throughout the world.

Cheese is a way of preserving milk to make it last longer and travel more easily. It is concentrated, and thus very nutritious: A little goes a long way.

Like wine, coffee, and other ancient foods, the origin of cheese is a mystery. Legend says it originated by accident: Travelers in the Near East poured milk into pouches made of sheep's stomachs and hung them from their saddles. At the end of a day's journey, they found the milk had turned to tasty curds and thirst-quenching whey. The motion and heat, together with rennet from the sheep pouches, were ideal conditions for the first step in the production of cheese.

Although there are many variations in the way cheese is made, the fundamentals are the same. First, milk—usually cow's, goat's, ewe's, or a combination of the three, whole, skimmed, or enriched with added cream—is coagulated into curds, either naturally or with the aid of rennet. The curds are then broken up, finely for hard cheeses and into larger pieces for soft cheeses. The whey is drained or pressed out. For fresh cheese, such as American cottage cheese or French *fromage à la pie,* the process stops here.

342

For other cheeses, the curds are then placed in molds of characteristic size and shape. The moisture is allowed to drain again for soft cheese. It is expelled by pressure when making the hard cheeses. The curds then ferment and are attacked by fungi which live off the products of the fermentation. Some fungi are responsible for a cheese's characteristic flavor. These in turn are attacked by other micro-organisms which maintain a kind of balance and are responsible for the type of crust which forms on a cheese.

Today, these micro-organisms, which differ for each cheese, have been identified. For some varieties, they are manufactured and innoculated into the cheese, a method which accelerates the process and ensures uniformity.

Until such recent discoveries, however, cheese making retained an aura of mystery. Through long apprenticeship, generations of cheese makers knew by instinct when the curd was just right to be cut or molded, when the molds should be pressed, how long they should be salted, and how often they should be turned. Even today, with our understanding of what is happening during the various stages of cheese making, we still do not know why a cheese made in Wisconsin by the same process used in Normandy turns out differently. Despite science, nature still plays its part.

In France, laws rigidly control the name of each cheese by the district in which it is made, just as the *Appellation Contrôlée* designates the origin of French wines. As with wines, labeling is important, for the underlying soil, herbage, altitude, and animal breed determine texture and flavor as much as the species of microbe and the method of processing.

Blue-Veined Cheese

The name Roquefort is applied only to cheese made within clearly defined boundaries in the Department of Aveyron in south-central France. The first law to protect its name was passed in 1666, but Roquefort had a long history before that date. In the first century A.D., according to Pliny, it was being sold in the streets of Rome.

Its origin remains speculative. The story goes that over 2,000 years ago, a shepherd left his lunch in one of the Roquefort caves. When he returned several months later, he found the moldy remains superbly delicious. In attempts to repeat his experience, the secrets of Roquefort were discovered.

There are many factors which make Roquefort the only cheese

of its kind in the world. It is made of the milk of sheep which graze on the high barren pastures of the Causses, long narrow plateaux which crown a series of mountain ranges in south-central France. It is ripened in the cool damp caves of the Combalou, a mile-long limestone formation in the heart of the town of Roquefort.

Geological history created a labyrinth of fissures within the formation which interconnect these caves. These fissures, typical of limestone formations, run vertically as well as horizontally, and act as air passages, creating a constant wind which draws cool moist air from the surface of an underground river below the Combalou and circulates it through the caves. The result is a constant temperature of about 40° F. and a uniform humidity year round: perfect air conditioning for the development of *penicillium roqueforti* (bread mold), the blue-green mold which attacks the curds and gives Roquefort its inimitable flavor.

It is no wonder that Roquefort is known as the King of French cheeses!

Similar cheeses, the Blues, are made in other districts and other countries, but true Roquefort has the red sheep emblem on its label. It has a greyish rind with a firm, crumbly, light yellow center, evenly veined with blue.

For the connoisseur, Roquefort reaches its peak only after a year of ripening. However, it is put on the market after a month or two. This is the one cheese which should never be allowed to stand at room temperature. Return the unused portion immediately to the refrigerator, putting it in a cheese or butter compartment where the temperature should be about 35 to 40 degrees, the temperature at which Roquefort was born.

Soft Cheeses

Camembert is an infant as French cheeses go. The process of its manufacture was perfected in the late eighteenth century by a local farmer's wife in the little village of Camembert, in the department of Orne in Normandy. It is the product of lowland cow herds feeding on lush Normandy grasses. It is a soft paste cheese from which little of the whey has been drained. The attacking fungus is *penicillium candidium,* which today is manufactured and sprayed on as a liquid in the large plants where Camembert is made. Cheeses made by the same process and called Camembert are produced all over France and in other countries as well, but each place of origin must be designated on the label.

Creamy yellow inside, with a whitish-yellow crust, Camembert comes in rounds as small as 8 ounces.

It was an unwritten law in my family that I was never to be sent to buy any soft-ripened cheese. I like my Camembert as white and as hard as chalk—a disgrace to a Frenchman!

Because different cheeses are best made at different seasons and because the fermentation rate varies so in France, there are definite seasons for eating each cheese at its peak. In the United States, however, one must rely mainly on when they are available in the markets.

Soft cheeses should be nursed to their full maturity in a cool place, then eaten as soon as possible. Harder varieties will keep longer; they should be well wrapped, then placed in a closed container before refrigerating.

Bries have been made in the Seine et Marne Department, just to the east of Paris, for over a thousand years. Subject to awards and rhapsodies throughout the centuries, Brie has been lauded as the "Royal Cheese," and called the "gentle jam of Bacchus."

Several towns in the district are noted for their own variations: Meaux, Melun, Provins, and Coulommiers. The best, the Brie of Meaux, comes in thin flat rounds up to 2 feet across. The others are smaller and slightly thicker, but of much the same quality. They have a greyish crust and a soft, creamy, light yellow paste inside.

Coulommiers is made in the same area as the Bries of Coulommiers, but by a different process. The 12-ounce wheels are covered with a white, slightly greyish crust. The inside is a soft pale yellow. They have a mild fresh flavor when young, and a nutty flavor when fully ripened. They are packaged in thin wooden boxes.

Époisses is made throughout central France. During the curing process, it is seasoned with black pepper, clove, fennel, salt, and brandy.

Semi-Soft Cheeses

Port-Salut* was first made by a group of Trappist monks who had settled, following their exile in Switzerland during the French Revolution, near Laval in Brittany. They chose for their home an old abbey they named the *Abbaye de Notre Dame de Port-du-Salut*, the port of salvation. Like Gruyère and Emmenthal, which it is said the monks were trying to copy, Port-Salut is made with scalded curds.

*Also called Port-du-Salut.

At first the monks produced just enough for their own consumption, then gradually, enough for local sale. By the 1870's they had herds large enough so that they could send cheese to Paris, where it immediately came into great demand.

For many years the formula of Port-Salut remained a secret. Today, the cheese is made commercially by many manufacturers to whom the Trappists have sold the rights. Saint-Paulin is a similar cheese made by firms which do not have a legal right to the registered name. Port-Salut is also made in Wisconsin. It is an excellent cheese, but very different from the Trappists' product.

A French cheese widely available in the United States today is Bonbel, found in many supermarkets along with a similar variety, Baby Bel. Although not typical French cheese, these both have a pleasant, mild flavor. They are sold under the trademark "La Vache Qui Rit" (the laughing cow), and are sealed in paraffin.

Pont-l'Évêque, literally meaning "Bishop's Bridge," is named after a small town in Calvados in the heart of the Normandy apple country. It is a semi-soft cheese, having about the same consistency as Camembert, its sister cheese. It is a great companion for a glass of cider. Pont-l'Évêque comes in small golden squares of about 7 ounces, cross-hatched with the pattern of the straw mats on which it has ripened. It is packaged in wood chip boxes.

Reblochon is a high mountain cheese from Haute-Savoie in the French Alps. It is a semi-soft, yellow cheese with a reddish-brown crust and mild, nutty flavor. The "hard milk of the Alps," as the natives call it, comes in small, flat rounds which traditionally weigh about a pound. "Reblochon" means "second milking," as this cheese was once the product of the day's second yield.

La Tomme (which means "cheese" in the dialect of Haute-Savoie) au Marc de Raisin is another interesting variety from Savoie. Its rind is formed of dried grape skins and seeds from local wine pressings, which give its solid white cream a breath of Bacchus. It is one of the smaller cheeses, coming in rounds weighing 3 1/2 to 4 pounds.

Semi-Hard Cheese

The "Swiss" cheeses are used often in French recipes because they melt smoothly without separating and have a distinctive, yet mild, flavor. In France and Switzerland, "Switzerland Swiss" is called Emmenthal, for it was first, and is still chiefly, made in the Valley of Emme in the Canton of Berne.

Swiss cheese is one of the most difficult kinds of cheese to make. Control of the quality and composition of the milk, propagation and use of the essential bacterial starters, and the details of refinement* are complicated procedures that require the services of a skilled cheese maker and special equipment.

Because of this, Swiss cheese has always been produced co-operatively, the farmers bringing their milk twice a day to their local cheese maker. If the milk is not absolutely fresh, it changes the flavor of the finished cheese.

In the factories, huge copper kettles hold 2,000 to 3,000 pounds of milk. An outer jacket around the kettle forms a chamber for hot steam which heats the milk.

True Swiss has eyes 1/2 to 1 inch in diameter, 1 to 3 inches apart. They are produced by one of several bacteria used in its manufacture. In some imitation Swiss cheeses, the holes are bored into a finished cheese. Beware of counterfeits!

Gruyère, the second most famous cheese from Switzerland, is very similar to Emmenthal, although it has a sharper flavor. It comes in smaller rounds, weighing from 55 to 110 pounds. (Rounds of Emmenthal weigh closer to 200 pounds.) Gruyère may also have eyes, but they are smaller than those of true Swiss.

There are French varieties of both these Swiss cheeses, made on the French side of the Alps: Emmenthal Français, Beaufort, and Comté, all second to none.

The Gruyère, well known in America, which comes in individual foil-wrapped triangular portions, is a processed cheese made from a mixture of Swiss cheeses. Like all processed cheeses, it goes through a series of operations which homogenize and sterilize it, and stop the ripening process. When buying Swiss cheese, always buy it in chunks rather than in slices. It keeps better.

Hard Cheese

The large, barrel-shaped Cantal, up to 15 inches in diameter and often over 100 pounds, is a hard, yellow, fairly strong cheese.

*Refinement (*affinage*) is a very delicate operation in cheese making, the goal of which is to bring the cheese to the proper maturity by regulating the temperature, humidity, and drainage. For some cheeses, the process includes adding spices or herbs. For others, like Swiss, it includes controlling the level of carbonic gases that produce the holes. Refinement often takes place in special cellars (*caves à fromages*). Goat cheeses are refined outdoors in special screened cages, while other types of cheese are refined resting on beds of straw.

It too was praised by Pliny in the first century. The very best is
made from the milk of cows pastured in the alpine meadows of
Auvergne in the Department of Cantal in central France, and labeled Central Haute-Montagne. Like most hard cheeses, Cantal is
an excellent traveler, lasts a long time, and is good eating year
round.

Other Cheeses

GOAT CHEESE: There are many goats' milk cheeses, fromages de chèvre, produced throughout France. They can always be distinguished from other cheeses by their flavor. They are mild, white, and creamy, somewhat like a hard cream cheese, and should always be eaten with butter. Among those which are well known are Banon, Valençay, and Chabichou.

BOURSAULT: The most recent revolution in cheese making was the creation of Boursault, which is very rich in butter fat. At first it was unrefined, prepared with garlic, pepper, and herbs. Later it was refined and copied by Boursin. Both trade names now are produced by the same firm.

If I were to record all the cheeses I particularly enjoy, the list would go on and on. It is a rewarding world to explore. Over 100 French varieties are available in the United States, and of course, there are Swiss, Dutch, English, Norwegian, Italian, and other cheeses as well. Given a little knowledge, one can soon begin to distinguish cheeses made from cow and goat milk, from raw and scalded curds, from highland and lowland herds.

Cheese is a treat at any time. To savor its true flavor, it should usually be served at room temperature. Remove it from the refrigerator 2 hours before serving. (The exception to this is Roquefort, which should be served chilled.) When serving cheese as an afternoon snack or an hors-d'oeuvre, furnish several small dishes of herbs and spices in which to dip cheese cubes. Try freshly ground black pepper, cumin, or fresh or dried chopped dill, parsley, or thyme. Accompany it with unsalted nuts, sticks of celery, slices of crisp apple, and, of course, crusty French bread and butter.

However, nothing brings out the true quality of a cheese better than wine; reciprocally, nothing enhances a wine better than cheese. Personally, I prefer red wine with all cheeses, but it is traditional to have a light wine, a dry white, or a rosé, with a mild cheese; a full red with a mild, tangy cheese; a robust red with a pungent cheese. It is a marriage which has lasted through the ages.

Relatif aux Salades

ABOUT SALADS

WHATEVER the meal, light luncheon or formal dinner, in France a green salad is always served after the main course. *La Salade Verte* can be anything leafy and green—lettuce, chicory, endive, dandelion, watercress, Escarole, Romaine, Chinese cabbage, spinach.

Any number of other vegetables may be prepared *en vinaigrette* as appetizers: artichokes, carrots, cabbage, beets, cucumbers, leeks, tomatoes. Both types of salads may be served at the same meal.

When making the vinaigrette dressing, which is simply vinegar and oil with condiments, the condiments should always be sprinkled in first, then the vinegar added, and last the oil. Oil and vinegar always seem to mix better if the oil is added to the vinegar, not the vinegar to the oil. I think it makes a decided difference in taste!

With all the vinegars in the market, it can be confusing to decide which one to purchase: Champagne vinegar, *Framboise* vinegar, garlic, shallot, tarragon vinegar, "old vintage" vinegar, sherry vinegar . . . the list goes on and on. I find that a vinaigrette dressing is just as appetizing prepared with plain red wine vinegar. I prefer to add fresh herbs myself when I want them.

Use the kind of oil that suits your taste. The key to a vinaigrette dressing is the use of wine vinegar, not the kind of oil that is used. Peanut oil is generally used in the northern part of France, and olive oil in the southern part. It is important to note that a good olive oil should have a green tint. Also available are almond oil, avocado oil, and walnut oil (all very expensive). As with vinegar, one can start a collection of oils for experimentation, but any vegetable oil will make a good dressing. Keep oil in a cool place, but not in the refrigerator.

Always choose a bowl large enough so that you can toss your salads thoroughly, without worrying about throwing them out of the bowl.

Make the dressing for a green salad in the bowl in which the salad will be served. As the greens should not rest in the dressing, place the salad fork and spoon in the bowl first, then gently break leaves into bite-sized pieces onto these utensils when you are ready to bring the salad to the table. (The greens can be washed and prepared ahead and refrigerated, wrapped in a cloth towel or in a colander.) Toss thoroughly just before serving.

The flavor of vegetable appetizers, in contrast, is improved if they are allowed to marinate in the dressing for a short time. Most of these may be made several hours to a day ahead.

À Propos de Café

A SHORT HISTORY OF COFFEE

IT wasn't until the seventeenth century that coffee was introduced to France. It became an overnight sensation when the Turkish ambassador to the court of Louis XIV popularized his native custom of serving coffee as a social gesture. By the eighteenth century there were coffee houses throughout Europe. The ability of coffee to ease fatigue and enliven the mind was well demonstrated by statesmen, philosophers, writers, painters, and men of science who gathered around the coffee table and practiced the lively art of conversation.

The oldest of these coffee houses, *Le Café Procope,* is still open at its original location, although today it is only a mediocre restaurant. Established in 1686 by one Francesco Procopio, a gentleman from Palermo, this café was frequented over the years by such men as Voltaire, whose table may still be seen there, La Fontaine, Rousseau, Balzac, Victor Hugo, Verlaine, Diderot, Robespierre, and the American ambassador to France, Benjamin Franklin.

Although coffee houses are no longer gathering places for "*les beaux esprits,*" they are still congenial spots for good conversation and good coffee. Often my parents and their friends, during a Sunday afternoon stroll, would walk half-way across Paris to a café noted for its excellent coffee, brewed only from beans roasted on the premises.

From legends concerning the origin of coffee, one fact seems clear: The discovery of making the seeds of a large evergreen shrub, *Coffea Arabica,* palatable, was made by Moslems in the Middle East, where the coffee bush is native, before the eleventh century. It is said that a herdsman noticed his goats cavorting day and night after they had eaten the fruit of the coffee bush. Such a stimulant interested devout Moslems, who often found themselves dozing during their long prayers.

For several centuries after its introduction into Europe, Arabian coffee, sold under the name *moka,* was the best coffee one could buy. Today, most coffee comes from Central and South America, where the plant, transplanted from Arabia many years ago, flourishes. *Café du Brésil* was roasted in the *épiceries fines,* the fancy groceries, throughout Paris when I was a child. We always knew from the aroma which floated over a wide neighborhood, where to go to purchase our pound, freshly roasted.

Coffee is a flavorless bean as it comes from the bush, and the coffee aroma perishes quickly once it is released by roasting. It disappears still faster once the roasted bean is ground.

Each morning, one of us would sit on a kitchen chair with the coffee mill between our knees and grind just enough for breakfast. For this meal, powdered chicory was mixed with the ground coffee. Mother had a porcelain drip pot. She would stand over the stove spooning on a tablespoon of hot water at a time, allowing it to slowly soak down through the coffee, extracting as much of the essence as possible. The brew was poured into bowls or very large cups, with an equal amount of hot milk. For us children, sugar was a must. Although today I am the only one in our home who drinks coffee, I still grind my own beans, bought as freshly roasted as possible.

In contrast to the breakfast cup, after-dinner coffee is *le café noir,* a brew unadulterated by chicory, cream, or milk. To dilute it by one drop is sacrilege! This is not just an epicurean whim. Coffee aids digestion if taken black after a meal. Nutritionists' tests have proven that coffee mixed with milk is not as easily assimilated, and that it stimulates digestion only after that process has already begun.

"*Le café noir*" is always served in a *demi-tasse,* a small cup holding 1/3 to 1/2 cup at most. Drinking *café noir* from a regular-sized cup is like having *Coquilles Saint-Jacques* in a casserole instead of scallop shells. It should taste exactly the same, but it does not.

The reputation of a French housewife as a hostess depends as much upon her coffee as on her cooking. To have it said that her *café noir* is "*jus de chausettes,*" the French equivalent of dishwater, would be an insult of the highest order.

To get a good brew for after-dinner drinking: Use an earthenware drip-type pot. Put fresh cold water in your kettle and bring it to a rolling boil. Measure 3/4 to 1 full cup of coffee into your pot (depending on the relative strength you like), and place the pot over low heat. Add 3 cups of boiling water, 1/4 to 1/2 cup at a time, waiting until the first measure has dripped through entirely before adding the next. Do not allow coffee to boil. Pour into a heated serving pot; keep hot in a pan of hot water over low heat.

Serve it after the dessert course; sit back, relax, and feel it soothe. For special occasions, serve *une petite tasse de café* "*avec la goutte,*" with a tear-drop of brandy, or "*un canard,* a sugar lump dipped in brandy until saturated. It is a perfect culmination to a dinner with good company and lively conversation.

Alimentation de Luxe

LUXURY FOODS

TO shop at an *Alimentation de Luxe* for food is like shopping at *Dior's* for a dress. In France, stores under this name sell only the best and most deluxe foods.

The items discussed here are specialties of France, products which may be added to any meal for a touch of elegance. They are foods which are good to know something about, although you certainly won't use them every day.

Many products could come under this heading, but these are ones that bring particular delight to our home. They may be found in food specialty stores or on the import counters of some supermarkets.

Les Truffes

TRUFFLES

Looking at the black, wrinkled, warty truffle as it is dug from beneath an oak on a hillside of the Périgord, the uninitiated might well wonder why this subterranean fungus is ranked among the delicacies of the world. But for those who have once sampled its incomparable flavor and been exposed to its penetrating aroma, its fame is no longer a mystery. What remains a mystery is its growth.

How this delicacy was first discovered we do not know. We do know that they were revered by the Romans, who called them children of the gods, daughters of the earth; they dedicated them to Venus, goddess of love, and believed them to be an aphrodisiac. In the eighteenth century, Brillat-Savarin asserted that these black diamonds of the kitchen made women more loving and men more lovable.

There are other regions of the world where truffles are found, but the Périgord region in the district of Dordogne in southwestern France produces the most prized variety. Here, after the autumn frosts, the farmer begins his hunt for the diffident truffle. Sometimes with a dog, but most often with the aid of a trained pig (preferably a pregnant sow, who seems to have the keenest scent), he combs the hillsides; the pig strains at her leash, grunting loudly. When she stops and roots, she is distracted with a handful of corn and the farmer carefully digs the truffle.

For a memorable experience, treat yourself to a small tin, about 3/8 of an ounce. Sliver pieces into sauces, salads, omelets, garnishes, and stuffings. Place slices under the skin near the breastbone of poultry that is to be roasted. A little goes a long way. When you know what the Romans were talking about, you may become a devotee yourself.

Foie Gras

Literally "fat liver," *foie gras* is an epicurean delight which also dates from Roman times. According to Pliny, a consul named Metelus Scipio hit upon the art of fattening geese so that their livers swelled. But the practice may well be far older than the Romans, for there is evidence that Egyptians and Greeks were masters of the art long before the Empire.

The process requires that for the last several weeks of a goose's, or a duck's, life it be closely confined without opportunity for exercise, and force-fed with the aid of a funnel, through which mashed corn is stuffed down its throat several times a day. The bird becomes a veritable fat factory. In the end a goose liver may weigh up to 4 pounds.

Foie gras has a firm, velvety smooth texture and a pinkish, white color. In France it is often eaten fresh. In the United States it may be purchased canned: *au naturel,* augmented with truffles, or made into a pâté. In *foie gras aux truffes,* the truffles have been slipped through the liver so that each slice will contain a piece. *Pâté de foie gras* is a finely ground mixture of 75 percent liver with 25 percent salt, spices, and other meat.

Foie gras comes in tins of many sizes and shapes. Try a small one; chill it; serve several thin slices on a lettuce leaf. To cut it smoothly, dip a knife in hot water between each slice. Canned *foie gras* will keep almost indefinitely. Once opened, however, it will keep only a day or two.

A taste of this bitter-sweet delicacy will make you wise in the world of gastronomy!

Épicerie Fine

THE GOURMET SHOP

MARRONS GLACÉS: *Les épiceries fines* and *les confiseries* (the confectionary stores) hold a particular temptation for me—glazed chestnuts. Just the thought of them puts me in a happy mood. A tiny bag of broken ones was always the treat I'd choose when I had extra spending money; and a festive season never seems complete without a *bonbon* dish filled high with perfect whole ones. *Marrons glacés* are made by a long slow boiling in sugar syrup. They usually come from south-central France, where chestnuts grow in profusion. In France they come in bulk by the pound, broken ones selling for half price. For export, only perfect ones are individually wrapped and packaged in tight tins. Look for them in food specialty stores for a special treat.

BAR-LE-DUC: This is a jam exquisite in both taste and color, made of currants or gooseberries whose seeds are removed by hand. For a special treat, use this jam for filling *petits fours* and other delicate pastries. It is a specialty of Bar-le-Duc, a town in Lorraine, east of Paris.

FRUITS À L'EAU DE VIE: These are whole fruits preserved in brandy or a liqueur, put down at the peak of perfection. The choice includes apricots, cherries, chestnuts, raspberries, tiny tangerines, *reine-claudes, mirabelles,* and *quetsches* (green gage, yellow, and purple plums). Traditionally they are served in glasses with very short stems; the fruit eaten first with small silver spoons, and the liqueur sipped from the glasses. They provide a delightful variation of the after-dinner drink.

BISCUITS POUR CHAMPAGNE: Hard, finger-shaped biscuits with a delicate sweetness, these can be served with Champagne, sweet wines, or desserts such as chocolate mousse, caramel custard, or ice cream.

CRÊPES DENTELLES: A delicate *crêpe* rolled into crispy fingers, these are a specialty of Brittany. They come individually foil wrapped, packaged in tight tins. They are delicious with afternoon tea or coffee, or with delicate desserts.

PETIT-BEURRE: Hard and semi-sweet, these biscuits are an institution in France. They are always on hand in the French home for teething children, for morning and afternoon snacks, and to accompany desserts. French law regulates that they must be made with pure sweet butter.

Les Fleurs Cristallisées

CRYSTALLIZED FLOWERS

"Violettes, oeillets, lilas, roses, mimosa, lavande, feuilles de menthe. . . ." It could be the cry of a Paris street vendor, calling attention of passers-by to his cart of beautiful flowers. But the sound of these names always brings to my mind another world—the world of my kitchen. There, these flowers have been captured and preserved by being crystallized in sugar. A more delicate, delightful confection I cannot imagine! I use them for a last exquisite touch on special desserts, cakes, or ice creams. They are as delicate to the palate as to the sight.

Each flower brings its own memories, and with use, will gradually create its own occasions. Yellow mimosas always remind me of the straw boxes filled with their blooms sent to us, along with orange blossoms and tangerines, by fortunate friends who spent their winters on the Riviera. Opening those boxes in the dusk of a cold Paris afternoon, I melted in the warmth and sunshine of that far-off place.

This same warmth overtakes me in my kitchen when I happen to glance at my pantry shelves brightened with their bouquet of containers. These colorful little boxes can be purchased in most shops specializing in such delicacies or in department stores where there are special sections of imported foods.

If you are of a romantic turn and have the inclination, you can crystallize your own flowers. It is a meticulous labor of love and I prefer to leave it to the specialist. In France, crystallized flowers are produced in the south, where acres and acres of flowers are cultivated for the perfume industry. My friend Jean, however, successfully preserved a whole spring meadow of violets. Here is how they are done.

INGREDIENTS

a couple of dozen violets
1 egg white
1 tablespoon water
1/2 teaspoon almond extract
sifted granulated sugar

METHOD

Pick bouquets of purple meadow violets in full bloom. Wash gently under running faucet; allow to dry thoroughly.

Cut, or nip off with thumb and forefinger, the stems directly under the blossoms, being careful not to damage petals.

Add water and extract to egg white and gently stir with fork until the cohesiveness of the white is broken.

Using an artist's soft paint brush (a number 2 or 3 is good), coat thoroughly each violet petal with egg white. (If the blossom is dipped into egg white it will become saturated, the petals will fold together, and the sugar will adhere too thickly.)

Place coated blossoms on waxed paper. While still wet, sprinkle lightly but thoroughly with fine sugar. Allow to dry completely before placing in lidded container for storage.

Angelica

This confection is the candied stem of the angelica plant, a tall, stout-stalked member of the parsley family which grows widely in temperate zones. Early considered a "plant of the holy spirit," it was named for its angelic healing qualities. Its roots are still used in medicines and as the base of Chartreuse and other liqueurs. The candied stems have a pleasant flavor.

Angelica can be purchased in shops specializing in gourmet foods, where it is plentiful around Thanksgiving and Christmas. It may seem expensive, but you use only a little at a time, and one package lasts for years. It keeps best in a tight tin box.

Angelica may be used as it comes from the package, sliced in strips, or it may be softened and turned into decorative shapes. To soften, cut off desired amount and soak in very hot water, changing water two or three times until angelica is pliable (about 15 to 20 minutes). Remove from water, dry on a paper towel.

For added flavor, soak in small amount of Kirsch or rum for 24 hours.

WEIGHTS AND MEASURES

dash	= 1/8 teaspoon		1 cup	= 1/2 pint
3 teaspoons	= 1 tablespoon		2 cups	= 1 pint
4 tablespoons	= 1/4 cup		4 cups	= 1 quart
16 tablespoons	= 1 cup			
			4 quarts	= 1 gallon
8 ounces	= 1 cup		8 quarts	= 1 peck
16 ounces	= 1 pound			

SOME IMPORTANT EQUIVALENTS
FOR INGREDIENTS

STAPLES

1 pound flour = 4 cups
1 jumbo egg = 1/4 cup
2 jumbo eggs = 1/2 cup
3 jumbo egg yolks = 1/4 cup

4 jumbo egg whites = 2/3 cup
1 pound butter = 2 cups
1/4 pound butter = 1/2 cup
  or 8 tablespoons
1 pound butter, clarified =
  1 1/4 to 1 1/2 cups

CONDIMENTS

18 turns pepper mill = scant
  1/2 teaspoon
10 turns pepper mill = scant
  1/4 teaspoon
12 small sprigs parsley,
  chopped = about 3
  tablespoons

1 large garlic clove = 1
  teaspoon, chopped
7 garlic cloves = 4 heaping
  teaspoons, chopped
3 medium shallots, chopped
  = 2 tablespoons

OTHER INGREDIENTS

1/2 pound raw mushrooms,
  sliced = almost 3 cups
1/2 pound fresh mushrooms,
  sliced and sautéed = 1 1/2
  cups
1 pound fresh mushrooms,
  sliced and sautéed = 3 to
  3 1/2 cups
4 ounces Swiss cheese =
  about 1 cup, grated, well
  packed

1 pound meat = 2 cups,
  cubed
1 pound nuts in shell = 2
  cups shelled nuts
1 pound dried chestnuts,
  cooked = 1 quart well-
  packed purée
1 pound fresh chestnuts,
  cooked = 2 cups purée

METRIC EQUIVALENTS

Since cooking in the future will be done in metric terms, I am including some conversion tables that should meet home kitchen requirements. For the sake of convenience, numbers have been rounded off, but that will make no difference in the taste or quality of the dishes presented in this volume. Abbreviations used are: cm = centimeters; ml = milliliter; g = grams; and kg = kilogram.

SPOONFUL EQUIVALENTS BY VOLUME

1/8 teaspoon	=	.5 ml	1 tablespoon	= 15 ml
1/4 teaspoon	=	1.5 ml	2 tablespoons	= 30 ml
1/2 teaspoon	=	3 ml	3 tablespoons	= 45 ml
3/4 teaspoon	=	4 ml	4 tablespoons	= 60 ml
1 teaspoon	=	5 ml		

CUP EQUIVALENTS BY VOLUME

1/4 cup	=	60 ml	1 cup	= 250 ml
1/3 cup	=	85 ml	1 1/4 cups	= 310 ml
1/2 cup	=	125 ml	1 1/2 cups	= 375 ml
2/3 cup	=	170 ml	2 cups	= 500 ml
3/4 cup	=	180 ml	3 cups	= 750 ml
			4 cups	= 1.000 ml

WEIGHT EQUIVALENTS

1 ounce	=	28 g	1 pound	
4 ounces	=	115 g	(16 ounces)	= 450 g
1/2 pound	=	225 g	1 1/2 pounds	= 675 g
3/4 pound	=	340 g	2 pounds	= 900 g
			3 pounds	= 1.350 kg

EQUIVALENTS OF POT AND PAN SIZES BY VOLUME

5 to 6 cups	= 1.5 liters	2 quarts	= 2	liters
1 quart	= 1 liter	3 quarts	= 3	liters

EQUIVALENTS OF LINEAR PAN SIZES

1 inch	=	2.5 cm	10 inch	= 25	cm
5 inch	=	12.5 cm	12 inch	= 30	cm
8 inch	=	20 cm			

METRIC EQUIVALENTS, CONT.

OVEN TEMPERATURES

150° Fahrenheit =   65° Celsius
200° Fahrenheit =   93° Celsius
250° Fahrenheit = 121° Celsius
275° Fahrenheit = 135° Celsius
300° Fahrenheit = 149° Celsius
325° Fahrenheit = 165° Celsius
350° Fahrenheit = 175° Celsius
375° Fahrenheit = 190° Celsius
400° Fahrenheit = 205° Celsius
425° Fahrenheit = 218° Celsius
450° Fahrenheit = 230° Celsius
500° Fahrenheit = 260° Celsius

Fortunately, an hour will remain 60 minutes, so if anything is overcooked you won't be able to blame it on the metric system.

GLOSSARY

À POINT: Precise or perfect timing for broiling, sautéing, poaching, roasting, or browning.

BAIN-MARIE: Water bath.

BEURRE BLANC: A butter sauce to accompany fish made with a reduction of shallots, white wine, and vinegar.

BEURRE CLARIFIÉ: Clarified butter.

BEURRE ESCARGOT: A mixture of butter, chopped fresh garlic, and chopped fresh parsley. Sometimes includes chopped shallots.

BEURRE MANIÉ: A mixture of butter and flour made into a paste to thicken a sauce at the end of cooking.

BEURRE NOISETTE: Butter, regular or clarified, heated to a light brown color. At this stage it develops a hazelnut aroma. Often fresh lemon juice is added to it.

BLANCH: To drop ingredients in boiling water in an open pot very briefly, as parboiling. Used to remove skins from tomatoes, onions, fruits, almonds.

BOUQUET GARNI: Herb bouquet usually composed of fresh parsley sprigs (fresh thyme sprigs when available), and bay leaves.

BRAISER: To simmer food gently in its own juice without evaporation.

BRIOCHE SHAPE: A traditional ball shape form topped with a smaller ball. Named for a traditional French roll.

BRUNOISE: Finely diced raw vegetables.

CHARLOTTE MOLD: A straight-walled, metal baking pan with handles, usually fitted with a lid.

CHINOIS: A conical strainer with a long handle, made either of solid metal or of wire mesh, used for extracting liquid.

CHIQUETER: Making indentations around edge of dough with the back of a knife blade.

CRÈME SAINT-HONORÉ: A pastry cream to which beaten egg whites have been added.

CROUTON: Has several meanings: 1) The heel of the long stick of French bread. 2) The heel of French bread or a piece of the crust cut lengthwise and rubbed with garlic, then immersed in salad dressing. 3) Small cubes or slices of bread sautéed in clarified butter or roasted in the oven.

DÉGLACER: A step in the preparation of a sauce, whereby a small amount of liquid is added to the skillet or pan in which meat or poultry has been sautéed or roasted.

DORURE: A coating mixture of egg yolks, water, and salt used for glazing.

DUXELLES: Chopped mushrooms and onions.

ENTREMETS: A light sweet dish which may be served after the roast and before the pastry in a formal meal.

FRAISER: A procedure to distribute butter more thoroughly when making dough.

GASTRIQUE: A reduction of vinegar, wine, and herbs.

GLACE: Frosted, iced, glazed.

GOUTTIÈRE: A sheet of metal 10 × 10 inches with accordion ridges about 1 inch high, onto which small pastries are flipped to give them a curved shape.

HÂTELETS: Skewers with fancy heads with varying motifs, used to decorate roasts and seafood.

HAUTE CUISINE: Refined cooking, the elements of which include developed technique, creative imagination, and a presentation that is pleasing to the eye as well as the palate.

LIAISON: A mixture of egg yolks with heavy cream or sour cream (or both), to which hot liquid is added.

LUT: (also called *repère* or *repaire* in culinary language): A mixture of flour and water made into a paste to seal molds or pots.

MACÉRER (Macerate): To steep ingredients, mostly fruits, in liquor or brandy.

MARINER (Marinate): To immerse (or steep) fish, seafood, meat, poultry, or game in a pungent mixture of wine, herbs, vegetables, and spices.

MEAT GLAZE: May be either jellied juices of a roast or several cups of strong beef, chicken, or veal stock reduced to only a few tablespoons.

MIREPOIX: A combination of *brunoise* (finely diced vegetables). Usually carrots and onions, although sometimes turnips, leeks, chopped boiled ham, and bay leaves are added. Used as a base to flavor certain dishes.

PARIS-BREST: A pastry ring made with cream puff paste and filled with *Crème Saint-Honoré.*

PÂTE À BABAS: A batter-like dough which has risen twice.

PÂTE À BRIOCHE: Light, feathery yeast dough which has risen three times.

PÂTE À BRIOCHE COMMUNE: A dough with a heavier texture than the above which has risen only twice.

PÂTE BRISÉE (Broken dough): A French pastry dough.

PÂTE À CHOU: Cream puff paste.

PÂTE À FONCER: Similar to *pâte brisée* except that egg is added to it. Used for *pâté, croustade,* and meat or fish *en croûte.*

PETITS FOURS: Small pastries which may or may not be coated with icing.

PISTOU: A mixture of crushed fresh tomatoes, garlic, and basil, bound with olive oil.

ROUX: A binding of hot butter and flour.

PRALINE: A combination of almonds, hazelnuts, or walnuts and granulated sugar, cooked until sugar turns to caramel, then crushed to a powder and used to flavor pastry creams and ice cream.

SAUTÉ: To cook or brown quickly in a small quantity of hot fat.

SOUFFLÉ MOLD: A shallow, straight-walled baking dish, usually.porcelain, although pyrex and metal are used.

TERRINE: A glazed earthenware mold with a lid.

TROUSSER (To truss): Binding the legs and wings of a bird tightly together against the body with strings so that it will hold its shape during and after cooking.

VANNER: The action of constantly moving a pan on burner to incorporate butter or *beurre manié.*

Index